Routedge Revivals

Social Welfare in Africa

First published in 1987, this book analyses social welfare in the major countries of Africa, at that time. For each country it considers the ideological framework underlying the social welfare system and describes the historical development of both the system and the political and socio-economic context. Each chapter looks at the structure and administration of the systems in place and how these are financed. Contributions examine the nature of the different parts of the welfare system, surveying social security, personal social services, and the treatment of the following key target groups: the aged; those with disabilities and handicaps; children and youth; disadvantaged families; the unemployed; and the sick and injured. Each chapter concludes with an assessment of the effectiveness of the system considered. In this book, particular attention is paid to the role of foreign aid agencies and to missionaries, and to the special problems of poverty and famine in Africa.

Social Welfare in Africa

Edited by
John Dixon

First published in 1987
by Croom Helm

This edition first published in 2016 by Routledge
2 Park Square, Milton Park, Abingdon, Oxon, OX14 4RN
and by Routledge
711 Third Avenue, New York, NY 10017

Routledge is an imprint of the Taylor & Francis Group, an informa business

© 1987 John Dixon

The right of John Dixon to be identified as editor of this work has been asserted by him in accordance with sections 77 and 78 of the Copyright, Designs and Patents Act 1988.

All rights reserved. No part of this book may be reprinted or reproduced or utilised in any form or by any electronic, mechanical, or other means, now known or hereafter invented, including photocopying and recording, or in any information storage or retrieval system, without permission in writing from the publishers.

Publisher's Note
The publisher has gone to great lengths to ensure the quality of this reprint but points out that some imperfections in the original copies may be apparent.

Disclaimer
The publisher has made every effort to trace copyright holders and welcomes correspondence from those they have been unable to contact.

A Library of Congress record exists under LC control number: 87024364

ISBN 13: 978-1-138-94689-7 (hbk)
ISBN 13: 978-1-315-67054-6 (ebk)
ISBN 13: 978-1-138-94690-3 (pbk)

SOCIAL WELFARE IN AFRICA

Edited by
JOHN DIXON

CROOM HELM
London • New York • Sydney

© 1987 John Dixon
Croom Helm Ltd, Provident House, Burrell Row,
Beckenham, Kent, BR3 1AT
Croom Helm Australia, 44-50 Waterloo Road,
North Ryde, 2113, New South Wales

Published in the USA by
Croom Helm
in association with Methuen, Inc.
29 West 35th Street,
New York, NY 10001

British Library Cataloguing in Publication Data

Social welfare in Africa. — (Croom Helm
    comparative social welfare series).
    1. Public welfare — Africa
    I. Dixon, John, *1946–*
    361.96   HV438
    ISBN 0-7099-4505-1

Library of Congress Cataloging in Publication Data

ISBN 0-7099-4505-1

For Tina, Piers and Aliki

To my parents-in-law,
Gordon and Ditha Slowey

Printed and bound in Great Britain by Mackays of Chatham Ltd, Kent

TABLE OF CONTENTS

ACKNOWLEDGEMENTS

PREFACE

CONTRIBUTORS

ETHIOPIA
Quentin F. & Emmy Lou Schenk — 1

GHANA
Yvonne Asamoah & D.N.A. Nortey — 22

IVORY COAST
Adama Bakayoko & Sylvestre Ehouman — 69

KENYA
Wacira Wa Gethaiga & Lorece P. Williams — 100

MAURITIUS
Mohipnarain Joynathsing — 121

NIGERIA
A.O. Sanda — 164

SOUTH AFRICA
Brian McKendrick & Erzsebet Dudas — 184

TANZANIA
W.J. Mallya & H.A. Mwankanye — 218

ZAMBIA
Elizabeth E. Brooks & Vukani G. Nyirenda — 247

ZIMBABWE
Joe Hampson & Edwell Kaseke — 279

APPENDICES — 307

INDEX — 348

ACKNOWLEDGEMENTS

The idea of a six-volume global series on comparative social welfare was my dream in 1983; the task of identifying contributors and commissioning some 60 chapters has been a regular nightmare ever since. The production of this, the third volume, marks the halfway point of the project. To achieve this target is gratifying. It makes the light at the end of the metaphorical tunnel seem both brighter and more accessible.

The translation of this capacious idea into a publishing reality is the result of the efforts of a hard-working team. The conceptual framework that permeates the entire series was developed with the valuable assistance of Dr Hyung Shik Kim. The search for contributors has been made considerably easier by the generous efforts of countless people, most of whom I have never met, whose assistance I sought to identify national experts. To name the 600 or so people and organisations I have contacted is quite impossible, but to all of them go my sincere thanks. Having an enthusiastic and perspicacious publisher has also been invaluable. Mr Peter Sowden at Croom Helm has provided me with encouragement and latitude, both of which are essential in a project involving some 60 contributors spread throughout the world.

Financial support for this project has been generously provided by the International Fellowship for Social and Economic Development Inc, a non-profit organisation with the following objectives:

- to undertake and to advance the study and research of social and economic policy, administration and development in the Third World;

- to organise conferences, seminars, workshops and lectures;

- to promote, organise and sponsor the publication of worthwhile research on social and economic policy, administration and development in the Third World; and

- to advance the planning, implementation and evaluation of social and economic policy in the Third World.

Further information about IFSED can be obtained from the Director, IFSED, PO Box 228, Belconnen, ACT, 2616, Australia.

As editor of this volume I must, first and foremost, thank all the contributors who have, individually and collectively, made it possible. They have accepted my nit-picking queries and editorial liberties with more good humour than I deserve.

To Mrs Cheryl Leeton goes my thanks for typing the manuscript in its various drafts and in its final form. The artwork was done by Mr Karl Rudeiger of the Instructional Media Centre at the Canberra College of Advanced Education, and I thank him.

To my long-suffering wife, Tina, goes my appreciation for putting up with me throughout the preparation of this manuscript. Without her support and understanding it would have undoubtedly taken much longer to complete.

For any errors of fact and for all opinions and interpretations, the authors and the editor accept responsibility.

John Dixon

PREFACE

This is the third of a six volume series that will be completed by the end of 1988. The first volume, Social Welfare in Asia (eds John Dixon and Hyung Shik Kim), appeared in 1985. The second volume, Social Welfare in the Middle East (ed. John Dixon), appeared in 1987. The forthcoming volumes are:

- Social Welfare in Developed Market Countries (eds John Dixon and Robert Scheurell)

- Social Welfare in Latin America (eds John Dixon and Robert Scheurell)

- Social Welfare under Socialism (eds John Dixon and David Macarov)

Once completed, this series will have described and reviewed the welfare systems of some 55 countries in a way that facilitates a comparison of their features.

It is important to recognise that any comparative study must be placed in the context of the interlocking nature of the dominant social value or traditions, and of a variety of socio-economic and political forces, all of which interact with the prevailing patterns of social need and available resources to determine the fabric of particular welfare systems. Thus a comparative social welfare study, if it is to be useful, must place particular welfare systems in their particular cultural, social, economic, political and ideological environments. It must also acknowledge that different cultures create a different framework of reference from which to perceive human welfare and the institutions and programmes that have evolved to meet at least some human needs. It is pointless to attempt to compare countries that are fundamentally different, hence the regional focus of this tightly structured anthology.

Social security is defined as:

> the whole set of compulsory measures instituted to protect the individual and his family against the consequences of an unavoidable interruption or serious diminution of the earned income disposable for the maintenance of a reasonable standard of living (Rys 1966, p.242).

Thus it includes compulsory employer liability (with or without insurance); provident funds; social insurance (benefits subject to contributing conditions); social assistance (benefits subject to residence qualifications and an income or means test); and universal programmes (benefits subject only to residency qualifications). The social security boundary is, however, blurred in many countries, for elements of fiscal welfare (that is, a system of tax rebates or taxable income deductions that reduce the tax liability of particular target groups) and occupational welfare programmes (for example, occupational superannuation, non-statutory sick pay entitlements, free or subsidised health care for employees and their dependants) may impinge on social security in some instances. Where this is significant, details are included. Health insurance arrangements are also included.

The personal social services are characterised by service functions that have a major bearing upon personal problems, individual situations of stress, inter-personal helping or helping people in need, and the provisions of direct services in collaboration with workers from statutory and voluntary agencies. Accordingly, the term 'personal social services' will be used in such a way as:

- to distinguish them from cash benefits;

- to refer to various forms of services in kind that are provided, in the main, in response to recognised 'personal' needs; and to include service provisions that usually require the assistance and help of qualified personnel, such as social workers or probation officers.

It should be noted, however, that the adoption of this terminology in the context of a developing society may cause some conceptual and practical problems. Thus it is necessary to be eclectic in what should be included under the rubric 'personal social services'.

All monetary values are expressed in national currency units. No attempt has been made to convert these into a common unit by means of official currency exchange rates. The currency units for the countries included in this anthology are:

Ethiopia	:	Dollar
Ghana	:	Cedi
Ivory Coast	:	Franc
Kenya	:	Shilling
Mauritius	:	Franc
Nigeria	:	Pound
South Africa	:	Rand
Tanzania	:	Shilling
Zambia	:	Kwacha
Zimbabwe	:	Dollar

REFERENCE

Rys, V. (1966), 'Comparative Studies in Social Security: Problems and Perspectives', <u>Bulletin of the International Social Security Association</u>, 19, 7-8 (July-Aug), 242-68.

CONTRIBUTORS

Dr Yvonne Asamoah is a Senior Lecturer in Sociology at the University of Ghana, Legon, Ghana.

Dr Adama Bakayoko is an Assistant Professor in Econometrics in the Centre Ivoirien de Recherches Economiques et Sociales at the Universite Nationale Cote d'Ivoire, Abidjan, Ivory Coast.

Dr Elizabeth Brooks is the Head of Social Development Studies in the School of Humanities and Social Sciences at the University of Zambia, Lusaka, Zambia.

Erzsebet Dudas is a Senior Social Worker with the Department of Health Services and Welfare (House of Assembly), South Africa.

Mr Sylvestre Ehouman is a Technicien de Recherche in the Centre Ivoirien de Recherches Economiques et Sociales at the Universite Nationale Cote d'Ivoire, Abidjan, Ivory Coast.

Dr Wacira Wa Gethaiga is an Associate Professor in the Afro-Ethnic Department of the California State University of Fullerton, Fullerton, California, USA.

Reverend Joe Hampson is the Principal of the School of Social Work, Hare, Zimbabwe.

Mr Mohipnarain Joynathsing is the Head of the School of Administration at the University of Mauritius, Reduit, Mauritius.

Mr Edwell Kaseke is the Dean of Studies at the School of Social Work, Hare, Zimbabwe.

Dr Brian McKendrick is the Head of the School of Social Work at the University of Witwatersrand, Johannesburg, South Africa.

Mr W.J. Mallya is a Tutor at the National Social Welfare Training Institute, Dar es Salaam, Tanzania.

Mr Haynes A. Mwankanye is a Tutor at the National Social Welfare Training Institute, Dar es Salaam, Tanzania.

D.N.A. Nortey is a social worker in Ghana

Dr Vukani Nyirenda is the Secretary of the University of Zambia, Lusaka, Zambia.

Professor A.O. Sanda is the Dean of the Faculty of Administration at the University of Ife, Ile-Ife, Nigeria.

Mrs Emmy Lou Schenk is a freelance writer.

Professor Quentin F. Schenk is in the School of Social Welfare at the University of Wisconsin-Milwaukee, Milwaukee, Wisconsin, USA.

Professor Lorece P. Williams is in the Worden School of Social Services at Our Lady of the Lake University of San Antonio, San Antonio, Texas, USA.

ETHIOPIA
Quentin F. and Emmy Lou Schenk

THE WELFARE SYSTEM ENVIRONMENT

Ideological Environment

Feudalism and Modernisation. Ethiopia has only recently begun to emerge from a system in which the welfare of the populace depended entirely on the beneficence of the rulers of the local areas, whether they be the old nobility, the church leaders, the patriarchs of the villages, or the Emperor himself. While other areas of Africa were being wrenched into the modern era by the invasion of European colonists, Ethiopia managed to ward off European colonisation and thus maintained its age old isolation from the world along with its nearly feudal system of government.
   At the beginning of Second World War, things began to change. In 1935, the Italians invaded. They defeated Haile Sellassie, and proceeded to occupy the country from 1936 until their defeat in 1941. There was armed resistance to Italian domination throughout their stay, and this resulted in the execution of most of Ethiopia's educated elites. However, it may also be said that the Italians made many improvements in the country's infrastructure (including the building of roads and bridges and introduction of the telephone system). Thus when Emperor Haile Sellassie regained his position, a return to the pre-War status quo was impossible. The traditional geographical isolation of Ethiopia had broken down, and the introduction of the ideology of modernisation from the West was underway.
   In some ways, Haile Sellassie welcomed the idea of modernisation. He had spent the War years in England and was impressed with the need to change Ethiopian society. However, his efforts in

Ethiopia

this direction were constantly stymied by the Coptic Church, by those elites who had managed to survive the Italian occupation and who, in general, saw little or no reason for change, and, perhaps most of all, by his own vacillating efforts. Throughout his reign, Haile Sellassie was unable to resolve the conflict between his heartfelt desire to transform Ethiopia into a modern state and his equally heartfelt desire to maintain total domination of the country. These two aims were, of course, completely contradictory.

From the present perspective, it is easy to criticise Haile Sallassie particularly in regard to welfare. Sometimes, to those who viewed his regime, it seemed that his idea of a welfare programme consisted of little more than throwing bread to crowds of grovelling peasants from the windows of his Rolls Royce. Even so, it should be remembered that he did initiate many changes in the country, and that his vacillation was by no means irrational, for the changes he inaugurated eventually resulted in his overthrow.

Haile Sellassie outlawed slavery, brought in experts to unify and nationalise the legal code, introduced the concept of universal suffrage, and promulgated a constitution which allowed for a representational form of government. He brought women into the government in high ranking positions. He encouraged the development of hospitals and clinics, community development programmes, and the first tentative beginnings of welfare programmes for the handicapped, the aged, the lepers and the homeless children.

One of his major efforts was to initiate a system of universal public education from the elementary levels through the university. At its best, however, the school enrollment rate during Haile Sellassie's reign was minimal. In the larger cities, 52 per cent of the boys and 16 per cent of the girls were in school. The rural rate was 9.5 per cent of the boys, and a dismal 0.5 per cent of the girls (Lefort 1983, p.291). (There has been some improvement in these figures since the revolution. In 1977-8, the Ministry of Education estimated that 28.8 per cent of all primary school aged students were in school (see Bailey 1980, p.92).)

Under Haile Sellassie's auspices, potential leaders were sent abroad for graduate education, and came back to Ethiopia with Western concepts and techniques, which they wanted to apply to Ethiopia. Some of these included that modernisaton should improve the lot of not merely the rich elites, but also of the country's poorest citizens. From the standpoint of Ethiopia's traditional elites, this concept was heretical if not actually traitorous.

Haile Sellassie also sought aid and manpower from foreign nations who were interested in trying to move Ethiopia into the modern era. Because of the strategic location of Ethiopia in the Middle East, the struggles of the great powers to implant their own versions of modernisation were often occasioned more by the powers' felt need to maintain a presence in the area than they were for humanitarian reasons.

The United States was the first great power to achieve major influence in Ethiopia, so the initial development of the modern infrastructure followed the American pattern. This included the system of education from the elementary level to the university, the organisation of the central government, agricultural development, the location of American companies in Ethiopia to exploit its resources, and the beginnings of the welfare system. In fact, of all the countries in Africa, Ethiopia has the most distinctly American flavour in its efforts toward modernisation. This is especially true in higher education, where the plans emerge for strategies for modernisation.

In 1974, the monarchy was replaced with a military government which stated its commitment to develop a modern free nation with social services available to all the people (Lefort 1983, p.284). This might have been a major step in the effort to eliminate the old feudal patterns and establish modern ones. However, the new government was modelled along the socialistic lines of the Eastern Bloc, and this alignment soon resulted in the drying up of most of the sources of financial aid from the Western Bloc.

Ethiopia has obtained significant amounts of military assistance from its new allies, but the Eastern Bloc has not substantially increased its support of welfare much over its pre-revolutionary commitment. Furthermore, the combination of the continuing war with Somalia, the seemingly endless civil war between Ethiopia and Eritrea, and the government's day-to-day struggle to maintain its own power, has frustrated most efforts toward the formation of a modern welfare state. Little

Ethiopia

progress has been made in recent years to expand those types of welfare services which are a vital element in the creation of a modern society.

The Influence of the Church. Though tradition states that the Coptic Church was introduced into the country during the time of the Apostles, it is more likely that it did not become the state religion until the conversion of King Azana in the fourth century (Pankhurst 1961, p.33). Whichever is true, the Coptic Church in Ethiopia is certainly one of the oldest forms of Christianity. Begun before the Council of Nicea, and buffered from other forms of Christianity both by its location on an impenetrable plateau, and by the Moslem held territories which border it to the north, the Coptic Church has had, until recently, neither reason nor opportunity to update its theology or social philosophy. The Coptic Church taught, and, in spite of the present Marxist Government, probably still teaches, that poverty and pain are gifts of God to be endured, not eliminated, for the more one suffers in this life, the more blessed he or she will be in the hereafter. Thus, as far as the Coptic Church is concerned, welfare programmes are at best unnecessary and at worst heretical in that they might thwart the will of God.

Although Christianity has always been a minority religion, the Coptic Church has been powerful in shaping social policy. Since the Abuna, the chief patriach of the Church, retained the power to crown the Emperor, the Church was always closely aligned with the monarch. It has remained throughout Ethiopian history the religion of the ruling Ethiopian classes. Because its tenets have never been watered down by even the vaguest tinge of humanism, the Church has consistently impeded progress toward establishment of modern welfare programmes. Although its power has eroded in recent years, particularly since the downfall of Haile Sellassie, its teachings still form a powerful ethic shaping Ethiopian attitudes toward poverty, suffering, famine and starvation.

Church Missions. Even though Ethiopia is nominally a Christian nation, its indigenous church is concentrated primarily in the highlands, the provinces of Shoa, Gojjam and Tigre. The majority of Ethiopians are either Moslem or pagan.

Ethiopia

The Western churches, both Catholic and Protestant, have long felt that the Coptic religion was so divorced from their own theology that it was barely Christian. The felt necessity to eliminate pagan practices and to modernise Coptic theology has, for many centuries, resulted in a sporadic Christian missionary presence in Ethiopia.

For instance, Portuguese Jesuits achieved much prominence in the country during the sixteenth century. They managed to convert the King Za Dengel to Catholicism, but the attempt to promote the new faith among Za Dengel's subjects resulted in civil strife. Za Dengel was soon overthrown and the Jesuits were promptly expelled from the country along with the many reforms which they had attempted to inaugurate. (Levine 1965, pp.20-21).

Changes began when Haile Sellassie consolidated his rule in the late 1930s. Even though he was an ardent follower of the Coptic faith (his name, which he took at the time of his coronation, means 'power of the trinity'), Haile Sellassie took help where he could get it; the foreign church missions were the first to offer. From the 1930s on they have been an important source of welfare services in Ethiopia. The missions are international in scope, and include a variety of sects from Anglican and Roman Catholic, through the spectrum of Presbyterian, Methodist, and Mennonite, to Seventh Day Adventists and Jehovah's Witnesses.

Haile Sellassie saw the church missions as both an agent for good, and as a way to help him solve one of his biggest problems, that of maintaining political stability in the countryside. Mindful of the fate suffered by Za Dengel, however, he carefully limited the evangelisation to the Moslem and pagan areas of the country. The missions were never allowed to seek converts in the Coptic areas; however, if they agreed not to evangelise they were sometimes allowed to provide services (and thus to make quiet witness to their faith) in these areas. As a result, the mission stations, isolated and small as they were, provided most of the welfare services that were available outside of the two cities of Addis Ababa and Asmara.

The mission stations included a wide range of services, such as health care, maternal care and education, general education and agricultural education. They always distributed food and thus

Ethiopia

became an important vehicle for the funnelling of food to the starving peasants during the accelerated rate of famine and starvation that has occurred during the past 15 to 20 years.

It was the missionaries who ultimately made the media aware of the massive starvation that was developing in Ethiopia. Since they had been for many years actually living out in the countryside, they had begun to perceive what was developing as early as the late 1960s. However, they were unable to speak freely about what was happening, for they knew if they publicised conditions which the central government preferred to ignore they would be ejected from the country and their stations closed

The Hyphenated Ethiopian. The 'Hyphenated Ethiopian' is a term used by educated Ethiopians to describe themselves in relation to the past and the future. Raised in a basically feudal system, they have been educated to be modern industrial technocrats. Forcibly uprooted from past ideologies, they find it difficult to anchor themselves in a modern present. Therefore, they feel 'hyphenated', or between two worlds.

Their own ambivalence, they say, slows their ability to create the structures and services necessary to ensure modernisation. This hyphenation alienates them from the traditional culture, yet makes them fearful to stride forcefully into the future. The events of the past two decades have served to bolster that ambivalence, rather than to eliminate it (Schenk & Sellassie 1977).

Socio-Economic Environment

Poverty and Famine. Ethiopia is considered the poorest country in the world. Its Gross National Product (GNP) per capita in 1983 was US$120 (World Bank 1985). Its birth rate and mortality rate are among the highest in the world, but the former is falling while the latter is rising (World Bank 1985).

For the past two decades at least 200,000 people per year died of starvation, and the recent worsening of the famine pushed that figure over a million in 1985. In fact, of a population of some 41 million, one-fifth faces starvation (Shepherd 1975, p.88; Wolf & Brown 1985, pp.104-7). Although the birth rate has been falling in recent

Ethiopia

years the population is expected to reach 64 million by the year 2000 (World Bank 1985). With only about 10 per cent of government expenditure (latest available figures are for the early 1970s) being directed to housing, social welfare and health, the outlook for decreasing the rate of absolute poverty and starvation looks bleak (World Bank 1985).

Resource Depletion and Economic Development. The drought and famine which have swept East Africa destroyed Ethiopia's physical ability to sustain itself. Cyclical drought, overgrazing, erosion, malnutrition, disease, poor agricultural productivity dictate that Ethiopia will be dependent upon foreign resources and goodwill for at least the rest of the century (see Table 1). Even recently, as much as 50 per cent of the highlands were covered with trees - today they are barren. If overpopulation, overgrazing, deforestation, and erosion are not halted, Ethiopia will never again be able to feed its own population, a population which is presently malnourished at best and starving at worst (Shepherd 1975, pp.69-71).

Economic development is hampered by the lack of adequate transport and communications, trained manpower and by dislocation caused by political change. Development aid in the early 1980s, on a per capita basis, was the lowest for any of the UN-designated Least Developed Countries.

Historical Origins

The development of modern welfare programmes, as we know them in the industrialised countries, has yet to take place in Ethiopia. Those programmes which do exist are embryonic in nature, and render services primarily in the two largest cities of Addis Ababa and Asmara.

Even though a few rudimentary programmes were inaugurated before the Second World War, under the auspices of the missionary presence in Ethiopia, it can safely be said that the history of welfare in Ethiopia begins after the war was over. Since the early 1950s, however, there have been international efforts to establish permanent sectarian and non-sectarian welfare organisations throughout the nation. Even so, the advent of the civil war, which found the two cities on opposite sides of the conflict, weakened efforts to establish urban welfare programmes. With the

Ethiopia

onset of famine and starvation, there has been a steady increase in the presence of international agencies providing emergency relief on a temporary basis, but these make little effort toward the strengthening of the permanent structure of welfare programmes throughout the nation.

TABLE 1 : ETHIOPIAN SOCIO-ECONOMIC DATA

POPULATION (millions) (mid 1983)	40.9
GDP (US$) (1982)	4,270 million
DISTRIBUTION OF GDP (%) (1982)	
. Agriculture	48
. Industry	16
. Manufacturing	11
. Services	36
GDP GROWTH (1973-82) (% pa)	2.3
AGRICULTURAL OUTPUT GROWTH (1973-82) (% pa)	1.2
GNP PER CAPITA (US$) (1983)	120
AVERAGE ANNUAL RATE OF INFLATION (1973-82)	4.4
EXTERNAL PUBLIC DEBT	
. US$ (1983)	1,223
. % of GNP (1983)	25.9
AVERAGE ANNUAL GROWTH OF POPULATION (1973-83) (%)	2.7
CRUDE BIRTH RATE (per thousand people) (1983)	41
CRUDE DEATH RATE (per thousand people) (1983)	20
PERCENTAGE OF POPULATION OF WORKING AGE (15-64 yrs) (1983)	52
PERCENTAGE OF WORKFORCE IN AGRICULTURE (1981)	80
URBAN POPULATION AS PERCENTAGE OF TOTAL POPULATION (1983)	15
LIFE EXPECTANCY (1965)	
Male (years)	43
Female (years)	47
INFANT MORTALITY RATE (aged under 1) (1965)	166
DAILY CALORIE SUPPLY PER CAPITA AS PERCENTAGE OF REQUIREMENTS (1982)	93

SOURCE: World Bank 1985.

Ethiopia

International Relief Efforts : Non-Governmental.
A number of organisations with international programmes had an ongoing presence in Ethiopia even before famine and starvation became an epidemic. These include: The Ford Foundation, CARE, and OXFAM. More recently, with the increasing concern over the ongoing famine and starvation, organisations like the USA for Africa Foundation have been set up to raise funds and channel resources to Ethiopia and the surrounding affected areas.

The Ford Foundation concentrated on the strengthening of educational and governmental services. It gave a number of large grants to the national university, for medical, business, social science and outreach educational services. It also furnished consultants to various governmental agencies, including those ministries responsible for the development of welfare programmes.

Ethiopia was one of the first countries in which CARE established a presence after it was founded. It has channelled substantial relief supplies over the years, for it early recognised that Ethiopia was one of the areas with serious potential for starvation and famine. In 1985, CARE expanded its efforts to include long term development projects to increase the capability of the farmers in crop production.

Likewise, OXFAM, the British relief organisation, has long had a presence in Ethiopia, beginning shortly after the Second World War. It not only sent relief supplies to Ethiopia, but also sent volunteers who were dispersed throughout the nation as their numbers permitted. Like the missionaries, OXFAM volunteers have also long been predicting the advent of serious, ongoing famine in the rural areas, especially in the north. However, until recently, their warnings were largely ignored.

In the mid 1980s, the media discovered the famine in Ethiopia. Suddenly pictures of starving children began to appear during the dinner hour on the television screens of more fortunate nations. For the first time people outside of East Africa really saw what famine means in terms of human suffering. A great outcry of horror arose. Something had to be done! Nobody argued with that. On the other hand, because of the Marxist leanings of the Ethiopian government, the Western Bloc, in particular the United States, was

Ethiopia

somewhat less than enthusiastic about pouring money into Ethiopia.

A private initiative was needed, and musicians in the United States and Great Britain took the leadership. Performers in both countries recorded songs, all proceeds going toward organisations for relief. These efforts, variously called Band Aid, Live Aid, and USA for Africa, have resulted in the shipment of millions of dollars of food and other supplies to Ethiopia.

At the same time, partially because of the celebrities' interest in the situation and resultant publicity, pressure grew on the governments to send food and medical supplies. Missionary groups like World Vision also increased their relief efforts.

At present the famine has abated slightly. Conditions in the countryside are by no means good, but they are better than they were. The pictures of starving children have once again disappeared from the television screens. The media have gone on to newer and more picturesque crises.

Since the outpouring of aid was the result of the development of a media crisis, one cannot help but wonder what will happen now that the 'crisis' has been declared to be over. Celebrities like Harry Belafonte and Quincy Jones have spoken of the need for a continuing effort to make improvements in the lot of the Ethiopian people, most specifically to improve agricultural methods. It is to be hoped that they will continue to back up their words with action.

International Relief Efforts : Governmental. Many nations have furnished services to Ethiopia over the years since the Second World War. These include the United States, Sweden, India, Yugoslavia, Germany, England, Israel, Romania, Russia and China. The United Nations has also been active in the country.

The United Nations furnished consultants especially to assist in the preparation of social workers to establish and field the emerging social services. UN personnel served in the University, in the various governmental ministries, and some were even out in the provinces training personnel in such activities as community development, recreation centres, and the like. UNESCO, UNICEF and the FAO have also provided services and consultants.

Ethiopia

The United States sent Peace Corps volunteers, who served throughout the nation. Peace Corps volunteers assisted in the development of primary services such as provision of water supplies, elementary health practices, education, road construction, and farming practices. The United States also provided support for the education of social service personnel through grants to the University, as well as through scholarships to send individuals to United States universities to prepare them for service back in their own land (Schenk 1969a, pp.1-7).

Sweden did pioneering work in basic education in the rural areas of Ethiopia. Swedish volunteers built schools, and developed a far reaching literacy programme. It concentrated its efforts in the development of a programme of universal elementary education for the country, working at all levels of government from the national Ministry of Education to the specific school programme in the local community.

India's presence was small, but it offered scholarships to college graduates to study social work in its institutions of higher learning. India also had a small famine relief programme which it operated in a province outside Addis Ababa.

Yugoslavia co-operated with the national ministries to prepare the plans for development, commonly known as the five-year plan. An important part of the plan was the projections for social programmes, and the allocation of resources necessary to implement these plans. Most of these plans existed on paper only, for neither the manpower, the commitment, nor the financial resources materialised to put the plans into operation.

Yugoslavia also furnished considerable manpower, equipment and educational resources to expand the medical services in Ethiopia.

Germany had a small programme of agricultural education and famine relief in Ethiopia. England and Russia assisted in the strengthening of secondary education, as well as in some famine relief efforts. Other countries furnishing some assistance in the welfare area include Israel, Romania and China, who assisted in strengthening health services, as well as some famine relief.

Political Environment

Socialist Ethiopia has been ruled since November 1974 by a Provisional Military Administrative

Ethiopia

Council (PMAC) chaired by the Head of State. A General Congress (with 80 members) decides policy, which are executed by a Standing Committee of eight elected from the Central Committee of the Congress.

The PMAC appoints a largely civilian Council of Ministers, which it tightly controls.

Local government is carried out by Kebelles (or urban dwellers' associations) and peasant associations, of which there are some 1,200 of the former and 30,000 of the latter.

THE WELFARE SYSTEM AN OVERVIEW

Welfare Administration

Central Government: The Ministry of National Community Development. This state agency is responsible for programmes in social welfare and labour and has the following objectives:

- to develop and carry out (and with cooperation with other ministries and public authorities, and other public and private organisations and institutions) programmes of rehabilitation and assistance for the poor, the physically and socially handicapped, victims of natural and other disasters, and other persons who, without their own fault, are unable to care for themselves;

- to develop and carry out programmes for the reforming and rehabilitation of delinquent minors, including the establishment and operation of curative educational institutions for such persons;

- to encourage the development of programmes intended to provide recreation and other facilities to the youth of the nation; and

- to develop and carry out, in cooperation with other authorities concerned, programmes to facilitate the securing of employment by persons seeking the same, the protection of labourers from accidents and disease, the improvement of working conditions, and the regulation and supervision of child and female labour.

Ethiopia

Social Welfare Organisation. The following non-governmental organisations provide services mainly in the Addis Ababa area:

- Ethiopian Child and Family Welfare Association
- Ethiopian Cooperative Union for the Blind
- Ethiopian Council of Social Welfare
- Ethiopian Women's Welfare Association
- Ethiopian Red Cross Society
- Fund for the Disabled Association of Ethiopia
- Young Men's Christian Association (YMCA)
- Young Women's Christian Association (YWCA).

Missions. The following missions provide welfare programmes in Ethiopia:

- Baptist General Conference Mission
- Ethiopian Orthodox Mission
- Ethiopian Union Mission of Seventh Day Adventists
- Lazarist Mission
- St Mary's Charity Mission
- Swedish Evangelical Mission
- Presbyterian Mission of Ethiopia.

Financing Social Welfare

Social Security. The workmen's compensation scheme operating in Ethiopia is financed by participating employers who carry the entire cost through the direct provision of benefits.

Personal Social Services. The government's current expenditure on social welfare is not known but in the early 1970s it was some four per cent. The principal source of funding for voluntary agencies and missions is international charity.

THE AGED

Because of the high birth rate and relatively low life expectancy the aged do not constitute a significant welfare target group. As in many Third World countries the aged are considered in Ethiopia to be primarily a family responsibility.

Social Security
The only social security programmes aimed at the aged in Ethiopia are occupational retirement

Ethiopia

benefits for public employees, including employees of nationalised industries.

Personal Social Services
There are virtually no personal social services aimed at the aged in Ethiopia. The Ministry of Labour and Social Affairs operates development centres in a number of districts, which provide a variety of outreach services to, amongst others, the elderly.

Evaluation
The welfare of the aged in Ethiopia is considered to be primarily a family responsibility. Only those in selected employment receive any social security protection and the provision of personal social services to this group is severely limited.

CHILDREN AND YOUTHS

Because of Ethiopia's high birth rate its population structure is heavily biased in favour of the young. Indeed the government places a great deal of emphasis on child welfare, especially with respect to children who have lost their parents in the wars that have occurred in recent years.

Personal Social Services
A number of social welfare organisations provide assistance to children and youths.

Institutional Care. The Ethiopian Child and Family Welfare Association provides food, shelter, clothing and rehabilitative training to destitute children and youths in hostels and training centres. The Ethiopian Orthodox Mission operates orphanages and youth centres. St Mary's Charity Mission operates a boarding school for orphans and otherwise destitute children located in Addis Adaba.

Some 10 homes and hospitals exist in Addis Ababa to provide services for handicapped, neglected, abandoned or delinquent children.

The Swedish Mission operates a home for children of lepers in the Wollega region.

Rehabilitation of Delinquent Minors. The Ministry of National Community Development operates programmes designed to reform and rehabilitate delinquent minors. This includes the

Ethiopia

establishment and operation of curative education institutions for such people.

Youth Facilities and Services. The YMCA and YWCA both seek to develop a balanced adulthood through the promotion of social, recreational, educational and spiritual activities amongst young men and women of all races and regions. Unlike many social welfare agencies both organisations have branches outside Addis Ababa (for example in Asmara, Bahr Dar, Ambo, Adwa and Sebata).

Social Security
Ethiopia provides no social security benefits to or in respect of children or youths.

Evaluation
Although Ethiopia has a young age structure and a growing population under age 15, the range of welfare services available to this group is extremely limited. Institutional care is available to a limited degree in Addis Ababa but is virtually absent throughout the rest of Ethiopia.

THE HANDICAPPED

The number of handicapped or disabled people in Ethiopia is not known, although it is likely to be in the order of 4 - 6 million people.

Personal Social Services
The Ministry for National Community Development and a variety of voluntary welfare agencies provide a limited range of programmes aimed at the handicapped.

The Blind. The Ethiopian Cooperative Union for the Blind seeks to improve the living conditions of the blind by establishing training schools, which give vocational education, and by helping the blind find employment.

Centres for Disabled. The Ethiopian Orthodox Mission operates a number of centres for the disabled.

Vocational Rehabilitation. The Fund for the Disabled Association of Ethiopia provides rehabilitation and training programmes for the disabled, largely in Addis Ababa. The Baptist

Ethiopia

General Conference Mission operates a leprosarium for the care, teaching and rehabilitation of leprosy patients in the Shoa region.

The Intellectually Handicapped. The mental hospital in Addis Ketema, a district of Addis Ababa, has approximately 450 beds. It is not only the only mental hospital in Addis Ababa, a city of over one million people, it is also the only mental hospital in the entire country.

Social Security
The workmen's compensation programme established in 1960 provides permanent disability benefits to all covered employed persons who suffer a work injury. Employers must provide support to workers, and their families, if they suffer a fifty per cent or more disability as a result of work injury. The enabling legislation specified neither the amount of benefit provided in such cases nor any time limits on the provision of such benefits.
   The employer is also expected to cover the cost of necessary medical care, hospitalisation, pharmaceuticals and related expenditures.

Evaluation
The handicapped and disabled in Ethiopia probably number 4-6 million. Those living within Addis Ababa have access to limited services, which are not available to those living in other parts of Ethiopia.
   Those disabled as a result of work injuries are given some social security protection under the workmen's compensation programme. Uniquely, employers are required to provide such workers with unspecified support for an unspecified period of time.

NEEDY FAMILIES

The juxtaposition of poverty and famine placed the Ethiopian family unit in severe risk. International relief aid from government and non-government sources has been provided to Ethiopian families, but misery and suffering continue to prevail.

Personal Social Services
A number of government and non-government programmes operate in Ethiopia to provide support

Ethiopia

to needy families, particularly the victims of natural and other disasters. Unfortunately the sheer magnitude of the poverty and famine that prevails in Ethiopia makes these programmes most ineffectual.

The Ethiopian Women's Welfare Association seeks to relieve the distress of the destitute and the widowed by fostering improvements in child care and social welfare services, by establishing centres for home economics, education, clinics and community centres, which become the focus of cooperation of people in various districts and provinces, thus creating other programmes of relevance to needy women and families.

The Ethiopian Red Cross Society aims to prevent and alleviate suffering with complete impartiality, without discrimination as to race, nationality, class, religion or political opinions.

The Baptist General Conference Mission supports the hospital and dresser school for assistance to indigent patients.

St Mary's Charity Mission operates home services for the poor, free meals for the poor and a food distribution centre in Addis Ababa.

The Presbyterian Mission of Ethiopia operates medical, agricultural, educational and literacy programmes in the western regions of Ethiopia.

Community Centres. A number of community centres operate in Addis Ababa to organise local community groups or 'iders' as they are called in Amharic. This effort has been greatly expanded since the 1974 revolution. The centres aim to work towards elimination of common problems, render family welfare and women welfare services, render adult education services, provide recreational and leisure time activities, improve sanitation practices, and provide basic amenities within the community serviced by the 'ider'.

District Development Centres. The Ministry of Community Development operates district development centres in a number of regions. These provide a community-focused base for local self-help activities.

Social Security

Funeral Grants. Under the workmen's compensation programme survivors of workers who die as a result

Ethiopia

of work injury receive a lump-sum grant covering the reasonable cost of funeral expenses.

Maternity Leave. The 1975 labour decree requires employers to provide 45 days of maternity leave after confinement.

Evaluation
The plight of families in Ethiopia is staggering. A combination of famine and poverty make the problems confronting government and non-government agencies concerned with family welfare immense. The government's focus has been on the creation of community centres in Addis Ababa and district development centres in other parts of Ethiopia. These have become a focus for community-based self-help programmes.

THE SICK AND INJURED

The scope of modern health services in Ethiopia has been greatly expanded since 1960, but they still reach only a small part of the population. In 1978 Ethiopia only had 530 doctors, 87 hospitals with a total of 8,874 beds, and about 1,350 clinics and health centres. With foreign assistance, however, health centres and clinics are steadily expanding into the rural areas, but in times of famine Ethiopian health services are totally inadequate. In 1977 free medical care for the needy was introduced.
In Addis Ababa there are some 30 clinics, health centres and hospitals, which exist to provide a wide range of services to the mentally ill, mothers and children, veterans, lepers and so forth. Even though Addis Ababa has the best health care in Ethiopia the facilities are woefully inadequate for the task at hand.

Social Security
The 1975 labour decree requires employers to provide full pay during the first month of sick leave and half pay during the second and third months, provided the employee has worked continuously for 45 days.

Evaluation
The Ethiopian health care system is very undeveloped and totally incapable of coping with the health needs of the Ethiopian population. In the late 1970s there were over 69,000 people per

Ethiopia

physician, only marginally below the 70,000 per physician recorded in the mid 1960s. This constitutes about 12 times the average for low income countries (World Bank 1985).

THE UNEMPLOYED

The concept of unemployment is virtually meaningless in Ethiopia where the juxtaposition of resource depletion over population has created a great deal of surplus labour. With 80 per cent of the workforce engaged in agriculture, it is inevitable there is a high level of disguised unemployment in that sector. Those in employment in the formal sector in the urban centres have access to no social security protection.

Young people seeking their first jobs have limited access to vocational training centres operated by social welfare agencies largely in Addis Ababa.

The Department of Labour within the Ministry of National Community Development has developed job-search programmes to assist the unemployed gain work.

ASSESSMENT OF THE ETHIOPIAN WELFARE SYSTEM

Ethiopia is one of the poorest countries in the world. Its human problems far outstrip its capacity to cope with them. In fact, it is unable to provide the resources necessary to sustain life of many of its citizens, leave alone to provide welfare programmes which might eventually raise the overall standards of living. Ethiopia must rely upon foreign resources, which have also proved inadequate to alleviate the famine and starvation.

These circumstances, plus the fact that organised welfare programmes are a recent development in Ethiopia and are still viewed with a certain amount of suspicion by the peasants, mean that welfare programmes have little impact outside of the city of Addis Ababa. The civil war has decimated what services previously existed in the other large city, Asmara. Even though the present government has increased its efforts to expand welfare programmes and services, that which they are able to provide is but a mere drop in the bucket in relation to the need which exists.

Foreign assistance has helped, but often help has been short term in nature, provided only to

Ethiopia

deal with the immediate crisis brought to world attention by the media. Unfortunately, this kind of response seldom makes it possible to cope with the long term aspects of the massive human problems which Ethiopia faces (Schenk 1969a; 1969b; 1969c).

If Ethiopia is to free itself of dependence on foreign resources, it is imperative that some method be developed to slow population growth, regenerate depleted resources, merge the ideology of modernisation into the existing culture, and provide for the cooperation between the Ethiopian government and foreign powers to accomplish these ends.

REFERENCES AND FURTHER READING

Abatena, H. (1970), A Report on the Study of Children and Youth of the Shanty Towns and Slums of Addis Ababa, Kampala: UNICEF, 4.

Bailey, G. (1980), An Analysis of the Ethiopian Revolution, Athens, Ohio: Center for International Studies, Ohio University.

Ginsberg, E. & Smith, H. (1967), Manpower Strategies for Developing Countries. Lessons for Ethiopia, New York: Columbia University Press.

Lefort, R. (1983), Ethiopia: An Heretical Revolution?, London: Zed Press.

Levine, D. (1965), Wax and Gold, Chicago: University of Chicago Press.

Pankhurst, R. (1961), An Introduction to the Economic History of Ethiopia, Addis Ababa: Lalibela House.

Schenk, Q. (1969a), Final Report, Committee for the Study of the College on Social Sciences and Development Administration, Addis Ababa: Haile Sellassie I University Press.

_____ (1969b), Some Observations on International Voluntary Services. Addis Ababa: Haile Sellassie I University Press.

Ethiopia

_____ (1969c), 'The Welfare Function in Ethiopia - Development of Policy, Plans, Programs'. Proceedings, Seminar on Welfare Services in Ethiopia, Addis Ababa: Haile Sellassie I University Press.

_____ (1972), The Ethiopian University Service of Haile Sellassie I University, An Experiment in the Merger of Higher Education and National Youth Services, Addis Ababa: Haile Sellassie I University Press.

_____ (1977), 'Alienation of Youth as an Unintended Consequence of Military Assistance in Africa'. Journal of Sociology and Social Welfare, 4 (3&4), 534-43.

_____ and Sellassie, S. (1977), Western Education and Social Change in Ethiopia, (mimeo).

School of Social Work (1966), Directory of Social Welfare Organisations and Social Services in Ethiopia, Addis Ababa: Haile Sellassie I University Press.

Schwab, P. (1985), Ethiopia, London: Francis Printer

Shepherd, J. (1975), The Politics of Starvation, New York: The Carnegie Endowment for International Peace.

Wolf, E. & Brown, L. (1985), 'Seeds of Hope in a Dying Land', Audubon, 87 (2), pp.104-7.

World Bank (1985), World Development Report 1985, New York: Oxford University Press.

GHANA
Yvonne Asamoah and D.N.A. Nortey

THE WELFARE SYSTEM ENVIRONMENT

Ideological Environment
Ghana is a country with abundant human and natural resources. The challenge is to find the means to harness these so that all citizens can benefit positively from the fruits of their labour.
Values concerning social justice, individual freedom and the worth and integrity of the individual have been expressed since independence. However, specific political ideologies and prevailing economic circumstances dictated the extent to and manner in which these values were translated into policy. The ideologies also provided the framework within which each government made decisions about retaining, discarding, modifying or expanding welfare services.
The current government recognises the crucial link between socio-economic development and the development of human resources. The provision of services and programmes that will maximise popular participation, minimise economic and social dependency and create equal opportunity is viewed as a legitimate state responsibility.

The Colonial Legacy. Ghana emerged at independence with the rudiments of a formal welfare system that reflected both the ideology and basic structures of the system in the United Kingdom. Early programmes were based on what was perceived as the prevailing social problems and potential local revenues. Fortunately, the colonial administration recognised the need to develop rural areas as well as attend to urban social problems. Ghana's current social welfare organisation reflects this dual perspective (see HMSO 1960, Drake 1962).

The Family System and the Spirit of Voluntaryism and Mutual Aid.
Ghana has a strong tradition of close family ties, community support and a spirit of voluntaryism. The family and community play essential roles in meeting the basic security needs of the people and continue to supplement the formal welfare system. Although forces of change have to some extent altered traditional family patterns, the system of mutual rights and obligations still remains strong.

Tribal societies and voluntary groups that serve as mutual aid providers and/or offer assistance in times of crises help meet the security needs of individuals in both urban and rural areas. Members' contributions are sometimes used for development projects in their home towns.

Indigenous institutions have helped to minimise the negative consequences of rapid social change. In the absence of a programme of public assistance and with the limited coverage under the formal social security system, these institutions will continue to be a focal point in meeting human needs.

Self Reliance.
In the early days of independence, Kwame Nkrumah stressed the theme of self reliance (Nkrumah 1961, p.169) and this has continued to be reflected in the policies of succeeding governments. The present goal is to attain the highest level of social and economic development possible through the efficient utilisation of resources and individual effort. To achieve this, individuals are encouraged to initiate activities in their homes, communities, schools, and workplaces that will foster productivity, eliminate waste, and improve living standards.

National Integration and Cultural Plurality.
Efforts to develop a sense of national identity and a nation free of all forms of ethnic, tribal and religious discrimination began at independence (Nkrumah 1961, p.167). Preserving cultural uniqueness while at the same time encouraging national loyalty remains a challenge.

Ghana continues to preserve its rich cultural heritage through support of traditional institutions. Traditional leaders are involved in both the development and implementation of welfare and related policies at all levels.

Ghana

Fundamental Human Rights. Fundamental rights of individuals were enshrined in the three constitutions of Ghana (1960, 1969, 1979). Specific guarantees included the individual's freedom of movement, assembly, expression and conscience; equal treatment under the law; protection from undue harassment, forced labour, servitude, inhumane treatment, deprivation of life and property and physical and moral hazards; entitlement to a fair hearing in criminal cases; and equal access to all special care and facilities provided by or at the expense of the State (Ghana 1969a, 1979a; Rubin 1961 pp.247-66).

Issues concerning personal guarantees and human rights have been addressed by every regime since independence. Current provisions relating to human rights and racial discrimination are embodied in Provisional National Defence Council's Law Number 42 (Ghana 1982b 1(b),(d)).

Focus on Social Security. The priority of the colonial administration was to provide services to alleviate suffering and promote social education. Social insurance schemes were seen as impractical in the absence of a sufficiently large wage-earning population and adequate funds to administer the scheme (HMSO 1960). It became increasingly clear after independence, however, that provisions under existing labour legislation were insufficient and that more comprehensive measures were required.

Historical Origins
The British colonial administration supported the development of welfare services in the colonies through a series of Colonial Development and Welfare Acts in the 1940s (see Hill 1962; Wicker 1958). Since then, there has been a progressive expansion of personal social services and social legislation.

Social Security Legislation. The Social Security Act of 1965 (Act 279) provided the initial framework for the formal social security system. The Act was superseded by the Social Security Decree of 1972 (Ghana 1972b) which set up the Social Security and National Insurance Trust (SSNIT). Legislative Instrument 777 (Ghana 1972c) provided for the payment of unemployment benefits and Legislative Instrument 818 (Ghana 1973) established rules and regulations for employers,

Ghana

accounting and financial procedures, and administration.

Other legislation, passed in the 1960s, includes the Workman's Compensation Act, 1963 (Act 174), Industrial Relations Act, 1965 (Act 299), and the Labour Decree, 1967 (NLCD 157). Rules relating to collective bargaining, arbitration, trade union organisation, discrimination in employment, compensation for work-related injuries, employment contracts, public employment centres, employment of minors, and general working conditions are specified.

The Formal Welfare Structure and Personal Social Services. In 1943 a Secretary of Social Services was appointed to undertake coordination of social welfare in the Gold Coast. A Department of Social Welfare and Housing, established in 1946, initially assumed major responsibility for the personal social services. At the same time, provision was made for a school to train local staff. During the 1950s, several structural and administrative changes were made reflecting attempts to consolidate services under appropriate ministerial jurisdiction. A Rehabilitation Section was added in 1961 (see Ghana 1953, 1957).

The Community Development service began following an experiment in mass education and literacy in 1948. The success of the first experiment prompted the government in 1949 to declare that the acceleration of economic and social development through the people's own energies was the settled policy of the government (DuSautoy 1957, p.113). The first mass education programme, launched in 1952, served as a model for future programmes. Emphasis was placed on literacy, stimulation of local leadership, voluntary effort, and self help. Increased agricultural production, promotion of public health, improvement in housing, development of small-scale industries, communal project work, and special campaigns were emphasised as the programme continued to expand (Ghana 1953; DuSautoy 1957, pp.124-5).

The Formal Structure and Child Welfare Services. Provision for the proper guardianship and care of orphans was embodied in the Gold Coast's juvenile delinquency legislation. A juvenile court and probation system and approved schools were introduced during the 1940s. The Department of

Ghana

Social Welfare and Community Development had statutory responsibility for juveniles below the age of 17 who had committed offences, who were seen to be in need of care and protection or who were exposed to physical and/or moral danger (see Ghana 1953; HMSO 1960). Alternatives to institutional care included foster care and placement with 'fit persons'.

Minimum standards for day nurseries were established by the Department. Through grants-in-aid to voluntary agencies, services were provided to assist mothers in the care of their families and to care for children with special needs. The Ministry of Education initiated a school welfare service in the 1970s designed to serve school children, parents and staff in the pre-university education system (Ghana 1977a, p.345).

Personal Social Services for Adults and Families. Services for adults under the formal system have consisted primarily of counselling, marital reconciliation, aftercare and probation, hospital welfare and care for the destitute in special homes. Care of the non-destitute aged was the responsibility of their families (Ghana 1957).

Community or neighbourhood centres made their appearance during the War years, and the Department of Social Welfare and Community Development provided some assistance. Many of the centres were run by private organisations and were used as meeting places for women's groups and for leisure activities.

Voluntary Organisations and Personal Social Services. Voluntary organisations, some of which pre-date the Second World War, offered services for the youth, the blind, the crippled, lepers, women and children. Some were set up by non-Ghanaians and were affiliated with overseas bodies; others were initiated by Ghanaians and affiliated with church groups or missionary societies. Tribal organisations, which developed mainly in towns, operated as mutual aid associations and met the need for both economic security and social companionship (see Assimeng 1981, p.144; Little 1965; Peil 1977, p.288).

Youth Movements and Services. Youth movements date back to the first youth conference held in 1930 (Ghana 1976, p.11). Some of the indigenous movements eventually grew into mass movements with specific political orientations. Imported youth movements reflected the goals and philosophies of the parent organisations and offered informal education. A Youth Employment and Vocational Guidance Service for school leavers and non-residential vocational training centres for boys and girls in urban areas were set up in the 1950s (Ghana 1957, p.6).

Trade Union Movement and Personal Social Services. Trade unions started in Ghana in the early 1920s and responsibility for union activities now rests with the Trade Union Congress (TUC). The TUC provides a number of social services for its members such as clinics, vocational schools, literacy classes, consumer cooperatives and credit unions (Ghana 1977a, p.76).

Political and Socio-Economic Environments

The Political Context. Ghana has experienced several changes of government since gaining independence in 1957. The latest change took place on 31 December 1981 ushering in the Provisional National Defence Council (PNDC). Public services and programmes are carried out through Ministries headed by Secretaries appointed by the PNDC, through other government-established bodies, and through directives issued by the PNDC (see Ghana 1982a; 1982b). Administratively, Ghana is divided into 10 regions headed by Regional Secretaries appointed by the government, and each region is divided into smaller administrative districts.

The PNDC saw as its major task the establishment of social and political foundations within which the task of economic recovery could begin. Defence committees were set up in communities and work places in order to ensure 'the wider participation of the masses in the task of rehabilitating the country and democratising its institutions' (Ghana 1983, p.6).

The Economic Context. Ghana experienced severe economic hardships in the 1970s. While some hardships have been attributed to earlier ill-conceived economic and political decisions and mismanagement, many resulted from adverse developments in the international economy (see

Ghana

ACARTSOD 1983; ILO 1983; OAU 1985; UNICEF 1984; World Bank 1984).

By 1980, Ghana was in an economic crisis. The results were a decline in per capita income, inability to service external debts, severe increases in the costs of production, over-inflation of the local currency, and the inability to maintain an acceptable level of essential social and public services. There was a mass exodus of both skilled and professional and managerial level workers (see Novicki 1984a; Ghana 1983, p.24; World Bank 1984, p.1).

Efforts to abate the crisis led to the launching of the Economic Recovery Programme (ERP) in 1982. The objectives were to restore incentives for production, increase availability of and improve the distribution system for essential goods, increase availability of foreign exchange, lower the rate of inflation, rehabilitate physical infrastructures, and restructure economic institutions (see Novicki 1984b; Ghana 1983, pp.24-25; World Bank 1984).

By 1984 there appeared to be an improvement in economic performance which resulted in an estimated drop in inflation from 40 per cent in 1984 to 12 per cent in 1985. To date, however, export earnings still do not exceed import requirements, and organisation and management limitations have resulted in a slower improvement rate than originally projected. Of particular concern is the high rate of expenditure on wages, salaries, allowances, pensions in the public sector, institutional feeding, drugs, maintenance and repairs leaving little for development expenditure (Ephson 1986, pp.67-85; Ghana 1986b, pp.1-3).

Measures proposed for the period 1986-88 including continued adherence to policies outlined in the ERP, policy reforms with regard to key productive areas, wages and employment, and continued external assistance are expected to result in improvements in education, health and the social services (Ghana 1985g).

Demographic Features. The population now stands at 12,205,574, an increase of 42 per cent since 1970, with a rate of growth of 2.6 per cent. The rural population is 68.7 per cent of the total, and the urban population continues to increase – from 23.0 per cent (all regions) in 1960 to 31.3 per cent in 1984 (Ghana 1984). It is estimated that the urban population will exceed 50 per cent of the total population by the year 2000 (World Bank 1984, p.26).

Ghana has an estimated crude birth rate of 47 per thousand and an estimated crude death rate of 14.6 per thousand. The infant mortality rate is estimated at 98.3 per thousand. Life expectancy at birth is 50.3 and 53.7 years for males and females respectively (UN 1986, pp.156, 337).

If the present rate of population growth continues, it is estimated that the population will reach 24 million by the year 2000, and if the present fertility rates continue, 50 per cent of the population will eventually be below 15 years of age (World Bank 1984, p.26; UNICEF 1984, p.155). Recognition of the adverse effects continued high rates of population growth will have on economic and social development is reflected in Ghana's official population policy (Ghana 1969b).

In 1981, out of a total population of about 10 million United Nations projections estimated the working population as follows: agriculture 53 per cent; industry 20 per cent, services 20 per cent (World Bank 1985, p.214). (UNICEF (1984) places estimates for agriculture at 60 per cent and includes crops, livestock, fisheries and forestry.) During the 1970s the labour force grew by an annual average rate of 2.4 per cent, and 18 per cent of the total labour force was counted as 'unemployed' (World Bank 1984, p.26).

Ethnic and Religious Composition. By law, references to ethnicity cannot appear on any official document, hence it is difficult to obtain recent data on ethnic distribution. The only official record available on ethnic composition is a post enumeration survey taken in 1960 when the population was 6,772,815. The main language groups identified were the Akan (44 per cent of total population), Mole-Dagbani (16 per cent), Ewe (13 per cent), Ga Adangbe (eight per cent), Guan (four per cent), Gurma (four per cent), Grusi (two per cent), Yourba (two per cent) (Ghana 1960d). Ghanaian society is both matrilineal and patrilineal depending on the ethnic group. In the matrilineal system, lineage is traced through maternal descent and property is inherited through maternal relatives. The opposite prevails under patrilineal descent.

Religions include Christianity, Islam, and

Ghana

traditional religion. Many different religious sects have mushroomed in the past several years (see Assimeng 1981; Baeta 1967; Peil 1977).

THE WELFARE SYSTEM : AN OVERVIEW

The key elements in the welfare system in Ghana are (1) social security and income protection schemes, (2) labour and other legislation, (3) services sponsored and financed by government, (4) services offered by voluntary organisations.

The Structure and Administration of the Welfare System

The Provident Fund. The Social Security and National Insurance Trust (SSNIT) is the primary social security institution and is administered by a board of directors (Ghana 1972b, Parts III, IV).

The 1972 Decree applies to every employer having five or more workers and to every worker to whom the Social Security Act of 1965 applied, unless otherwise specified. It does not cover workers in agriculture or fishing and those in the informal sector such as petty traders, motor mechanics, and private artisans. Also excluded are persons with diplomatic status, employees in foreign missions, and workers whose conditions of service entitle them to non-contributory gratuity and pension such as senior members of the universities and officers in the armed forces (Ghana 1972b, Part VI).

The Social Security Bank, established as a subsidiary of SSNIT in 1977, grants loans to business enterprises for financing of productive investments in the economy. It also grants personal short and long-term loans and operates a consumer credit scheme for members of the Social Security Fund and/or customers of the Bank.

Personal Insurance. Any Ghanaian may elect to be privately insured either through the State Insurance Corporation or through private carriers. The State Insurance Corporation offers life, fire, marine accident, motor and property insurance and protection against natural disasters. Agricultural insurance is available on a limited basis only, and many problems are yet to be resolved with regard to assessment of the risks involved to enable adequate coverage at a premium farmers can afford (SIC 1979).

Ghana

Labour and Other Legislation. Various Ministries or government bodies have responsibility for administration or provision of workmen's compensation and other services under legislation designed to protect specific population groups. Ultimate jurisdiction rests with the courts.

Government-Sponsored Personal Social Services. The Department of Social Welfare has primary responsibility for administering welfare and rehabilitation services. The services are decentralised, and each region has a similar structure that includes a Regional Director and professional social work staff.

The Department of Labour is responsible for enforcement of labour legislation. It also monitors compliance with international conventions that have either been ratified or are supported by government. The Department operates public employment centres, vocational guidance and disablement resettlement services, and undertakes inspection of factories.

The Department of Community Development is responsible for improving standards of living in both urban and rural communities with emphasis on voluntary participation. Services are delivered by professional staff and trained volunteers.

School welfare services, under the Ministry of Education, are provided by a cadre of professional social workers attached to regional and/or district offices throughout the country. Currently, welfare needs of both school pupils and staff are addressed.

Ministries responsible for specific welfare services frequently draw on resources from other ministries including those of Health; Education; Agriculture; Youth, Culture and Sports; Information; and Works and Housing. Special commissions set up by the government work cooperatively with the Ministries responsible for welfare activities. Professional bodies and interprofessional organisations support and promote welfare activities through research and recommendations.

Voluntary Services. Voluntary organisations including the Christian Council of Ghana and the Planned Parenthood Association of Ghana have been instrumental in implementing Ghana's official population policy (Ghana 1969b). Service organisations such as Rotary Club, American

Ghana

Women's Association, British Women's Association, and Association of University Women, gear programmes toward individuals and communities. The following organisations direct their programmes toward specific population groups: Boy Scouts, various church-related youth organisations, YWCA, YMCA, Girl Guides Association, Ghana Society for the Blind, Society of Friends of Lepers, Child Care Society, Cripples Aid Society, Society for Friends of the Mentally Retarded, Society for the Deaf, and the Society for the Prevention of Tuberculosis. Ghana Red Cross Society and St John's Ambulance Brigade focus on citizen preparedness and emergency relief.

The Private Sector and Enterprise-Based Social Services. All employees or workers and their families in the private sector are eligible for any services offered or financed by government with the exception of those that are specific to employees in the public sector. These include persons who may or may not be covered under the social security system. Some employers in both public and private sectors provide welfare services for employees over and above those required by law. These include transportation, clinics, educational programmes for workers and their families, subsidised housing, canteens, supply of basic commodities at controlled prices, child care, recreational and credit facilities. Others encourage worker cooperative ventures such as small scale farming, the produce from which is shared. Unfortunately these services often suffer from lack of coordination and insufficient management and funds.

Financing Social Security and Personal Social Services

Social Security. The Social Security and National Insurance Trust (SSNIT) is responsible for all monies paid into the Fund. Benefits, administrative and other costs are disbursed from the Fund.

The primary source of finance for SSNIT is the contribution of members. The government does not pay any direct subsidy but supports the Fund indirectly through payment of contributions of its employees who are members of the Fund. Other sources of income include donations, legacies, revenues and rents from movable and immovable property owned by the Trust, penalties levied on defaulting employees and unclaimed amounts of contributions. SSNIT also acquires interest from government stocks and bonds, the only investment avenue open to it according to law (Ghana 1972b, Part V, VII; Ghana 1973, Part IV, 37(1)).

Deductions are made by employers from workers' salaries at source. The rates of contributions into the Fund are as follows: employer - 12.5 per cent of worker's salary per month; worker - five per cent of salary per month; self-employed - 12.5 per cent of monthly income. Deducted contributions are considered as being held in trust for the worker until such time as they are remitted to the Fund. Where any contribution is not paid within the prescribed time, a sum equal to three per cent of the unpaid amount is charged to the employer and can be recovered as a debt. No employer can reduce, directly or indirectly, the pay or emoluments of any member for reason of his liability for any contributions to the Fund. The Decree protects members' contributions from attachments, and benefits received by any member, nominee or heir are non-taxable (Ghana 1972b, Parts VII, VIII).

According to statistics available, in 1981 the number of contributors represented 63.7 per cent of the projected labour force, or 14.6 per cent of the total population. During the decade ending in 1981, the coverage increased from 27.0 per cent of the labour force to 63.7 per cent with an average crude annual growth rate of about 17.2 per cent (SSNIT 1986).

Personal Social Services. Programmes that fall under the goverment-administered social welfare services are financed through a system of subventions. Monies are made available to the Ministries after submission of their estimated requirements for operation of programmes, payment of salaries, benefits, and administrative costs. Decisions about monies to be allocated are made by the Ministry of Finance and Economic Planning. Allocations are based on available central revenues collected through personal and corporate taxation, export earnings, savings and investments.

Funds provided for community development activities are expected to be supplemented by the community's contributions in terms of materials (where possible), communal labour, special levies and voluntary contributions. This principle has prevailed since the beginning of the service and continues to exist (see DuSautoy 1958).

In addition to subventions, government departments often benefit from funds contributed for special projects from organisations such as the United Nations, individual countries, national and international foundations, or private agencies.

Voluntary associations affiliated with parent organisations outside the country may receive some funding from that source on a regular basis or in relationship to specific projects. Other revenues are collected locally through membership dues, special fund-raising activities, or donations. The Ghana National Trust Fund, established during the Nkrumah regime, operates like a communty chest for voluntary agencies affiliated with it. Fund-raising activities are conducted throughout the year and funds are disbursed to the registered beneficiaries based on the recommendations of the Board of Trustees.

THE AGED

Traditionally the family insured a person throughout life. The family is gradually shifting from being a productive unit to a consumptive unit; consequently members have to rely more on their own efforts to meet their needs.

With the increase in wage employment and increased migration, the number of persons in close proximity on whom one can depend has become smaller. In the urban setting, productive activities generally take place outside the family thereby potentially reducing the quantity of social interaction among family members. This may have adverse consequences for the aged in the household who may require more than financial assistance. Increased opportunities brought about by industrialisation and technological advancements have attracted the young and the not-so-young able bodied to the urban areas, leaving older kinsmen behind in a setting where opportunities are limited and amenities relatively scarce (see Apt 1975b; Assimeng 1981; Peil 1977).

This pattern does not suggest that extended family obligations are not adhered to. Despite the dispersion of the family over many towns and cities, contacts are still maintained and family obligations are accepted (see Assimeng 1981; Kumekpor 1975a; Oppong 1974). This is seen clearly during specific life cycle events such as birth, marriage and death when members of the extended family return home, discuss their needs, and seek assistance from others who may be economically better off.

The aged hold a very special position in the traditional family structure. Some aged persons, however, are indeed without family support and are destitute (see Apt 1975b).

Of immediate concern is the establishment of a system that will enable workers to generate enough money to provide for themselves when they are no longer able to work. If the trend toward more conjugal family patterns continues, this issue is a compelling one.

Social Security
Retirement benefits are provided for some categories of workers in wage employment.

Provident Fund Benefits. At the age of voluntary retirement (recently set at 45 years for men and women) a member of the provident fund is entitled to a superannuation benefit. Members who opt to continue working after the superannuation has been paid must continue to make contributions (together with the employer) until further voluntary retirement or until mandatory retirement age (60 years) is reached. At this time the balance of the superannuation is paid.

The superannuation benefit is a lump sum equal to total employee and employer contributions paid in plus at least three per cent compound interest. A total of 4,255 persons received this benefit in 1983 (Ghana 1972b, Part IV (40); SSNIT 1985).

Pension Scheme Benefits. A pension scheme is available for persons whose conditions of service entitled them to receive gratuity and pension prior to the introduction of the social security scheme, senior members of the universities and other establishments, and members of the armed forces. Upon retiring, the worker receives a lump sum gratuity payment plus monthly payments. The amount paid is equal to a fixed fraction of the worker's emoluments for each completed month of pensionable service. If death occurs before retirement age, nominees or their personal representative are entitled to a gratuity. In addition, widows receive a pension equal to one-quarter of the deceased's annual pension emolument. Under certain conditions, parents of the deceased are entitled to receive pensions (Ghana 1950). As of January 1986, the rate of pension is 75 per cent of the pensioner's basic monthly enrolment.

Food Allocation. Retired persons are entitled to purchase periodically a specified quantity of essential commodities at controlled prices.

Subsidised Health Care. All medical facilities under the jurisdiction of the Ministry of Health are available to the aged (Ghana 1972d). Those in hospitals for the physically and mentally ill benefit from the services provided by trained hospital welfare staff under the Ministry of Social Welfare. Some elderly patients are forced to remain in hospital longer than their illness requires because their relatives are reluctant to take them home.

Personal Social Services

Counselling and Supportive Services. Services offered by the Department of Social Welfare help put the aged in touch with resources and help them re-establish ties with kin. Emergency relief may be provided from donated sources and voluntary organisations.

Destitute Homes. The Department of Social Welfare maintains a destitutes' infirmary for destitutes who are either aliens or elderly Ghanaians who have lost touch with their families. A study of Ghanaians admitted during a ten-year period revealed the following as contributing factors to their situation: loss of children and close relatives through death; loss of contact with the extended family through migrations; inability of surviving relatives to house and care for them (Apt 1975b, p.177).

Rural Services. The aged in rural communities benefit from the various programmes run by the Department of Community Development. The focus is on improved nutrition, meal preparation, health and sanitation, and small scale farming methods. Mobilisation squads made up of unemployed or underemployed persons and volunteers assist aging farmers at fees lower than those charged by individual farm labourers.

Ghana

Voluntary Organisations. Voluntary organisations and church groups assist the aged with specialised needs (for example, the blind, crippled, lepers). Some aged join mutual aid associations. Associations for retired persons are beginning to appear.

Evaluation

When one considers the per capita income of Ghanaians - estimated at US$486.00 for 1985 (Ewusie 1986) - and the cost of living, it is clear that superannuation benefits under the provident fund scheme are inadequate. Benefits have little positive effect on the socio-economic situation of the majority of recipients. Wage earners may have obligations to members of their families who are not protected under any scheme. These obligations do not cease when a worker retires. At present the average lump sum benefit paid under social security is less than one year's salary for the majority of workers. The inadequacy of benefits discourages the dependents of a deceased person from applying for survivor's benefits. The benefits hardly compensate for the expenses incurred in trying to obtain them.

Most retirees use their benefits on non-income generating pursuits such as children's education, home repairs, daily maintenance and health. Opportunities for small scale investment are very few and the size of the benefit precludes such investment in the few areas available (see SSNIT 1980).

Retirees under pension schemes have slightly better prospects for insurance against old age because of the monthly payments they receive in addition to a lump sum. Workers not covered by provident fund or pension schemes have virtually no safety net except that provided by their families. Fortunately, however, retired workers may become involved in agricultural pursuits that can meet their subsistence needs and provide some income for the future.

The provident fund scheme has an indirect effect on the standard of living of both contributors and non-contributors. Monies accumulated in the Fund are a resource at the disposal of the government for financing general development programmes. Contributors also benefit from consumer credit facilities offered by the Social Security Bank. Through investments the Social Security Bank helps create new employment opportunities for the labour force.

The provident fund scheme is under review. Proposals include raising benefit levels; instituting a prepaid health insurance scheme into which members pay until retirement and which, after retirement, enable them to enjoy free medical treatment; providing for workers not now covered, especially farmers and fishermen; and converting the provident fund system into a pension scheme that will allow for adjustment against inflation.

General improvement in the economy will lead to an increase in the purchasing power of the aged and will enable the government to consider alternative social security arrangements. In the meantime, primary responsibility for meeting the needs of the aged will remain with their families with support from voluntary organisations and formal welfare services.

THE DISABLED AND HANDICAPPED

Prior to the introduction of formal and informal services, the disabled and handicapped were cared for by their families. In many cases, care was minimal and was sometimes harsh - stemming from concerns about stigmatisation of the entire family by the known existence of a handicapped member. Some of the disabled, ostracised by their communities, took to begging or became totally destitute (see Danquah n.d.).

Voluntary organisations and the churches pioneered services for the disabled and handicapped. In Ghana early support was provided by organisations based in the United Kingdom (HMSO 1960). They played a major role in raising public consciousness about the need for a systematic approach.

Despite cooperative efforts between voluntary agencies and the Ministries, services were fragmentary and inadequate. Many destitute and abandoned children and destitute adults rounded up under the Control of Beggars and Destitutes Ordinance were found to be physically handicapped (see Addo 1962; Gold Coast 1957).

Recognising the growing magnitude of the problem, the government appointed a committee to study the situation. The result was the John Wilson Report, which recommended the integration of the disabled and handicapped through a comprehensive programme of registration, training and rehabilitation (Addo 1962, p.96; Ghana 1960b). The emotionally disturbed and mentally ill were not as fortunate in having early champions of their cause, and services for these groups developed more slowly.

Social Security
Disability compensation for employed persons is provided under the social security regulations and through the Workmen's Compensation Act. All workers in the public service are entitled to temporary or permanent disability allowance.

Provident Fund Benefits. An invalidity benefit is paid when a member of the Social Security Fund is rendered incapable of any normal gainful employment due to a permanent physical or mental disability and has retired from employment on that basis. An application must be endorsed by the employer and a medical officer, and confirmation by a medical board is required. The benefit paid is a lump sum equal to the total employer and employee contributions plus at least 3 per cent compound interest. In 1983 a total of 98 persons received benefits under this scheme (Ghana 1972b Part IX 1(b)); SSNIT 1985).

Workmen's Compensation Benefits. The Workmen's Compensation Act of 1963 applies to workers in commerce or agricultural establishments with 10 or more workers. The employer bears the entire cost.

In cases of permanent total incapacity, the worker receives a lump sum equal to 54 months' earnings. An additional amount of one-quarter of the above is paid in cases requiring constant attendance. Rates for permanent partial disability are specified according to the degree of injury. Temporary total or temporary partial disability benefits may be paid in a lump sum or monthly and equal two-thirds of the difference between the previous monthly earnings at the time of the accident and monthly earnings the employee is earning or is capable of earning after the accident. There is a ceiling on benefits for temporary disability and a maximum duration of 24 months. The employer must bear the expenses for surgical, hospital and nursing care and the supply of drugs and prosthetic devices or appliances up to a specified amount (Ghana 1963, (4), (5), (6), (7), (8), (14), (28)).

Ghana

Personal Social Services
A wide range of personal social services is available for the physically disabled and handicapped and fewer for the mentally handicapped and mentally ill. The focus is on rehabilitation and re-integration into the society through gainful employment.

Registration. Registration of the disabled and handicapped is undertaken periodically by the Department of Social Welfare. By 1980 41,849 disabled persons were registered. Of an estimated 1980 population figure of roughly 12 million, the rate of disability, according to registration figures, was 3.49 per thousand of all ages. Of the 41,849 registered, 21,288 (50 per cent) were crippled, 6,862 (16.4 per cent) were deaf and 13,699 (32 per cent) were blind. There were 27,946 males (66.8 per cent) and 13,903 females (33.2 per cent). The registered number is an underestimate of the total disabled population and falls short of the 100,000 estimated as far back as 1960 and the 169,759 reported in the 1970 census (Ghana 1970; UNICEF 1984, pp.291-3).

Disabled children (under 15 years) in 1980 formed 26.8 per cent of the registered total of 41,849. Of these, 7,079 (63 per cent) were crippled, 2,925 (26 per cent) were deaf and 1,231 (11 per cent) were blind. The majority registered were in the 6-15 year category. The major causes of disability in the 0-40 year population group are poliomyelitis, trauma, leprosy, tuberculosis and other infections of the bone, cerebral palsy, chronic osteomyelitis; blindness due to onchocerciasis, and deafness as a result of ostitis media and birth problems. Accidents are a major cause of physical disability (UNICEF 1984, pp.294-6). Mental retardation has been attributed to chromosomal defects, birth trauma, minor brain damage, post meningitis and encephalitic brain damage, complications resulting from malaria, and negative environmental conditions such as neglect (UNICEF 1984, pp.296-7).

Rehabilitation. Rehabilitation centres have been established in each region for disabled men and women. Courses are provided in carpentry, joinery, tailoring, dressmaking, crafts, leather work, home management, food and nutrition and metal work. The rehabilitated disabled are helped to re-settle as self-employed persons or in

Ghana

wage-earning employment. A Disablement Resettlement Service assists in finding work for disabled persons. Legislative Instrument 632 (Ghana 1969c) requires employers to have a quota of their labour force employed in sedentary jobs which trained disabled persons can fill. In 1984 the number listed in the labour force was 417 (400 males and 17 females). In the same year, 25 additional disabled persons (19 males and six females) were placed in employment (Ghana 1986a). Sheltered workshops are operated for the severely handicapped, and Industrial Rehabilitation Units provide short, intensive courses in preparation for work in the industrial sector. Counselling services are rendered by professional social work staff of the Rehabilitation Division of the Department of Social Welfare.

Institutional Care. Institutional care is provided for mentally disabled and handicapped children and adults who have either been rejected by their families or who are too ill to live on their own. Severely retarded children reside in psychiatric hospitals which are under the supervision of the Ministry of Health. Mentally ill adults also receive services rendered by the Ministry of Health and may be hospitalised (voluntarily or involuntarily) or seen on an out-patient basis (Ghana 1972d).

Formal Education. The Ministry of Education is responsible for the formal education of disabled and handicapped youth. The Ministry provides special education for the deaf, blind, crippled and mentally retarded, and has begun to implement plans for integrating the disabled in schools with the non-disabled. There are courses for the training of teachers. Private schools, run by individuals, supplement the services of the Ministry of Education.

Voluntary Organisations. Voluntary organisations continue to play a major role in rehabilitation through provision of services, funds and training facilities.

Rehabilitation Aids. Special devices and equipment may be obtained through government agencies and voluntary organisations. Special limb-fitting centres and an orthopaedic centre also provide assistance.

Ghana

Evaluation
The government has assumed a major responsibility for the disabled and handicapped and has continued to expand its efforts to reach as many as possible. Negative social attitudes continue to prevail and no doubt account for the under-registration of all age groups and categories of the disabled. These attitudes also adversely affect the way disabled persons view themselves and their role in society.

Both voluntary organisations and government agencies have been hampered by lack of funds. Tools for work in the rehabilitation centres and for distribution to those who have completed training are often not available. Other problems include lack of markets for goods produced in the centres, lack of qualified teachers, lack of appropriate materials and inadequate facilities.

Benefits provided through social security arrangements are inadequate to sustain a worker during a crisis period. More attention needs to be paid to access to physical facilities in public places. Provisions in Legislative Instrument 632 must be enforced in order to expand employment opportunities. Screening for early identification of children at risk must be intensified.

With continued social education, it is possible that families will be prepared to assume more responsibility for the care of their mentally disabled kin who, with some assistance, could be re-settled in their home environments. This would enable existing resources to be used for those who do not have family supports and/or for those for whom family supports are inadequate.

NEEDY FAMILIES

Ghana has no statutory definition of a 'needy family'. In the absence of a government-sponsored social assistance programme that requires a definition of need in terms of income relative to family size and cost of living, the term 'needy' remains a relative one.

Assessment of need is fraught with difficulties. Although it can be reasonably assumed that persons in low paying jobs or persons unemployed or underemployed would face the most severe financial problems, this is not always the case. There are two factors that must be taken into account when assessing the degree of neediness. The first is the nature and extent of

Ghana

a person's extended family obligations. The second is the nature and extent of the actual or potential resources to which a person has access (for example, family members obligated to assist in times of crisis or on a regular basis, inheritable property and other direct and indirect sources of income, legal or illegal).

The economic crisis of the past few years has had the net effect of eroding real incomes and reducing the standard of living for a very large segment of the population. Data available on income levels, disease patterns, health status, environmental conditions, and mortality rates indicate that many people are unable to meet their basic need requirements in the areas of nutrition, health, education, housing and water supply (see Ofosu-Amaah 1975). The various estimates of per capita income which range from less than $400.00 to $486.00 underscore this situation (see Ewusie 1986; World Bank 1985, pp.171, 174).

There are differences between urban and rural poverty. Incomes in rural areas tend to be lower and seasonal (creating hardships during the lean season) and there are relatively fewer amenities, services and employment opportunities. Although urban dwellers may have higher incomes, these incomes have to be shared by many who have migrated and are living with them under crowded conditions. Urban dwellers do have the advantage of having more access to essential services, particularly health services.

Groups hardest hit by poverty in the rural areas include small-scale farmers and fishermen, daily and casual labourers, rural artisans, self-employed labourers on family farms, the aged, disabled, and underemployed. Those hardest hit in the urban areas include workers earning less than the minimum wage, the unemployed, manual workers, small scale self-employed, the aged, and low wage earners entirely dependent on their salaries (see UNICEF 1984, pp.90-3). The poor and needy spend nearly all their income on food leaving little for other essentials (such as housing, educational fees, clothing and transport). Low wage earners entirely dependent on their salaries often become victims of 'loan sharks' and may experience chronic indebtedness.

Social Security
Individual family members benefit under provisions in the social security and labour legislation.

Ghana

Life Insurance/Survivor's Benefits. One per cent of the employer's contributions to the SSNIT is put aside each month for life insurance benefits. Nominees of members who die before claiming any superannuation, invalidity or emigration benefits are entitled to 12 months of the current salary of the deceased member plus the survivor's benefit. However, survivors of deceased members who stopped contributing to the Fund for a period of 12 months cannot claim the life insurance benefit (Ghana 1973 Part III, 28 (1)(2)(3)).

The survivor's benefit is a lump sum equal to total employee and employer contributions paid in, plus at least three per cent compound interest. The benefit is payable to nominated relatives or, if none, to other family members as prescribed (Ghana 1972b Part IX, 40 1 (c)(2)).

Non-members of the provident fund benefit indirectly through their relationship to family members who enjoy the provident fund benefits or as a beneficiary of a deceased fund member.

Pension Scheme Benefits. Breadwinners under the pension scheme, upon retirement, receive a lump sum gratuity plus monthly payments. If the breadwinner dies before retiring, his widow receives a gratuity payment plus a pension equal to one-quarter of the deceased's annual pension emolument, and children under 21 years, up to six, are entitled to a pension.

Paid Maternity Leave. Employers are required to grant paid maternity leave of 12 weeks to female employees. Employees are also entitled to paid sick leave as specified in collective bargaining agreements. These measures help protect families from income loss of breadwinners.

Subsidised Health Care. All government sponsored health facilities are available for the needy. In cases where extreme need is evident, consultation or hospital fees may be reduced or waived.

Food Supplementation. Needy families can take advantage of food supplements dispensed by government clinics and voluntary organisations especially for pregnant women and mothers of young children.

Ghana

Tax Exemptions. Recognising that the erosion of real incomes during the past decade made it increasingly difficult for heads of families to meet their obligations, additional tax reliefs were introduced in the 1984 budget. The selective minimum exemption system takes into account family and social obligations. Exemptions for married heads of household and families with children were raised. Low income earners were given reliefs which placed them in a lower tax bracket. Adequate measures for identifying household heads with dependents have not yet evolved thus making this measure difficult to implement.

Minimum Wage. The minimum wage has been adjusted periodically in an effort to keep pace with the rising cost of living.

Personal Social Services
Support services for needy families are provided on a case-by-case basis by the Department of Social Welfare and charitable groups. Specific families may benefit from emergency financial assistance from donated sources for specific purposes. No provision exists for long term care or financial supplementation for whole families.

Services in private health care facilities may be paid for on the basis of a sliding scale for those with demonstrated need. Individual employers also offer special services (essential commodities at controlled prices, free health care, transportation to and from work, educational supplements, day care services, bonuses and leave, risk, transportation and rent allowances) which are particularly helpful to those workers whose incomes, even at minimum wage level, are inadequate.

Evaluation
Needy families benefit from welfare provisions indirectly in terms of the access of individual family members to existing facilities, services and entitlements. Unfortunately, benefits under the social security provisions are too meagre to make much of an impact.

Maintaining the strength of the family is viewed as a highly desirable welfare objective that should be achieved primarily by increasing the productive and earning capacities of individuals rather than through remedial state-sponsored services. It is envisaged that

Ghana

results of collective productive efforts will lead to improvements in the quality of services necessary to maintain acceptable levels of education and health. Because the term 'family' in Ghana encompasses a wide group of persons who may be widely dispersed and may not be synonymous with 'household', family welfare programmes must be careful to identify the most appropriate unit for intervention (see Kumekpor 1975b).

CHILDREN AND YOUTH

The health status and general welfare of many Ghanaian children are cause for concern. Infant mortality rates show marked rural/urban differences. The majority of deaths occur in children under age five. The 10-19 year age group has the lowest mortality rates. The major causes of death in infancy are low birth weight, other diseases peculiar to the newborn, infections, malnutrition and anaemia. In the post-natal period, infections are the most important cause of death. In the 1-4 year age group, three-quarters of deaths are caused by infections, and malnutrition causes more deaths in this period than at any other time (UNICEF 1984, pp.152, 173, 184-5). Many children live under conditions of general poverty with inadequate housing, clothing and supervision.

Social Security

Provident Fund Benefits. Family allowances are not provided. Children and youths may receive payments on the death of a qualified member of the Social Security Fund if nominated as beneficiaries (Ghana 1972b Part IX 40(c)).

Pension Scheme Benefits. Under pension schemes for workers who are not members of the Social Security Fund, children, up to a maximum of six, are entitled to pension until they reach the age of 21 if the worker dies.

Workmen's Compensation Benefits. Minor children of a worker who dies as a result of work injury may be compensated with a share of a sum of 42 months' earnings for total dependents or as determined by the Court for partial dependents (Ghana 1963 3(a), (b), (c)).

Ghana

Maternity Leave. The Labour Decree requires employers in any industrial, commercial, or agricultural establishment to pay a female worker's earnings during 12 weeks of maternity leave - six weeks before and six weeks after confinement. A female worker nursing a child is permitted to take half an hour twice a day during working hours for this purpose (Ghana 1965, 42(a), (b), (g), (h)) or may be allowed to leave work early.

Child Labour. Children under 15 are barred from employment unless the employment is with the child's own family and involves light work of an agricultural or domestic nature only. Young persons (over 15 but under 18 years) may not be given night duty in industrial establishments and cannot be employed in any mine or underground work, except in cases of emergency (Ghana 1967 Part V, (42), (44), (45)). The engagement of children in work in the informal sector, with or without pay, is very common.

Subsidised Health Care. Maternal and child health services were introduced in the 1920s and have continually expanded under the auspices of the Ministry of Health. Services include immunisation, growth monitoring, maternal care, family planning, health education, school health services, pre-school feeding programmes and treatment.

Medical care is available in government hospitals, clinics and health posts. A small fee may be required in cases of hospitalisation or for drugs. Severe illnesses (for example, malnutrition) or illnesses that are a threat to public health may be treated free of charge. Government medical services are often supplemented by aid from international organisations.

Personal Social Services
The network of personal social services for children and youth reflects a high level of cooperation among government agencies and national voluntary and international organisations.

Food Subsidies. Nursing mothers and mothers with young children may receive free food supplements at the pre-natal and post-natal clinics upon presentation of a registration card. Voluntary organisations provide food subsidies in rural and urban areas.

Foster Care. Children who cannot be cared for by their parents or children whose parents believe they may receive better educational or occupational advantages elsewhere are often fostered with kin or non-kin (see Goody 1975, p.149). Kin fostering serves as a welfare system within the family structure. Statutory provisions provide for children under 17 years who are in need of care and protection, are exposed to physical and/or moral danger, or who are placed on probation to be fostered by fit persons with supplementation by the State (Ghana 1960a).

Institutional Care. Increased mobility and economic circumstances have necessitated alternatives to traditional fostering and arrangements for children without immediate or long term support. Children's homes, run by the Department of Social Welfare, are available. These homes cater for children from birth through adolescence who are orphaned or abandoned and for children of lepers, destitutes and mentally or physically ill parents (see Apt 1975a). Voluntary organisations often provide gifts of food and other items to supplement the Department's resources.

The state assumes care-taking responsibility only when it is affirmed that no relatives or interested parties are willing to accept this responsibility. A child's stay in the home is viewed as temporary and efforts are made to find permanent homes through adoption if necessary. Homes are also run by private organisations or churches. For example, the SOS Children's Village, affiliated with an international body, caters for abandoned children. Their policy, which has caused some controversy, does not permit adoption or return to relatives.

Adoption. Children may be adopted provided potential parents meet certain specifications. The Department of Social Welfare represents the interests of juveniles with respect to adoption orders. Rules governing adoptions are specified in law (Ghana 1962). In the past there have been more applications for adoption than children available (Ghana 1972a, p.11).

Day Care Centres. Day care centres are run by individuals, voluntary organisations, local authorities, and some employers, but are under the supervision of the Department of Social Welfare (Ghana 1978). The expectation is that the centres will be operated on a non-profit basis, but this is not always the case and conditions in some centres are very inadequate.

Support for Children Affected by Marriage Breakdown or Neglect. Parents or any person legally liable to maintain a child are expected to supply the child with the necessities of health, life and reasonable education. An application for maintenance may be brought by anyone who has custody of the child, or children themselves, against any legally responsible adult who neglects to discharge this obligation. An order may also be brought against a father for payment of maintenance during pregnancy and after delivery and for the expenses incidental to the birth or death of a child. Family Tribunals established in each magisterial district make judgements regarding complaints of paternity, custody and maintenance. No distinction is made between children born in or out of wedlock. The maintenance order expires at age 18 years or before if the child is engaged in gainful employment, or may be extended to 21 years for children in school (Ghana 1977b Parts I-III).

Anomalies in previous intestate succession legislation often created hardships for children when one or both parents died (see Bentsi-Enchill 1975). PNDC L 111 (Ghana 1985e; Ghana 1985f) ensures that children and spouses have access to the disposable property of those legally responsible for them and who die intestate or who have disposable property not covered in a will. This law is supplemented by three others relating to registration of customary marriage and divorce, administration of estates, and accountability of head of family designed to bring uniformity to marriage and inheritance patterns previously governed largely by customary law.

Non-Subsidised Health Services. Private health facilities are available and fees are charged. They are run by private doctors, midwives or non-profit making religious missions. Delivery by midwives or traditional birth attendants is common. Unfortunately, trained neonatal help is often non-existent under these circumstances, resulting in untreated birth injuries and neonatal infections. At times babies are delivered by

Ghana

untrained persons or by women themselves without assistance, placing the newborns at risk (see Neequaye & Nkrumah 1981; UNICEF 1984, p.186).

Out-of-School Care. Programmes for children and youths during holidays or after school are offered by voluntary organisations and through various Ministries. They include recreational activities, informal education and voluntary work camps.

Vocational Guidance and Youth Employment Centres. The Department of Labour provides vocational guidance and counselling services in conjunction with the Ministry of Education to children in second cycle schools and runs youth employment centres for unemployed youth.

Statutory Services for Juveniles. Children under 17 years who have committed offences or are believed to be inadequately cared for may be brought before juvenile court. Juvenile court case dispositions include caution and discharge, fines, probation, supervision and 'fit-person' orders, recognisance and repatriation. Probation officers or aftercare agents from the Department of Social Welfare supervise the youngsters while on probation or after discharge from probation homes or industrial schools (Ghana 1960a).

Evaluation
Despite the array of health and welfare services for children and youth, they are inadequate and suffer from lack of funds. Distribution is unequal and many rural children and youth are not adequately covered. Access to health services, which are concentrated in urban areas, may account for the lower infant mortality rates in urban areas.
    Poor health among children is often associated with lack of education of parents, poor environmental conditions and inadequate preventive measures. Educational programmes must aim to reach all communities and to educate children to be conscious of good health practices.
    Legislation relating to maintenance and inheritance procedures will be useful only if people are educated to become aware of their rights and to seek redress under the law. With an increasingly younger population (under age 15), more effort will be needed to keep the youths in school or place them in employment. Child labour

Ghana

laws are not enforced and many children engage in heavy domestic or agricultural work which not only affects their health but also prevents them from attending school regularly. Improvement in the overall economic situation will be necessary before families who now live in poverty and may be forced to abandon or neglect their children or use them to supplement their own labour will be able to provide adequate care. Until then, state-supported services, however inadequate, will continue to bear a large part of the responsibility.

THE SICK AND INJURED

Sick and injured persons in Ghana have access to a variety of services and health facilities, public and private. Benefits to offset income loss for sick and injured workers are available under the social security system and labour legislation.

Social Security

Provident Fund Benefits. Members of the Social Security Fund may apply for a sickness benefit after a five-day waiting period if they are medically certified as ill, have made at least 24 monthly contributions to the Fund, and have received no other emoluments from the employer during the illness (Ghana 1972b Part IX, 1(e)). A flat rate calculated on the basis of the worker's current daily income is paid for a maximum period of 26 weeks. No sickness benefits were paid in 1982 or 1983 (latest available figures (Ghana 1973 Part III, 24(4); SSNIT 1985)).

Paid Sick Leave. Employers usually pay full wages to their employees during the first three months of sick leave and pay up to 50 per cent of wages for up to an additional three months under collective bargaining agreements.

Work Injury Benefits. Employees in industry and commerce and in agricultural establishments of 10 or more workers are entitled to compensation for work-related injuries under the Workmen's Compensation Act. Workers earning above a certain amount are excluded. The injury must incapacitate the worker for at least five days and not have occurred as a result of the worker's misconduct. If the injury results in death, total dependents receive a sum equal to 42 months' earnings and partial dependents receive benefits as determined by the court but which cannot exceed the amount payable to total dependents. Any compensation paid before the death occurred is deducted. If the workman leaves no dependents, medical attendance and burial expenses, not exceeding a specified amount, may be paid (Ghana 1963 (2), (3)).

Workers are compensated for permanent total incapacity by a lump sum payment equal to 54 months' earnings (with a specified minimum) and a constant attendance supplement, where required, of 25 per cent of total disability benefits. Smaller lump sum payments are given in cases of permanent partial disability based on a fixed schedule (Ghana 1963 (6)).

Injuries resulting in a temporary incapacity, total or partial, entitle workers to periodical payments equal to two-thirds the difference between their average monthly salary at the time of the accident and the monthly salary they are currently earning or capable of earning, or a lump sum based on probable duration and degree of incapacity. A ceiling is placed on benefits and the duration of periodical payments is two years with the possibility of a six-month extension in special cases. Benefits cannot exceed those that would have been payable if permanent total incapacity had resulted.

Compensation is also payable for diseases if contracted while employed within a period of 12 months previous to the date of incapacity. Employers bear the costs in all categories of work injury for medical, surgical, hospital and nursing care; drugs and appliances up to a specified amount (Ghana 1963 (7), (28), (31)).

Health Care. Sick and injured workers have access to all health facilities (hospitals, clinics and health posts) available under the Ministry of Health. No special facilities are provided for workers, but individual establishments (public and private) may operate health programmes primarily for workers (and their families) in that establishment. A small fee may be required in government facilities for consultation, hospital admission or drugs.

Private medical practitioners and church missions offer a range of services and facilities for anyone able to pay the required fees. Traditional medical practitioners such as herbalists, bone setters, and diviners serve a wide clientele who either patronise them almost exclusively or in addition to medical personnel (see Appiah-Kubi 1978, 1981; Twumasi 1975).

Personal Social Services

Support services for the sick and injured are provided by families, the community, voluntary and other organisations or enterprises, and private hospitals and special clinics.

Hospital Welfare Services. Sick persons also benefit from services provided by trained social workers attached to government hospitals through the hospital welfare service under the Ministry of Social Welfare. The social workers assist patients in negotiating for their compensation entitlements, counsel them with regard to their adjustment to the illness, refer them to appropriate agencies for rehabilitation services, and work with their families to obtain the necessary financial or social support. Children who may lack adequate supervision during the illness of a guardian or parent(s) may be temporarily cared for in children's homes.

Mobile clinics provided by the Ministry of Health and other government (and voluntary) agencies deliver medical and dental services to rural areas. Special programmes under the Ministry of Health are directed toward the control of communicable diseases and include screening, immunisations and environmental services.

Family Support. Families support their sick relatives through the provision of meals for those who are hospitalised. This has become increasingly necessary over the past few years due to the limited resources in government-sponsored medical facilities. Families may also be required to pool their resources to cover hospitalisation payments, drugs and travel expenses and to make arrangements for child care in the case of incapacitated parents or guardians.

Community and Voluntary Support. Community support includes the rehabilitation and building of clinics in rural areas through self-help and voluntary contributions, proceeds from community farms, technical assistance from the Department of Community Development, and, in some cases, financial assistance from voluntary organisations.

Ghana

Voluntary organisations assist the sick by visiting hospitals and donating food and drugs. Public-spirited individuals, voluntary organisations, and private and state enterprises have recently initiated campaigns to raise funds for the rehabilitation of hospitals and clinics.

Some private organisations and state enterprises have 'adopted' specific hospital wards and embark on campaigns that include periodic cleaning, supply of drugs, sheets, and blankets to patients, and fund raising.

Evaluation

Despite current and past efforts and the consistently high allocations for health expenditures in national budgets, the health situation may still be viewed as very serious. Overall health coverage is low (about 30 per cent of the population has access to formal health care) and health care favours the urban areas. The continued decline in the value of the cedi has greatly reduced resource allocation to health in real terms and prevented the purchase of essential drugs and supplies (Ghana 1985g, p.33; UNICEF 1984, pp.317, 367-9).

Efforts to improve the situation include support for the primary health care programme (proposed in 1977), the basic structures for which are already in place. The overall philosophy of this programme is to reduce the rate of mortality and morbidity due to conditions which can be prevented, easily treated or controlled. All resources are being mobilised including traditional medical practitioners (see Bannerman, Burton & Wen-Chien 1983; Ghana 1979b).

In addition, methods for manufacturing drugs from local leaves and plants are being explored. Other measures include continued efforts to recover costs for services through the levy of fees, introduction of a health insurance scheme as an alternative means of financing health services, contributions from communities, and international assistance (see Ghana 1985g, p.24).

Benefits under social security arrangements are inadequate. Sickness benefits are minimal and the ceilings placed on work injury benefits are unrealistic in terms of present conditions.

Ghana

THE UNEMPLOYED

Protection of unemployed persons within the context of the prevailing socio-economic circumstances of African countries is a formidable task. The nature of the labour force, the extent and nature of and means for verifying unemployment, labour migration patterns, absence of well organised labour exchanges, and costs of administration create complications (see Mouton 1975). As the Ghanaian labour force continues to expand, both by natural increase and through migration, however, it is clear that some measures have to be provided to protect the unemployed.

Ghana has experienced a rapid increase in urban population. The percentage of urban population has increased from 23.0 per cent in 1960 to 31.3 per cent in 1984 (Ghana 1984, p.51). Between 1970 and 1980, the Greater Accra region had the second highest growth rate (3.3 per cent) of all regions (Ghana 1984, p.54).

It is estimated that 32 per cent of the population moved out of the rural areas during 1960-70. The urban areas attract not only the skilled and semi-skilled, but also those engaged in service-oriented jobs and petty trading. A large number of migrants obtained employment in the low productivity formal sector. However, given the slow rate of growth in the economy during the same period, many migrants could not be absorbed in either the formal or informal sectors (see World Bank 1984), thus swelling the ranks of the unemployed.

Urban drift places a severe strain on the infrastructures of the urban environment. Greater Accra has a density of 438 persons per square kilometre compared to 51 persons per square kilometre nationwide (Ghana 1984, p.51). Attempts to stem the tide by appealing to the migrants to return to the rural areas have not been effective (see Assimeng 1981, p.141). Underemployed and unemployed migrants move in with kinsmen, some of whom are aready leading a marginal existence.

A serious threat to the already acute unemployment problem and economic situation was posed in 1983 when 1.2 million Ghanaians deported from Nigeria returned home. Unfortunately, most of those caught in the first wave of deportations were the unskilled and semi-skilled. The rapid integration of the unskilled returnees into the society in non-urban areas through the efforts of

Ghana

a National Coordinating Committee helped to mitigate the urban unemployment problem (Ghana 1983, pp.12-13).

An additional threat was posed when victims of drought in the Sahelian region in 1985 began to pour into Ghana. These persons were also relocated as swiftly as possible into rural ventures in order to prevent strains in the urban areas.

Using the ILO definition of labour force, the working population (15-60 years) in 1970 was 3,331,618. In the same year, 198,571 persons were listed as unemployed. In 1983, 24,157 persons were registered with the Labour Department - 17,738 males and 6,419 females (all regions). The greatest number (47.9 per cent) was recorded in the Greater Accra District (Ghana 1985c).

Social Security

Ghana is one of a few African countries providing benefits for the unemployed (see RESDC 1983). Services are provided by the Department of Labour, which deals with registration, and unemployment benefits are paid under regulations stipulated in the Social Security (Unemployment Benefit) Regulations of 1972.

Provident Fund Benefits. An unemployment benefit is paid to a member of the Fund who has become unemployed and has made at least 36 monthly contributions. Two of these contributions had to be made during the last four months before becoming unemployed (Ghana 1972c).

A person who qualifies must register at the Labour Office. Unemployed persons do not qualify if they are no longer members of the Fund, left the job voluntarily, were laid off as a result of a labour dispute, are currently working part-time and earning more than 50 per cent of their previous basic pay, have refused to accept employment offered by the Labour Office or received redundancy or severance pay (or both) from the last employer or are receiving any other benefit from the Social Security Fund (Ghana 1972c, (1), (2))).

Beneficiaries receive 50 per cent of the average monthly salary during the 12 months immediately preceding unemployment. At the end of the third month of unemployment, they are entitled to a second benefit equivalent to 20 per cent of the previous monthly salary or C15.00 whichever is higher. A member can qualify for an unemployment benefit again only after 24 months of contributions (Ghana 1972c (3), (4)). Since this scheme began to operate in 1972, only three claimants have been paid (SSNIT 1985).

Benefits for Immigrants Terminating Employment.
Non-African aliens may obtain employment only in areas not restricted to Ghanaians. If employed, immigrants are entitled to all benefits to which a Ghanaian is entitled, including unemployment benefits, plus an emigration benefit if emigrating permanently.

The emigration benefit is paid only if members have not received superannuation or invalidity benefits. The benefit is a lump sum consisting of the member's and employer's contribution less the employer's payment to life insurance and social security, plus at least three per cent compound interest on the balance (Ghana 1972b Part IX). In 1983, 76 persons received this benefit (SSNIT 1985).

Personal Social Services
The unemployed have access to the full range of personal social services offered by government agencies and to those organised by voluntary organisations.

Public Employment Centres. These centres are operated by the Department of Labour throughout the regions. In addition, specialised Youth Employment Centres provide vocational guidance and counselling, both to unemployed youth and to those still in school. Job seekers in rural areas are often advised to obtain employment in those areas, and job seekers in the cities are encouraged to return to the rural areas in order to reduce urban unemployment (Ghana 1977a). Unemployment information centres are currently being expanded.

National Mobilisation Programme. The National Mobilisation Programme was designed to mobilise all available resources toward improving the economy through coordinated human effort. Its primary concern has been to initiate rapid development of the rural areas by improving infrastructures and to increase agricultural output. Many unemployed persons, including Ghanaian returnees and foreign immigrant drought victims, have been mobilised to assist in these efforts. Under the country's National Service Scheme, all persons, employed or unemployed, can be called upon to render service to the nation for two years in any capacity (Ghana 1983, pp.9-11).

Vocational Training Centres. The Department of Social Welfare operates vocational training centres that are open to Middle School leavers, dropouts from secondary and technical schools, and probationers. The centres offer training in agriculture, tailoring, woodwork, and light industrial skills. Vocational training centres are also run by the Ministry of Education.

Training Institutes. The Department of Community Development offers courses in wage-earning vocations. Technical vocational training is also offered to rural youth and adults.

Services Offered by Voluntary Organisations. Voluntary organisations run vocational training courses. Some unemployed persons, particularly the youth, may obtain sponsorship for these courses either from the organisation itself or from their kinsmen. Some courses are residential.

Evaluation

Unemployment has plagued the country since economic problems began to surface in the 1960s and is likely to remain until the economy becomes sufficiently vibrant to provide employment opportunities for the working-age population. High fertility rates compound the problem.

Government emphasis on encouraging the unemployed, underemployed and those in low productive occupations to engage in more productive pursuits (such as agriculture), and expanding the mining and industrial sectors will help. Decentralising public services, improving living conditions in rural areas and opening up job opportunities there may also help slow down urban drift.

The unemployment benefit scheme exists mainly on paper. The benefits are so meagre and the procedure so cumbersome that potential beneficiaries do not bother to apply.

Unemployment is viewed by some as a problem for which government should take full responsibility by providing benefits through tax revenues and not through employee/employer contributions. The money thus saved could be used for health insurance or housing schemes. The unemployment benefit is currently under review.

ASSESSMENT OF THE GHANAIAN WELFARE SYSTEM

The essential ingredients of the formal welfare system in Ghana have been in place for 40 years. New programmes and policies have evolved as new needs emerged. Political upheavals and economic problems have taken their toll.

Despite the negative features of the colonial past, the welfare institutions as a whole were based on humanistic values that transcend geographical boundaries and political ideologies. Ghana has built upon these institutions and continues to mould them into a set of structures that will preserve its traditional institutions while addressing the needs of citizens in a modern state. Priority will have to be given not only to those measures and policies that will stimulate economic development, but also to the social factors that might hinder the achievement of this goal, and to the short and long term consequences of economic development.

The set of compulsory measures designed to protect individuals and families from loss of income needs urgent attention. Ghana is one of the few African countries continuing to operate a provident fund social security scheme, and all evidence points to the need to revise this. One of its major shortcomings is that benefits are unrelated to the cost of living and lump sum benefits become exhausted within a very short time. The inadequacy is reflected in the relatively small numbers who collect benefits other than superannuation. Converting this system into a pensions scheme based on the idea of risk-pooling would better serve the income security needs of the insured.

Proposals to increase sick benefits to 50 per cent of monthly income for at least 24 months and instituting a pre-paid health scheme are steps in the right direction. These are positive measures that would protect income and help offset high expenditures required to man the health system.

On paper, the social security scheme appears to be comprehensive. However, in relationship to the total work force, only a small percentage are in wage employment and hence covered. The most important categories of persons not covered are farmers, fishermen and domestic service workers, and workers in small establishments whose employers do not elect to join the scheme.

Other measures requiring consideration are:

- Methods to ensure that employers do not default on their contributions need to be implemented.
- Administrative procedures need to be tightened and decentralised in order to reduce processing time. Efficiencies in birth, death and marriage registration, postal services, medical services and record-keeping will help to minimise delays in processing claims.
- Social education is required to encourage employers in small establishments to insure their workers and to encourage fishermen, farmers and others to take advantage of schemes developed for their beneift.
- Social security institutions must endeavour to maintain a high level of public trust. Any actions that might be construed as more beneficial to the institution's employees and/or wasteful of members' contributions will undermine this trust.
- Consideration should be given to increasing the interest paid on contributions through investment in non-government ventures. This is a proposal that is not without some risk.
- Existing labour legislation relating to work injury needs updating. The ceilings based on benefits and employer liability for medical expenses are unrealistic. A nation-wide scheme aimed at spreading employer liability over a wider pool might be considered.
- The unemployment scheme is not working and registration is ineffective. Decentralising unemployment centres will help as will new measures for identifying the unemployed. Unemployed persons who have not worked have no protection.

Social security schemes can never hope to carry the full burden of achieving social equality or raising the general standard of living. At present the system favours urban moderate and high income earners. Given the continued economic constraints the country is likely to experience, expectations about the impact of social security measures must remain modest. The scheme has so far had moderate success with redistribution of income among the wage or former wage earning categories (horizontal redistribution). Redistribution between groups (vertical redistribution) will not occur until presently unprotected groups are covered and basic structural and taxation reforms take place. These reforms will redistribute income and generate revenues needed for financing basic preventive and remedial programmes in health, education and welfare.

The personal social services aimed at those who are without income due to unemployment, lack of education or skills, those who have no means of earning an income and those who have the potential to earn will need strengthening. The dividing line between family and state responsibility will need continuous assessment. Individual employers must be encouraged to provide personal social services to alleviate the burden on government. It is doubtful that Ghana can support at this time family allowance schemes or social assistance programmes.

The challenge for the future is to develop a basic welfare system that will meet the needs of rural and urban dwellers in the formal and informal sectors. The system must guard against the perpetuation of dependency, give everyone equal access to the means for meeting basic needs, and preserve those traditional institutions that provide a natural cushion against destitution and hardship It is significant to note that Ghana's evolving welfare system takes cognisance of the vital interrelationship and delicate balance between the traditional and modern elements in the social structure.

REFERENCES AND FURTHER READING

Addo, J.S. (1962), 'Services for the Physically Handicapped', in Drake, St Clair & Omari, T.P. (eds), Social Work in West Africa, Accra: Department of Social Welfare and Community Development.

African Centre for Applied Research and Training in Social Development (ACARTSOD) (1983), Social Implications of the Lagos Plan of Action, Tripoli: African Centre for Applied Research and Training in Social Development.

Ghana

Appiah-Kubi, K. (1978), 'The Challenge of Traditional African Medical Practices to the Western Medical Systems and the Challenge of Western Medical Systems to Traditional African Medical Practice', an unpublished paper presented at the Annual Meeting of the African Studies Association, Baltimore, MD (Mimeo).

―――― (1981), Man Cures, God Heals. Religion and Medical Practice Among the Akans of Ghana, Totowa, New Jersey: Allanheld, Osmun.

Apt, N.A. (1975a), 'Children Without Parents: A Ghanaian Case Study', in Legon Family Research Papers, 4: Aspects of Family Welfare and Planning, Accra: Institute of African Studies, 80-4.

―――― (1975b), 'Urbanization and the Aged', in Legon Family Research Papers, 3: Changing Family Studies, Accra: Institute of African Studies, 177-83.

Assimeng, N. (1981), Social Structure of Ghana: A Study of Persistence and Change, Tema: Ghana Publishing Corporation.

Baeta, C.G. (1967), 'Aspects of Religion', in Birmingham, W., Neustadt, I. & Omaboe E.N. (eds), A Study of Contemporary Africa. Some Aspects of Social Structure, Vol. 2, London: George Allen & Unwin.

Bannerman, R.H., Burton, J. & Wen-Chien, C. (eds) (1983), Traditional Medicine and Health Care Coverage, Geneva: World Health Organisation.

Bentsi-Enchill (1975), 'Some Implications of Our Laws of Marriage and Succession', in Legon Family Research Papers, 3: Changing Family Studies, Accra: Institute of African Studies, 125-8.

Danquah, S.A. (n.d.), A Preliminary Survey of Beliefs About Severely and Moderately Retarded Children in Ghana, unpublished manuscript from a study conducted in Ghana in 1975.

Ghana

Drake, St Clair (1962), 'Social Problems in West Africa', in Drake St Clair & Omari, P.T. (eds), Social Work in West Africa, Accra: Ghana Publishing Corporation.

DuSautoy, P. (1957), 'The Gold Coast Community Development Service', in 1957 Yearbook on Education Around the World Education Bulletin, 1956, 9, 111-27.

_____ (1958), Community Development in Ghana, London: Oxford University Press.

Ephson, Ben (1986), 'Ghana: Three Years of Economic Recovery', West Africa, 13th January, 67-85.

Ewusie, Kwodwo (1986), Economic Trends in Ghana, 1980-84, Accra: Institute of Social and Economic Research.

Ghana (1950), Pensions Ordinance No. 42 of 1950, Accra.

_____ (1953), Welfare and Mass Education in the Gold Coast, 1946-1951, Report of the Department of Social Welfare and Community Development 1946-1951, Accra: Government Printing Deparment.

_____ (1957), Annual Report of the Department of Social Welfare and Community Development for the Year 1956, Accra: Government Printing Department.

_____ (1960a), Criminal Procedure Code, Act 30, Accra.

_____ (1960b), John Wilson Report, Accra.

_____ (1960c), 1960 Population Census of Ghana, Accra: Central Bureau of Statistics.

_____ (1960d), 1960 Population Census of Ghana Post Enumeration Survey, Accra: Central Bureau of Statistics.

_____ (1962), Adoption Act, 1962, Act 104, Accra.

_____ (1963), Workmen's Compensation Act, 1963, Act 174, Accra.

Ghana

_____ (1965), *Industrial Relations Act, 1965*, Act 299, Accra.

_____ (1967), *Labour Decree 1967*, NLCD 157, Accra.

_____ (1969a), *Constitution of the Republic of Ghana, 1969*, Accra.

_____ (1969b), *Population Planning for National Progress and Prosperity, Ghana Population Policy 1969*, Accra: Ghana Publishing Corporation.

_____ (1969c), *Quota of Posts for Disabled Persons*, LI 632, Accra.

_____ (1970), *1970 Population Census of Ghana*, Accra: Central Bureau of Statistics.

_____ (1972a), *Annual Report of the Department of Social Welfare and Community Development for the year 1972*, Accra.

_____ (1972b), *Social Security Decree 1972*, NRCD 127, Accra.

_____ (1972c), *Social Security (Unemployment Benefit) Regulations, 1972*, LI 777, Accra.

_____ (1972d), *Mental Health Decree, 1972*, NRCD 30, Accra.

_____ (1973), *Social Security Regulations, 1973*, LI 818, Accra.

_____ (1976), *Ghana '76. An Official Handbook*, Accra: Information Services Department.

_____ (1977a), *Ghana 1977. An Official Handbook*, Accra: Information Services Department.

_____ (1977b), *Maintenance of Children Decree, 1977*, SMCD 133, Accra.

_____ (1978), *Day Care Centres Decree, 1978*, SMCD 144, Accra.

_____ (1979a), *Constitution of the Republic of Ghana*, Accra: Ghana Publishing Corporation.

Ghana

_____ National Health Planning Unit (1979b), *An Approach to Planning the Delivery of Health Care Services*, Manual No. 1, Accra: Ministry of Health.

_____ (1982a), *Policy Guidelines of the Provisional National Defence Council*, Accra.

_____ (1982b), *Provisional National Defence Council (Establishment) Proclamation (Supplementary and Consequential Provisions) Law, 1982*, PNDCL 42.

_____ (1983), *Ghana, Two Years of Transformation: 1982-1983*, Accra: Information Services Department.

_____ (1984), *1984 Population Census of Ghana (Preliminary Report)*, Accra: Central Bureau of Statistics.

_____ (1985a), *Administration of Estates (Amendment) Law, 1985*, PNDCL 113, Accra.

_____ (1985b), *Customary Marriage and Divorce (Registration) Law*, PNDCL 112, Accra.

_____ Department of Labour (1985c), data supplied by Department of Labour on registered unemployed as of April 1983, Accra.

_____ (1985d), *Head of Family (Accountability) Law, 1985*, PNDCL 114, Accra.

_____ (1985e), *Intestate Succession Law, 1985*, Memorandum, Accra.

_____ (1985f), *Intestate Succession Law, 1985*, PNDCL 111, Accra.

_____ (1985g), *Progress of the Economic Recovery Programme 1984-1986 and Policy Framework 1986-1988*, Report Prepared by the Government of Ghana for the Third Meeting of the Consultative Group for Ghana, Paris, November 1985, Accra.

_____ Department of Labour (1986a), data supplied by Employment Information Branch.

Ghana

_____ (1986b), Press Statement by Dr Kwesi Botchway, PNDC Secretary for Finance and Economic Planning, 2nd January, Ghana Press Release No. 1/86.

Gold Coast (1957), *Control of Beggars and Destitutes Ordinance, 1957*, No. 36 of 1957, Accra.

Goody, Esther (1975), 'Delegation of Parental Roles in West Africa and the West Indies', in Goody, J. (ed.), *Changing Social Structure in Ghana: Essays in the Comparative Sociology of a New State and an Old Tradition*, London: International African Institute.

Her Majesty's Stationery Office (HMSO) (1960), *Social Welfare in the UK Dependencies*, London: Her Majesty's Stationery Office.

Hill, A.C. (1962), 'The Administrative Structure for Social Welfare in West Africa', in Drake, St Clair & Omari, T.P. (eds), *Social Work in West Africa*, Accra: Ghana Publishing Corporation.

International Labour Organisation (ILO) (1983), *Social Aspects of Development in Africa: The Role of Social Institutions*, Report I (Part I), Geneva: International Labour Office.

Kumekpor, T.K. (1975a), 'Marriage and the Family in a Changing Society', in *Legon Family Research Papers, 3: Changing Family Studies*, Accra: Institute of African Studies, 72-96.

_____ (1975b), 'A Reconsideration of the "Family" as a Unit of Welfare Planning', in *Legon Family Research Papers, 4: Aspects of Family Welfare and Planning*, Accra: Institute of African Studies, 13-26.

Little, K. (1965), *West African Urbanisation: A Study of Voluntary Agencies in Social Change*, Cambridge: Cambridge University Press.

Mouton, Pierre (1975), *Social Security in Africa*, Geneva: International Labour Office.

Ghana

Neequaye, J. & Nkrumah, F.K. (1981), 'The Epidemiology of Neonatal Tetanus in the Greater Accra Area', *Ghana Medical Journal*, 20 (3), 98-9.

Nkrumah, Kwame (1961), *I Speak of Freedom*, London: Panaf Books.

Novicki, Margaret A. (1984a), 'The Economics of the Rawlings Revolution', *Africa Report*, September-October, 42-7.

_____ (1984b), 'Interview, Fl. Lt. Jerry Rawlings Chairman of Provisional National Defence Council, Ghana', *Africa Report*, March-April, 4-8.

Ofosu-Amaah (1975), 'A Profile of Children Attending Child Welfare Clinics in Africa', in *Legon Family Research Papers, 4: Aspects of Family Welfare and Planning*, Accra: Institute of African Studies, 111-27.

Oppong, C. (1974), *Marriage Among a Matrilineal Elite: A Family Study of Ghanaian Senior Civil Servants*, Cambridge: Cambridge University Press.

Organisation of African Unity (OAU) (1985), *Africa's Priority Programme for Economic Recovery 1986-1990*, Geneva: Food and Agricultural Organisation.

Peil, Margaret (1977), *Consensus and Conflict in African Societies*, London: Longman.

Regional Economic Research and Documentation Centre (RESDC) (1983), *Social Security in Africa*, Lome: African-American Labour Centre, Organisation of Trade Union Unity.

Rubin, L. (1961), *The Constitution and Government of Ghana*, London: Sweet and Maxwell.

Social Security and National Insurance Trust (SSNIT) (1980), *Fifteen Years of National Social Security in Ghana 1965-1980, Achievements and Problems*, Accra.

Ghana

_____ (1985), Benefits Department, data on distribution of benefits under social security scheme, 1983, Accra: Social Security and National Insurance Trust.

_____ (1986), Data supplied by Actuarial Division.

State Insurance Corporation of Ghana (SIC) (1979), "SIC", A Look at Our Operations, Accra: State Insurance Corporation.

Twumasi, P.A. (1975), Medical Systems in Ghana, Tema: Ghana Publishing Corporation.

United Nations (UN) Department of International Economic and Social Affairs (1986), Demographic Yearbook 1984, Population Census Statistics II, New York: United Nations.

United Nations International Children's Emergency Fund (UNICEF) (1984), Ghana: Situation Analysis of Women and Children, Accra.

Wicker, E.R. (1958), 'Colonial Development and Welfare 1929-1957', Social and Economic Studies, 7 (4), December, 170-92.

World Bank (1984), Ghana, Policies and Program for Adjustment, Washington, DC: World Bank.

_____ (1985), World Development Report, London: Oxford University Press.

IVORY COAST
Adama Bakayoko and Sylvestre Ehouman

THE WELFARE SYSTEM ENVIRONMENT

Ideological Environment
The ideological environment of the Ivory Coast, like that of other sub-Saharan African countries, is the product of the integration of two different social realities: traditional rural values and modern industrial values. Before colonisation the Ivory Coast was a tradition-bound rural society. Most Ivorians highly praise their traditional African values. The social structure is dominated by the extended family system and ethnic and village loyalties, which provide a form of social security and an effective income redistribution system, one that goes beyond class and urban-rural distinction. Such loyalties can be found everywhere in the Ivorian society, but they are more apparent in public administration and some private enterprises. This is no coincidence, for, as in many African countries, solidarity and hospitality are a way of life in the Ivory Coast. Indeed, the spirit of hospitality and brotherhood is embodied in the Ivorian national anthem: '... land of hospitality ... the homeland of the genuine brotherhood ...' The traditional ethnic solidarity, even though valuable in essence, has gone far beyond acceptable limits. In some companies, for example, the majority of employees are either from the same or closely-related ethnic groups. This behaviour can be viewed as a way of reducing unemployment in one geographic area, but it does increase disparities between regions, which can generate regional social upheaval. The extended family system would be an excellent type of welfare system if the burden of maintaining a family or an ethnic group did not fall on the

shoulders of the few who have made it to the top of the social ladder in modern Ivorian society.

As the country has evolved from a purely traditional one to an independent and modern industrial society, many social aspects of life have had to change. It has, therefore, been necessary to produce new ideas and forms of social welfare that would fit this new environment. Firstly, when the country became independent there was a huge discrepancy in income distribution due to ecological differences between regions. This led to an influx of people to the rich southern region, resulting in unemployment in the cities of the south. The government, cognisant of these regional disparities, used the tax revenue from much more naturally-endowed southern forested regions to set up developmental programmes intended to reduce income disparities between the southern regions and the relatively resource-limited central and northern savanna regions. Industrialisation and urbanisation have proceeded hand in hand, along with a weakening of the extended family support system and thus there is a need for a public welfare system to obviate at least some of the social costs of development.

These, then, are the forces that have moulded the fabric of the Ivorian welfare system.

Historical Origins

When Portugese explorers first discovered the Ivory Coast, they found well-organised kingdoms in the northern and eastern parts of the country. Along the coast there were many small tribes. For many years this region served Europeans as a source of slaves, gold, and ivory. Many new peoples entered the area and gained power in the seventeenth and eighteenth centuries. In 1843 French trading posts were set up and protected treaties were signed with some local chiefs. The Ivory Coast became a French colony in 1893. After the Second World War a nationalist movement arose and the Ivory Coast gradually gained control of its own affairs. In 1958 it became a self-governing member of the French community. In the following year it joined with Dahomey (now Benin), Niger and Upper Volta (now Burkina Faso) to form the Conseil de l'Entente, a regional politico-economic association. In 1960 it became an independent republic closely bound to France.

The social security system in the Ivory Coast dates back to the early 1930s, with the

Ivory Coast

introduction of a workmen's compensation programme. It was developed further in 1952 by the introduction of law 52-1322 which defined the premises of the work code for the French colonies (see Charmantier & Rudmatten 1961; Cote de'Ivoire Journal Officiel 1964). This law was of great importance in the social development of French African colonies because it provided the basis of their future social security systems, including;

- the indemnity or compensation paid to workers during their leave from work for reasons of sickness;

- the indemnity to compensate for climatic risks; and

- the allowances paid during or after pregnancy in cases of pregnancy-related sickness.

It is indeed within the framework of that law that a family allowance system for wage-earners was established in 1955.

A social insurance programme was set up in the 1960s. It began by providing benefits for retired people in 1960 and was subsequently extended to cover work accidents and sickness benefits in 1985, when the management was transferred from a private insurance company to the Caisse de Compensation et de Prestations Familiaes (Family Compensatory and Service Provision Funds - CCPF) which also dealt with family allowance matters. The primary objective of the CCPF was to provide real and monetary benefits for Ivory Coast's residents, including:

- a grant to households;

- prenatal and motherhood allowances;

- family allowances; and

- daily allowances to compensate for a partial loss of wages or salaries resulting from maternity leave taken by employed women.

Growth in the expenditure on all these benefits increased rapidly in the early 1960s until the early 1980s because of the Ivory Coast's high birth rate and a rapid increase in the number of employed women.

Ivory Coast

The need to harmonise the management of social security led to the establishment of a social contingency fund, the Caisse Nationale de Prevoyance Sociale (National Fund for Social Contingencies - CNPS), which was established in December 1968 (see Iba 1984).

In 1968 the CNPS covered some 137,000 people, but by mid 1984 its coverage had increased to some 442,000 people, of whom 63 per cent were Ivorians, 29.6 per cent were other Africans and 7.4 per cent were non-Africans. Social security coverage is well below what it should be because of the lack of information on the part of both employers and employees and because illiteracy is still a reality in the Ivory Coast (Cote d'Ivoire, Ministere des Affaires Sociales 1985).

In the early 1960s special occupational welfare measures were introduced for government employees. In November 1962 a retirement programme for government employees (including magistrates) and their spouses and children was instituted. In April 1973 a mutual insurance company was established to help cover health care costs for government employees (including judges) and their families. This company also established solidarity funds to spread the social risk associated with accident and disease-related ailments.

The Political Environment

The Ivory Coast is a republic with executive power vested in the President, who is elected for a five-year term by direct universal suffrage. The Council of Ministers is directly responsible to him. Legislative power is invested in the unicameral National Assembly which has 147 members, directly elected (using two ballots if necessary) for five years. The ruling Parti Democratique de la Cote d'Ivoire (PDCI) is the only political party in the Ivory Coast.

The PDCI led the country to independence in 1960 under the leadership of President Felix Houphouet-Boigny as its leader and subsequently head of State. The Bureau Politique is the party's leading organ presided over by the President. It is the most important political body in the country, and, as such, it defines the main social, economic and political orientations for the Ivory Coast. Policy implementation is left to the various Ministries.

Ivory Coast

Socio-Economic Environment
The Ivory Coast lies on the West Coast of Africa between Ghana to the east and Liberia to the west, with Guinea, Mali and Burkina Faso to the north. Most of the country lies on a low plateau, rising gradually from the ocean towards the north. Dense forests grow in the south but give way to grasslands and scattered trees in the north.

Demography. In mid 1983 the population was estimated to be 9.5 million people (World Bank 1985). The population growth from 1920 to 1983 is shown in Table 1.

TABLE 1 : POPULATION GROWTH FROM 1920 to 1983

Years	Population	Annual Rate of Growth (%)
1920	1,825,000	1.4
1930	2,075,000	1.4
1940	2,350,000	1.4
1945	2,525,000	1.4
1950	2,775,000	1.9
1955	3,050,000	1.9
1960	3,865,000	1.9
1965	4,500,000	3.1
1970	5,500,000	3.1
1975	6,720,000	4.0
1978	7,800,000	4.0
1983	9,500,000	4.6

SOURCE: Cote d'Ivoire, Ministere de l'Economie et des Finances et du Plan 1978 and World Bank 1985.

The population of the Ivory Coast presents three essential characteristics, which are common to most developing countries:

- It grows rapidly at about 4-4.5 per cent each year and has tripled since the mid 1950s and doubled since the mid 1960s. It has been estimated that the population is likely to reach 17 million in the year 2000 (World Bank 1985).

Ivory Coast

- The consequence of this rapid population growth is that the Ivory Coast has a young population. Indeed, over 50 per cent of the population are less than 20 years of age. A predominantly young population may constitute a promise for a bright future, but, at the same time, it is a heavy burden for the present working generation in terms of the considerable investment it would require to ensure their health care and education.

- It is basically a rural population, albeit one that is urbanising quickly. The urban population represents about 44 per cent of the total population and the average annual growth was 8.5 per cent, some 1.84 times the total population growth rate over the same period (World Bank 1985). About one-third of Ivorians now live in agglomerations of more than 500,000 people (World Bank 1985).

Table 2 shows the population growth trend and structure for the Ivory Coast for selected years between 1960 and 1983.

The Ivory Coast indigenous population is made up of five main ethnic groups: the Akan, the Krou, the northern Mande, the southern Mande and the Burkinabe (Cote d'Ivoire 1979) (see Table 3).

The Mande in the north include the Malinke, the Bambara, and the Dioula. (The Mande group in the north has also ramifications outside the Ivory Coast, including Burkina-Faso, most of Mali, half of Guinea, Gambia, Sierra Leone and Senegal. The Mande in the south can also be traced back to Guinea, Liberia and Sierra Leone.)

The geographic distribution of the various ethnic groups constitutes a major policy parameter. The Krou group dominate the south-west region, while the Akan group is located in the mid-east and south-east of the country.

In addition to the five main ethnic groups there are a number of less well defined ethnic groups that do not belong to any particular ethnic category.

Thus it can be argued that the population of the Ivory Coast is a melting pot of ethnic groups from a variety of West African countries. This places a heavy burden on the government in terms of employment policies and fairness to each ethnic group.

Ivory Coast

TABLE 2 : TREND AND STRUCTURE OF THE POPULATION, IVORY COAST, SELECTED YEARS 1960-1983

Years	1960	1965	1970	1975	1980	1983
Pop'n mid-year (in '000s)	3,460	4,159	5,000	6,755	8,286	9,500
Age Structure (%)						
0-14 yrs	43.8	43.0	42.9	43.4	44.7	45.0
15-64 yrs	53.6	54.7	55.0	54.6	55.3	53.0
65 & over	2.6	2.4	2.2	2.0	2.0	2.0
Urban Pop'n % of Total Pop'n	19.3	32.2	27.6	32.6	39.6	44.0
Rural Pop'n % of Total Pop'n	80.7	67.8	72.4	67.4	60.4	56.0
Pop'n Density						
. per sq. km. of total area	10.7	12.9	15.5	20.9	25.6	29.5
. per sq. km. of agricultural land	61.2	75.7	86.7	103.9	120.1	-

SOURCE: World Bank 1985

Table 3 : DISTRIBUTION OF THE TOTAL IVORIAN POPULATION ACCORDING TO THE MAIN ETHNIC GROUPS AND SEX, 1975.

Ethnic Group	Population	Percentage
Akan	2,212,941	42.5
Krou	825,117	15.9
Mande of North	709,839	13.6
Mande of South	624,053	12.0
Burkinabe	800,098	15.3
Non-Defined Ethnic	31,588	0.7
TOTAL	5,203,588	100

SOURCE: Cote d'Ivoire, Ministere du Plan 1975.

Ivory Coast

The Religious Dichotomies. The Ivory Coast, like most other African countries, has been under the influence of European colonisation and Arab invasion over a long period of time. It is, therefore, understandable that it has three major religious groups; Christians, Moslems and those loyal to traditional African religions (Moreau 1982).

The Economy. Since independence the Ivory Coast has successfully developed its economy from a largely agricultural base, although agriculture remains the major economic activity.

During the 1970s, the Ivory Coast economy experienced an average annual growth rate of about 7.5 per cent, with a very low average annual rate of inflation of about three per cent. Since the late 1970s, however, the economy has suffered as a result of a weakening of commodity prices.

From the late 1970s the Ivory Coast has been subject to a series of external shocks: the coffee and cocoa boom in 1976 and 1977, a 40 per cent decline in the terms of trade following the sharp drop in coffee and cocoa prices in 1978, the increase in the price of imported oil and, more recently, the sharp increase in real interest rates on international financial markets. These shocks have led to rapid financial deterioration and to a severe slowdown in economic activity. The Ivory Coast experienced two consecutive years of recession in 1981 and 1982, in sharp contrast to the continuous record of economic growth since the early 1960s (World Bank 1980).

Agriculture is the major sector of the Ivorian economy (see Table 4).

TABLE 4 : STRUCTURE OF THE IVORY COAST ECONOMY IN THE LATE 1970s

	Gross Output	Exports	Imports	Domestic Demand	Value Added (at factor prices)
Agriculture	23.3	49.4	5.1	19.1	33.1
Industry	43.1	28.4	78.2	47.8	29.1
Services	33.6	22.2	26.7	33.1	37.8
TOTAL	100.0	100.0	100.0	100.0	100.0

SOURCE: World Bank 1980.

Ivory Coast

Some 53 per cent of the population are of working age (15-64 years) and for the decade prior to 1983 the workforce expanded at an average annual rate of growth of 3.8 per cent. The vast majority of those in employment are in the informal sector and not in receipt of wages (see Table 5). Indeed, in 1981, it was estimated that 79 per cent of the workforce was engaged in agriculture, four per cent in industry and 17 per cent in services (World Bank 1985).

TABLE 5 : STRUCTURE OF EMPLOYMENT IN THE IVORY COAST (1970)

	Formal Sector	Informal Sector		Total
		Salaried	Non-Salaried	
Number of Employees	255,800	334,730	1,590,710	2,181,240
Percentage	11.7	15.3	73.0	100.0

SOURCE: SETEF 1970.

In the past, substantial tax revenues from the agricultural sector have been used to create employment opportunities in other sectors, particularly industry. Nevertheless, unemployment exists. In 1973 it was estimated that some 80,000 people or three per cent of the workforce were unemployed. Assuming that this was an urban phenomenon it represents 15 per cent of the urban workforce. It should, however, be kept in mind that the employment level that can be measured with some degree of reliability represents only a small part of the overall workforce, namely the salaried employees in the modern sector. The informal sector in the urban areas provides substantial employment opportunities, as well as a form of social security, through its receptiveness to newcomers based on the extended family system. The deteriorating economic circumstances of the 1980s has undoubtedly resulted in higher levels of unemployment.

More than three-quarters of the unemployed in 1977 were illiterate or barely literate. Moreover, these unemployed people were neither formally trained for traditional farmwork nor

Ivory Coast

equipped to cope with specialised types of urban occupations. Nevertheless, the unemployed were seeking jobs in more congenial urban sub-sectors, where the work is to a large extent less strenuous than on the farm (Tuinder 1978).

The inflation rate in the Ivory Coast has increased markedly in the 1980s, so much so that for the decade prior to 1983 the average annual rate of inflation was 11.9 per cent, compared with the very modest average annual rate of inflation of three per cent for the decade prior to 1970. This acceleration in inflation is due mainly to the considerable increase in the price of imported consumer and producer goods.

THE WELFARE SYSTEM: AN OVERVIEW

The Structure and Administration of the Welfare System

The Ivory Coast welfare system covers basically government and private employees. Farmers remain outside the welfare system even though their contribution to the country's economic development is significant. Farmers are not covered by the social security system, although in 1956 a private company (the Agricultural Mutual Company) was created to allow farmers to protect themselves by means of voluntary insurance.

The only universal benefit ever provided by government to all Ivorians free of direct charges was a medical care system which survived until the early 1970s. This system was abandoned because of the heavy burden it placed on the government's budget because the public hospital system was unable to provide basic medicines for the growing number of patients seeking its services.

Social security administration is the responsibility of the CNPS under the general supervision of the Ministry of Labour and Social Affairs.

The National Fund for Social Contingencies (CNPS).
The CNPS is an independent public agency concerned with the administration of the Ivory Coast's social insurance system which contains the following branches: old age, invalidity and death; maternity; work injury; and family allowances. It also provides some welfare facilities. The fund is managed by a joint employer-employee board.

Ivory Coast

Ministry of Labour and Social Affairs. This Ministry is the body to which the CNPS is responsible. It also has part responsibility for the social security organisations concerned with public employees and for planning and developing the personal social services.

The Mutual Fund of Government Employees. This administers a contributory insurance programme covering pharmaceuticals, dental care and eye care. It was created in 1964 in order to improve living conditions of civil servants by means of mutual aid and solidarity. It is under the joint supervision of the Ministries of Finance, of Public Health and Population, of Labour and Social Affairs and of Public Administration (see Cote d'Ivoire, Journal Officiel 1964).

The Fund for Retirement. This fund provides retirement benefits for government employees who are either 55 years of age or who have completed 30 years of work for the government.

The Civil Pension Fund. This is a specialised fund that provides pensions for employees of the National Assembly and their dependants who have been employed for 20 years or more.
 The administration of the personal social services is jointly shared by government and the voluntary sector.

The Voluntary Welfare Sector. A wide variety of organisations operate in the Ivory Coast to provide a range of personal social services for children, the handicapped and needy families.

Social Security Financing
The cost of social security is met from a variety of sources including employer, employee and government contributions.

The National Fund for Social Contingencies (CNPS). Funding for benefits provided by the CNPS comes from five sources:

- Contributions by employers:
    - old-age invalidity benefits: 1.8 per cent of payroll;
    - cash maternity benefits and family allowances: 5.5 per cent of payroll; and

Ivory Coast

- work injury benefits: 2-6 per cent of payroll, according to industry risk.

(This contribution could also come in the form of a lump sum amount fixed by decree.)

- Contributions by employees:
  - old age, invalidity and death benefits: 1.2 per cent of earnings.

- Contributions by government:
  - maternity benefits and family allowances: earmarked yield of part of turnover tax.

(Maximum earnings for contribution (and work injury benefit) purposes is specified with respect to work injury, maternity and family allowance contributions. The current limit is 70,000 francs a month. A minimum earnings level for contribution purposes applies to family allowances, currently 20,000 francs a month.)

- Returns on investments:
  - interest earned on late payments of contributions.

- Donations.

Even though the CNPS has many financial sources, the major one is undoubtedly contributions from employers. Table 6 shows the relative importance of the contributions received for each branch of social security. The mean average rate of growth of contributions for the period from 1979 to 1983 was 4.2 per cent.

To ensure the achievement of financial equilibrium the Reserve Fund was established. Table 7 shows the different components of that fund from 1969 to 1982. Fifty per cent of these funds are deposited in development banks in order to be invested in different sectors of the economy. The balance goes into public securities yielding 12.5 per cent a year interest.

The Mutual Fund for Government Employees. This fund is financed by means of payroll taxes collected monthly on the basis of covered employees' real minimum wages. It is subject to a salary ceiling.

Ivory Coast

TABLE 6 : TRENDS OF THE VARIOUS CONTRIBUTIONS TO THE CNPS: 1979-83 (millions of CFA francs)

Year	Family Allowances	Work Injury	Age, Invalidity & Survivors' Pensions	Total
1979	8,347.0	3,746.7	6,174.4	18,268.1
1980	7,878.6	5,398.5	6,205.1	19,482.2
1981	8,766.8	5,650.1	6,872.0	21,288.9
1982	7,279.0	5,095.2	9,648.9	22,023.1
1983	8,394.3	5,691.2	7,463.8	21,549.3

SOURCE: Cote d'Ivoire, Ministere des Affaires Sociales 1985

TABLE 7 : MAIN COMPONENTS OF THE RESERVE FUND, 1979-82 (millions of CFA francs)

Years	Statutory Reserves	Technical Reserves	Social Funds Reserves
1979	2,209.9	709.551	308.202
1980	2,549.9	482.771	351.629
1981	2,571.5	208.995	343.602
1982	3,706.3	437.479	482.443

SOURCE: See Table 6.

Table 8 indicates the returns achieved on the Reserve Fund investments.

TABLE 8 : RETURNS ON INVESTMENTS BY CNPS: 1979-82 (millions of CFA francs)

Years	Financial Returns	Rents	Other Returns
1979	3,292.11	716.4	55.3
1980	5,308.6	776.7	27.9
1981	6,247.0	558.3	563.3
1982	7,460.2	419.5	940.8

SOURCE: See Table 6.

Ivory Coast

The Fund for Retirement. This is financed by means of both employer and employee contributions, which are set annually subject to an upper limit of nine per cent of earnings. The monthly contributions determined are shared between employers (60 per cent) and employees (40 per cent). A maximum earnings for contributions purposes applies. Contributions are paid by and in respect of all employees aged between 18 and 55 years. The contribution rate has been determined so that reserves can be accumulated for investment purposes.

Civil Pension Fund. Employees working for the National Assembly pay six per cent of their basic monthly salary as contributions to this fund, which attract an annual contribution from the National Assembly of 12 per cent of the employees' basic monthly salary. Additional resources also come from investment income, donations and exceptional subsidies by the National Assembly.

Financing the Personal Social Services
The cost of providing personal social services are shared by government and the voluntary sector. Annual budget allocations are made to the Ministry of Social Affairs which is responsible for providing a range of personal social services, as well as co-ordinating services provided by the voluntary sector. The network of voluntary agencies operating in the Ivory Coast draw their financial resources not only from government allocations but also from donations and other fund raising activities. Details of the level of funding are not available.

THE AGED

The aged do not constitute a major population category, because of the Ivory Coast's relatively young age structure, although with the significant reduction in the death rate which has occurred over the last couple of decades life expectancy at birth has risen to 52 years. Clearly, as the Ivory Coast undertakes its demographic transition the problem of the ageing is likely to become more evident.

Social Security
Social Security protection is provided for the aged by a variety of programmes.

Ivory Coast

The National Fund for Social Contingencies (CNPS). To qualify for an earnings-related pension, the covered employees must be 55 years old and have worked for at least 10 years in a company affiliated to CNPS; he must also have three years of contributions and have ceased any paid activity. The pension is equal to approximately 1.33 per cent of average earnings times the number of years of coverage, plus any periods of incapacity. Some periods of employment prior to the programme beginning in 1960 are also credited. For personal convenience, the pension can be obtained at age 50, but it will be reduced by five per cent for each year under age 55.

If the retired person has children under the age of 16 then his or her pension is increased by ten per cent in respect of each child, for up to three children, provided this sum does not exceed 30 per cent of the pension entitlement.

An old age settlement for workers over the age of 55 who are ineligible for a pension because they have less than ten years' covered employment is paid; the amount is equal to the total of all contributions paid into the fund.

A solidarity pension is provided for aged workers who, even though they have worked for ten or more years, have not been able to contribute to the fund because it was created after their retirement (CNPS 1983).

The Institution of Allowance and Retirement for West Africa. As a result of a convention which exists between the Ivory Coast and some other West African countries, including Togo, Benin and Senegal, each country pays an allowance to retired workers who have worked for ten years or more in one of the countries that are signatories to the convention (CNPS 1983).

The Fund for Retirement and the Civil Pension Fund. Public sector employees are granted a retirement pension upon reaching the age of 55 provided they have completed 30 years of work. The benefit provided is related to past earnings.

Personal Social Services
Contrary to the practices evident in Western societies, the family unit in the Ivory Coast accepts responsibility for the care of old people, in terms of shelter, food and medical care. Nevertheless, the tradition of such support is

Ivory Coast

breaking down as the family unit experiences financial difficulties which inhibit their ability to care for the elderly. There are, however, virtually no personal social services provided to the elderly in the Ivory Coast.

Evaluation

As in most Third World countries the elderly in the Ivory Coast are primarily a family responsibility. For those fortunate enough to be employed in covered occupations social security protection is available. However, this protection applies to a relatively small proportion of the elderly population.

The breakdown in traditional values, the growing incidence of nuclear families and harsh economic circumstances have all resulted in less family support being available to the elderly in the Ivory Coast. Old people, particularly those in the rural areas, do not have recourse to formal support systems to fill the gap left by the withdrawal of family support.

THE HANDICAPPED AND THE DISABLED

Responsibility for the welfare of the handicapped and the disabled is shared amongst families, voluntary agencies and the state.

Personal Social Services

There are only three institutions that take care of the handicapped and disabled in the Ivory Coast: the School for the Deaf and Dumb of Yopougon (Abidjan), the Centre for Blind People of Yopougon (Abidjan) and the Ivorian Institute of Mentally Handicapped Children of Vridi (Abidjan).

The School for the Deaf and the Dumb. This school was created on 4 February 1974 to provide basic education and practical training for the deaf and dumb in order to assist them earn a decent living. Young children with these handicaps, once accepted into the school, attend its primary school for six years, after which they go either to high school or technical school to become animal breeders, carpenters or dressmakers. The school provides room and board for all enrolled children. Admission is open to 12 people per year, which is the maximum of students in a classroom. Since the school opened in 1974, 112 children have entered this institution. According

Ivory Coast

to 1984 estimates 63 children are still studying of whom seven are at the centre for animal breeding. 42 children have so far graduated from this school.

From 1975 to 1978 the school was getting a subsidy of two million CFA francs from the Ministry of Social Affairs. This subsidy increased to six million CFA francs in 1978. Parents are also required currently to make monthly contributions of 10,000 CFA towards the cost of their handicapped children's education.

The Ivorian National Institute for the Promotion of Blind People. The idea of creating this institution was initiated by UNESCO, with the help of the Swiss organisation, CARITAS, in 1971, the International Year of the Book. Its objective is to rehabilitate the blind so as to make them independent. The Institute thus becomes a place for them to become aware of all their potentials and how best to make use of them. To gain entry into the Institute, applicants have to be declared blind, meet certain other requirements and be subject to a social investigation. Each year between seven and ten blind people enter the Institute.

The Institute provides the blind with training in three areas (Cote d'Ivoire, Institut National pour la Promotion des Aveugles 1980 and 1983):

- formal education from primary school to high school and to college using the braille method;
- practical training leading to paid employment upon graduation, especially farming, switchboard operating and basketry; and
- life skills training that teaches the blind how to work and live independently. (This programme reaches many blind people, especially those who are illiterate and who live in the villages.)

By 1982 70 blind people had graduated from the Institute, most of whom had completed some form of rural training (61 per cent) although a significant minority became switchboard operators (21 per cent) (Institut National pour la Promotion des Aveugles 1980 and 1983). The Institute is entirely financed by the Ministry of Social Affairs, although it receives some assistance from private organisations. From 1973 to 1984 the

Ivory Coast

Ministry contributed 50 million CFA francs annually towards the cost of the Institute. In 1985, because of the prevailing economic crisis, funding dropped to 42 million CFA francs from this source.

The Ivorian Institute for Mentally Handicapped Children. This Institute was created in 1969 by a group of parents of intellectually handicapped children. Its objective is to provide for the educational needs of such handicapped children.

Mentally handicapped children are admitted to the Institute at the age of five or six and remain there until they are 18 years of age. One of the basic requirements of admission is that the parents make a commitment to participate fully in the programme designed for their children. Thus the Institute does not provide residential services, children are with their families outside normal school hours. Another requirement for entry is that medical practitioners recognise that it is possible to improve the health status of the children attending the Institute. Since its creation in 1969 94 children have attended the Institute.

Parents of handicapped children are required to make a monthly contribution of 5,000-30,000 CFA francs, depending on the seriousness of the handicap suffered by the children. This requirement is not enforced and only a small proportion of parents pay these charges. The Ministry of Social Affairs provides an annual subsidy of 15 million CFA francs, about half that which it provided in the early 1980s, probably because of the economic difficulties being experienced by the nation as a whole. The Ministry also provides the Institute with nurses, instructors and other social workers whose tasks are to care for, train, guide and educate the handicapped children. Of those children who have graduated from the Institute two have been able to set up and manage their own businesses of raising chickens and rabbits (Fraternite Hedbomadaire 1984).

Social Security

The National Fund for Social Contingencies (CNPS). The CNPS provides invalidity pensions for permanently incapacitated covered employees aged 50 or over provided they have three years of

Ivory Coast

contributions and ten years of covered employment. The pension is identical to that provided for the aged, including the provision of children's supplements. An invalidity allowance for workers aged over 50 who have at least ten years' employment is paid if they are ineligible for a pension.

A permanent work injury disability pension is provided for workers participating in the work injury social insurance programme. In the event of a total disability the pension is equal to 100 per cent of average earnings. In the event of a partial disability the pension is equal to:

- average earnings multiplied by 50 per cent of the degree of incapacity for the proportion of disability between ten per cent and 50 per cent; and
- average earnings multiplied by 150 per cent of the degree of incapacity for the proportion of disability above 50 per cent. A constant attendance allowance of 40 per cent of the pension payable is also provided. Medical care, including hospitalisation, medicines, appliances, transportation and rehabilitation, is also provided.

Government Employees' Work Accident Programme.
Invalidity allowances are paid to government employees disabled as a result of work accidents or job-related sicknesses. The amount of this allowance is equal to a fraction of the minimum wage of the employee's particular wage category, but it cannot exceed 50 per cent of his or her income. This allowance is paid quarterly by government. If the cause of the infirmity is imputable to a third party then the state has full power to sue that party for reimbursement of the allowance.

Evaluation
The handicapped and the disabled are largely the responsibility of their families in the Ivory Coast. Those fortunate enough to be in covered employment receive modest social security protection. A limited range of personal social services are provided for the deaf and dumb, the blind and the intellectually handicapped, although it must be emphasised that only a relatively small number of handicapped people benefit from these services and facilities.

Ivory Coast

NEEDY FAMILIES, CHILDREN AND YOUTHS

As a result of the rapid population growth experienced by the Ivory Coast in recent years the proportion of people under the age of 15 has increased. In 1983 there were over four million people in this age category. In comparison with other countries with a similar level of socio-economic development, the Ivory Coast has a relatively high infant mortality rate (121 per thousand in 1983) and child death rate (20 per thousand in 1983) (World Bank 1985). It must also be recognised that the Ivory Coast has a relatively large percentage of its population residing in urban areas, thus placing additional strain on the traditional support system based on the extended family unit.

Personal Social Services

The SOS Villages. The first SOS village was built in Abogo Gare (Abidjan) by Father Martin, who first introduced a shelter for youth - Notre Maison - in Teichville in 1964. Fourteen years later a second SOS village was built in Aboisso in the south eastern part of the Ivory Coast.
Like all other SOS villages in the world, the two villages in the Ivory Coast provide abandoned children and orphans with a mother, a house, a village and a natural and healthy environment that fosters their emotion (see Gmeiner 1980, 1981a and 1981b). In certain areas of the Ivory Coast, especially in the south-east, the tenth child of a family is abandoned according to custom because, traditionally, they are believed to bring bad luck upon their families. It has often been difficult for SOS village officers to gain access to orphans because of the traditional extended family system. There is, therefore, a lengthy six-month inquiry before a child can be accepted into such a village. The inquiry consists of a social and police investigation, the results of which are studied by a national commission comprising fifteen members. This inquiry process recognises that there are some special cases (such as children abandoned at birth or the tenth child of an Agni family, who must be assisted immediately). Altogether there are some 130 children located in both SOS villages. They range in age from two months to 18 years and each is housed in the village under the supervision of a

Ivory Coast

non-married woman known as the mother of the house, who does the cooking and housework, with the assistance of the older children. She also monitors their homework. The two villages also conduct kindergartens that accept children from outside the village. Primary and high school education is provided for the children living in the village at schools located in neighbouring towns (SOS 1984; SOS en Afrique 1984a, 1984b and 1985). For those unable to complete their primary and high school education, professional training is available in such areas as farming, basketwork and carpentry. Upon reaching the age of 18, boys resident in the village are moved to a youth hostel inside the village compound.

The SOS villages are financed by SOS International through donations from the children's godfathers. The money is channelled in the Ivory Coast through the SOS Association of the Ivory Coast and the National Bureau of Co-ordination. A small government subsidy is also provided through the Ministry of Social Affairs, which also provides the village with nurses and kindergarten teachers.

Kindergartens for Needy Children. The CNPS has established kindergartens for needy children in order to give them an equal opportunity to develop. In 1980 there were 480 children registered at such kindergartens but by 1983 the number had increased to 710.

Foyers de la Femme. In order to provide education for women who have not had an opportunity to go to school, the CNPS provides education and training in home economics and dressmaking for the daughters and spouses of CNPS beneficiaries. Some 400 women benefited from this programme in 1983.

Vacation Camps for Children. Since 1956 the CNPS has organised vacation camps each year for children of its beneficiaries. In 1983 1,585 children aged between 7 and 14 attended such vacation camps.

Low Income Housing. The CNPS has built 438 housing units which it provides at a moderate rent for needy families that have a breadwinner in covered employment. (Cote d'Ivoire, Ministere des Affaires Sociales 1985).

Ivory Coast

Social Security

Survivors' Pensions.
The CNPS provides a survivor's pension to widows of deceased pensioners or covered employees who qualified for pension at their death. To be eligible for this pension the widow must have been married for at least two years and be aged 50 or more, or an invalid or caring for at least two children under the age of 16. The pension payable is equal to 50 per cent of the deceased's pension or pension entitlement.

Survivor pensions are also paid in respect of work-related deaths. Widows receive a pension equal to 30 per cent of the deceased's prior earnings.

Widows of government employees who die whilst on duty receive a life annuity equal to the invalidity allowance payable in respect of total disability. Administration of this programme is shared by the Ministries of Public Service and of Finance.

Orphans' Pensions.
Orphans of deceased pensioners or covered workers who have qualified for the pension receive an orphan's pension equal to 20 per cent of the deceased's pension or pension entitlement, provided they are under the age of 16 (21 if students). If there are more than five orphans then the deceased's pension or pension entitlement is shared equally.

Upon the death of a covered worker, where that death is work-related, orphans receive a proportion of the deceased's prior earnings (15 per cent for the first and second orphans and ten per cent for the remaining orphans). In the event of both parents being dead each orphan receives 20 per cent of the deceased covered worker's earnings.

Elderly Dependents' Allowances.
Surviving dependent parents and grandparents of deceased covered workers whose death is work-related, receive an allowance of 10 per cent of the deceased's prior earnings.

Funeral Grants (Work Injury).
Deceased covered workers whose death is work-related attract a lump sum funeral grant covering the cost of burial.

Maternity Benefits.
Women employed in covered employment and employed workers' wives receive a

Ivory Coast

maternity benefit equal to half pay for six weeks prior to confinement and eight weeks after (11 weeks if complications). The employer is required to pay half salary for this period. To qualify for such assistance covered employees must have three months' covered employment. A lump sum birth grant (18,000 francs) for each of the first three children. A maternity allowance (18,000 francs) and a prenatal allowance (13,500 francs) are also payable.

Family Allowances. Employees with one or more children aged between 13 months and 14 years receive a flat-rate allowance of 1,500 francs a month for each child, provided they have worked for three months and are currently working (or the widow of a pensioner). A one-time school allowance (4,500 francs per child) is also provided.

Evaluation

The family unit is still the basic social unit in the Ivory Coast. The processes of economic development and urbanisation are, however, bringing changes to the extent that traditional family support systems are unable to cope with the contingencies of modern life. The social security system focuses its attention on families with breadwinners in covered employment and covered families with children, urban nuclear families, whilst the limited range of personal social services available focus on children, especially those at risk. The very idea that families look outside the extended family support system for welfare support has not been widely accepted in the Ivory Coast.

THE UNEMPLOYED

Officially, an unemployed person is someone who has lost a job. Thus three categories of unemployed people can be identified: those who were laid off by their employers for economic and financial reasons; those who were laid off because of wrong behaviour at work; and those laid off because they were found guilty of mismanagement.

The unemployed are organised into three groups: managers, office workers, and blue-collar workers. Each unemployment group has a president who is allowed to forward grievances to the government.

Ivory Coast

Each unemployed person registers with the Ivorian Office of Manpower (OMOCI) where unemployment identification cards are issued.

Social Security
Until recently the Ivorian social security system did not embrace unemployment. In 1979, however, the Head of State created a solidarity fund in order to help the involuntarily unemployed. This development occurred in light of the numerous layoffs that were taking place in the early 1980s as a result of economic recession. The solidarity fund is financed from contributions from all workers in private and public institutions. Such workers contributed one per cent of their salaries, initially for a two year period ending 31 December 1983. But the economic recession that began in the early 1980s extended beyond that date; thus employee contributions to the solidarity fund are still being collected.

The solidarity fund provides benefits for unemployed workers who have been laid off by their employees because of economic and financial reasons. Only 3,000 people are benefiting from this fund. The unemployment allowance provided varies according to the unemployment category to which the unemployed person belongs. If they are involuntarily unemployed due to financial and economic reasons then they receive a monthly allowance of 75,000 CFA francs. If unemployment is due to wrongful behaviour at work then the allowance is reduced to 40,000 CFA francs a year. In all, 200 million CFA francs have been spent on unemployment relief (Cote d'Ivoire, Ministere des Affaires Sociales 1985).

Initially the solidarity fund provided unemployment relief for university and high school graduates who were seeking their first job. But because this form of unemployment did not fit with the official Ivorian government definition of unemployment and because the economic crisis caused an escalation in unemployment, the government has ceased providing first-job seekers with unemployment relief. Instead it is helping them find work (Fraternite Matin 1984).

In addition to the unemployment relief provided by the solidarity fund to blue-collar workers the government, through the Head of State, has donated 500 million CFA francs to 10,000 such workers.

Ivory Coast

Evaluation
The economic recession that has prevailed in the Ivory Coast since the early 1980s has led to an escalation in the number of unemployed people. Moreover it has made the task of finding employment more difficult for first-job seekers. In recognition of the strain that such an escalation in unemployment has on traditional family support systems the Ivorian government created a temporary unemployment relief scheme. This provides relief to the involuntarily unemployed although it discriminates against first-job seekers, those laid off work due to wrong work behaviour and those that are guilty of mismanagement.

THE SICK AND INJURED

The sick and injured in the Ivory Coast receive support from social security institutions and from their employers.

Social Security
The introduction of a sickness insurance branch of social security, based on the pattern of the industrialised countries, is not feasible in the Ivory Coast at the moment in view of the administrative structures needed. The CNPS has, alternatively, opted for its own medical centres, free medical treatment and pharmaceutical products.
  Within the framework of a construction programme of ten social and medical centres in 1984, the construction of two such centres has been accomplished, comprising dispensary facilities for delivering all medical care with the exception of hospitalisation and advanced surgery, and a pre-school education centre.

Occupational Sickness and Injury. According to the CNPS a works accident is defined as:

- any accident, irrespective of cause, which happens whilst working or as a result of work; and
- any accident occurring whilst travelling between home and work, provided that travel has not been interrupted or deviated for personal interest.

Occupation sickness is a sickness deemed to be a consequence of the particular employment. The

Ivory Coast

coverage of the CNPS's occupational sickness and injury programme extends to six population categories:

- all wage-earners from public establishments with financial autonomy, industry, agriculture and commerce;
- all apprentices;
- students in professional technical schools and those who are being retrained;
- members of production co-operatives and self-employed managers;
- directors of private corporations; and
- prisoners.

Once it has been established that a work accident or job-related sickness has occurred, the CNPS will cover the following expenses: free medical care, daily allowances, annuity to the victim, annuity to the eligible party, annuity to the spouse, annuity to the children and descendants and an annuity to the ascendants. These benefits accrue to covered employees and their relatives.

Temporary Work Accident Allowances for Government Employees. On 21 December 1964 legislation was enacted to provide temporary allowances to government employees suffering work accidents or job-related sicknesses. The allowances paid are equal to a fraction of the minimum wage of the wage category in which the sickness beneficiary belongs, but not so as to exceed 50 per cent of the beneficiary's income. This is paid quarterly.

Personal Social Services

The Blue Cross of the Ivory Coast. This institution was established in 1972 by the Blue Cross Switzerland. Its aim is to cure alcoholics by detoxification. From 1973 to 1984 some 2,000 patients have been treated and released from this institution. There are, on average, 120 patients a year and the recovery rate being experienced is 78 per cent. The therapy consists of 15 days' detoxification, psycho-therapy, sports and manual work. In addition, awareness meetings are held with patients about the side effects of alcoholism.

The Blue Cross of the Ivory Coast is funded by government and some private concerns. The goverment subsidy fluctuates between nine and ten million CFA francs a year. Occasionally the CNPS

Ivory Coast

also contributes, typically 1.5 million CFA francs in a year. Some para-statal companies like the Electrical Energy of the Ivory Coast, the Rail Road Company Abidjan-Niger and the Abidjan Transportation Company also contribute, typically some 250 thousand CFA francs a year. The government also pays the salaries of five nurses, two social assistants, a director, one doctor, a driver and a typist.

Evaluation
Covered employees suffering a work-related injury or sickness receive social security support from the CNPS in the form of a cash allowance and free health services. Those in uncovered employment have access to medical services compulsorily provided by employers under the 1964 labour code. (Farmers must contribute to the agricultural mutual fund in order to obtain any sickness benefits.)
   Non-occupational sickness is not a social security contingency that is covered by the Ivorian social security system.

AN ASSESSMENT OF THE IVORIAN SOCIAL WELFARE SYSTEM

Given that the Ivory Coast is a Less Developed Country with little experience in modern social security systems, it can be forcibly argued that it has made significant progress in setting up its social security system. It does, however, have its shortcomings. It does not adequately protect farmers (as farmers are typically illiterate, they cannot use effectively the agricultural mutual fund to voluntarily provide themselves with social security protection). Thus it can be argued that social security coverage needs to be extended to offer protection to more people. This can be done by decentralising the administrative arrangements through the creation of various regional and urban centres. To assist and facilitate this decentralisation the Ministry of Social Affairs has opened up the Ivorian Centre for the Training of Social Security Personnel. This Centre trains social security personnel who are very much needed to improve the quality of the services provided by the CNPS.
   The government is also working to broaden the scope of the Ivorian social security system. A sickness insurance programme for farmers is

currently being developed. It will involve significant contributions from farmers themselves, given that the government can no longer afford free medical care and other services.

The government is also contemplating a modification of the pension payment formula to allow retired people to obtain an acceptable level of pension. This is a long overdue reform. It is evident that social security is a political tool in the Ivory Coast. In 1984 5.42 per cent of the government's budget was spent on social security.

The personal social services are poorly developed in the Ivory Coast. Aside from the Institute for the Blind, which gets a substantial subsidy (compared to the other institutions), the School of the Deaf and Dumb is hardly equipped with the proper instructional material and funds to reach its goals. For the mentally handicapped, the funds usually come so late that it is almost impossible for the staff to undertake the programmes as scheduled. For example, because of limited funds, the student farmers at the Institute for the Blind have not received the 150,000 CFA francs which should be given to them in order to make a start in life. The instructional materials for the blind (special type of papers and typewriters and rulers) are all imported and therefore very expensive. With the high cost of those materials, a local small or medium size enterprise could efficiently provide the Institute with some of the basic material while the typewriters (Perkins Brailler) could still be imported. However, ways and means should be found to maintain those typewriters instead of having them sent back to France. Moreover, government officers should also meet very often with the Institute manager to evaluate the needs of the Institute.

Overall, the various Institutes taking care of the physically as well as emotionally handicapped should benefit from preferential rates on the part of the public utility companies in order to alleviate their financial problems.

The Ivorian welfare system, which is in its formative stage of development, has progressed far in the last twenty years. Its development in recent years has been adversely affected by the economic recession that has hindered the socio-economic development of the Ivory Coast. Confronted with a rapidly growing population, a strong trend towards greater urbanisation and

Ivory Coast

considerable ethnic diversity, Ivorian society is facing many challenges in the continued development of its welfare system.

REFERENCES AND FURTHER READING

Charmantier, A.P & Rudmatten, L.De (1961), <u>Lois Sociales, Securites Sociales</u>, Paris: Librairie Generale de Droit et de Jurisprudence.

CNPS see National Fund for Social Contingencies.

Cote d'Ivoire (1979), <u>Direction de la Statistique</u>, Juillet, Abidjan.

_____ (1980), <u>Inspection territoriale du travail et des lois sociales en Cote d'Ivoire</u>, 08868/ITLS-CI, Abidjan.

_____ Institut National pour la Promotion des Aveugles (1980), <u>Lumiere des Aveugles de Cote d'Ivoire</u>, Abidjan.

_____ Institut National pour la Promotion des Aveugles (1983), <u>Lumiere des Aveugles de Cote d'Ivoire</u>, Abidjan.

_____ <u>Journal Officiel</u> (1964), No. 44 du 17 aout, portant Code du Travail.

_____ Ministere des Affaires Sociales (1985), <u>L'Experience de la Cote d'Ivoire en matiere de Securite Sociale</u>, Abidjan.

_____ Ministere de l'Economie et des Finances et du Plan (1978), <u>La Cote d'Ivoire en chiffres, 1977-1978</u>, Abidjan.

_____ Ministere du Plan (1975), <u>Recensement de la Population</u>, Abidjan.

Fraternite Hedbomadaire (1984), 'Enfance Handicapee', 8 Mars, Abidjan.

Fraternite Matin (1984), 'Allocation Chomage-Ouvriers Compresses-Diplomes de l'Universite', 23 October, Abidjan.

Ivory Coast

Gmeiner, H. (1980), <u>Les Villages d'Enfants SOS, Institutions Modernes pour l'Education d'Enfants Abandonnes</u>, Innsbruck, Austria: Publications des Villages d'Enfants SOS.

―――― (1981a), <u>Les Villages d'Enfants SOS, Fixations des Objectifs - Genese - Organisation</u>, Sydney: F. Sochor, Zell am See.

―――― (1981b), <u>Impressions, Pensees, Croyances</u>, Innsbruck, Austria: SOS-Kinderdorf-Verlag.

Iba, B. (1984), <u>Seminaire organise a l'intention des inspections syndicaux de l'UGTCI par la Confederation Internationale des Syndicats Libres</u>, Abidjan: CNPS.

Moreau, R.L. (1982), <u>Africains Musulmans: communaute en mouvement</u>, (Editions Presence Africaine Paris et Inades Editions), Abidjan.

Mutuelle, A. (1984), <u>Les garanties offertes par la Mutuelle Agricole de Cote d'Ivoire</u>, Abidjan.

National Fund for Social Contingencies (CNPS) (1983), <u>Guide de l'Assure Social</u>, Abidjan.

SETEF (1970), <u>L'Image Base dans Ivory Coast the Challenge of Success</u>, Baltimore, Maryland: Johns Hopkins University Press.

SOS en Afrique (1983), <u>Nouvelles des Villages d'Enfants SOS</u>, No. 21, Innsbruck, Austria: SOS - Kinderdorf-Verlag.

―――― (1984a), <u>Nouvelles des Villages d'Enfants SOS</u>, No. 25, Innsbruck, Austria: SOS - Kinderdorf-Verlag.

―――― (1984b), <u>Nouvelles des Villages d'Enfants SOS</u>, No. 28, Innsbruck, Austria: SOS - Kinderdorf-Verlag.

―――― (1985), <u>Nouvelles des Villages d'Enfants SOS</u>, No. 29, Innsbruck, Austria: SOS - Kinderdorf-Verlag.

Toure, A. (1982a), <u>CNPS, Etude pour le Paiement des Points Supplementaires de Retraite Prevus a l'Article 2 du Decret No. 76/21 du 7 Janvier 1976</u>, September, Abidjan.

Ivory Coast

_____ (1982b), *Expose sur la CNPS*, September, Abidjan.

Tuinder, A. den (1978), *Ivory Coast: The Challenge of Success*, Baltimore, Maryland: John Hopkins University Press.

World Bank (1980), *Staff Working Papers, No. 647*, Washington DC.

World Bank (1983), *World Tables* (3rd edition) (Vol. 2, Social Data), Washington DC.

World Bank (1985), *World Development Report 1983*, New York: Oxford University Press.

KENYA
Wacira Wa Gethaiga and Lorece P. Williams

THE WELFARE SYSTEM ENVIRONMENT

Ideological Environment
Kenya, like most other African countries recently emerging from colonialism, inherited its ideas of social welfare from the former colonial power. It could be said that the people envisioned some type of utopia once the metropolitan powers left. The objectives in the struggle for independence included political equality; social justice; human dignity including freedom of conscience; freedom from want and exploitation; equal opportunity; and high and growing per capita incomes equitably distributed (see Kenya, Sessional Paper No. 10, 1963-5).

Kenya's welfare philosophy assumes the achievement of a modern developed society that will be just and egalitarian. It is determined by a number of social forces which include pre-colonial and colonial legacies which affect the implementation of present social welfare programmes.

The Pre-colonial Welfare Legacy. As with all African states, Kenya was made up of a territory occupied by over 40 ethnic groups all competing for territorial recognition. The societies were rural in nature and agricultural-pastoral in lifestyles. As such each was responsible for the social welfare of its group.

Colonial Welfare Legacy. Kenya, under the British, was administered for the benefit and welfare of the European. This was accomplished by manipulation of the social services, especially in the area of education. Europeans, Asians and Africans were taught in different schools with

Kenya

distinct curricula, the consequence of which was that the Europeans were prepared for decision-making and high salaries, Asians for skilled labour (and middle management) and Africans for unskilled tasks (Olorunsola 1972, pp.287).

Communal or Collective Spirit. African culture used to be most communal when and where economic life and the means of production were communally organised and controlled. In traditional society, the community provided all the needed support to its members. This spirit is still the dominant form of welfare for the majority of the population.

Self-Reliance or Harambee. Kenya's first President, Jomo Kenyatta, made self-reliance, or Harambee, a national policy. Harambee is a recognition of the government's inability to provide for the social needs of all the people. It remains a dominant theme politically.

Tribal Values. The tribal system does not permit the use of many services. Tribal groups are usually dependent upon members of the clan for the care of the sick, the handicapped, the aged, orphaned and homeless. Social services are provided by the missions who have been financed by funds from the government or from private organisations. Some modern Kenyans are in a period of transition and do accept the more Westernised version of social services.

Historical Origins
Kenya became independent on 12 December 1963, after undergoing a violent revolution, euphemistically called the 'Mau Mau' or 'Emergency', in the early-to-mid 1950s (MacPhee 1968, p.111). Among the many causes was the pre-independence political economy, which placed emphasis on European agriculture which was profitable because it existed in a monopolistic environment. Due to land confiscation, Africans were forced to be involved as labourers on European farms, dependent on wages and the goodwill of the farmer. Then and now, the struggle continues to be for land (Miller 1984, pp.5).

State of Welfare at Independence. At independence, the country inherited a welfare state designed for the colonials including high-cost European schools; supplemental and inducement pay to foreign expatriates; substantial housing allowances for civil servants and foreign inducement pay; all designed to attract more Europeans to colonial service. A small number of professional and lower-rank Asians, Arab and African workers received some of these benefits.

The new emerging government left intact most of the welfare benefits of the previous regime, but widened the welfare base to include a larger number of the new African elite. The process left out most of the African poor, thus retaining the same gap that existed between the Africans and Europeans.

The Government's Response. The basic philosophy of the government towards the building of the Welfare State was published 18 months after the attainment of independence.

In 1985 the government outlined the various steps it intended to take to achieve rapid economic development through increasing the national wealth; raising the standard of living; ensuring fair distribution of land; creating jobs; providing more and better schools and hospitals; and arranging for old-age retirement benefits and social security for all in Kenya (Kenya Sessional Paper No. 10, 1965). To this end the National Social Security Fund (NSF) was established.

The document essentially rejected the assumption that nationalisation of foreign owned industries would solve all social problems and opted for capitalistic development.

> Different societies attach different weight and priorities to these objectives, but it is largely in the political and economic means adopted for achieving these ends that societies differ. These differences in means are, however, of paramount importance because ultimate objectives are never fully attained. Every time one target is attained a new one becomes necessary. Indeed, we forever live in transition (Kenya Sessional Paper No. 10, para. 4, 1965).

Uhuru na Kazi - Freedom and Work. This was the promise made to people during the struggle for independence. The government is the largest employer in the nation. All government workers participate in some form of retirement benefits. Employers in the private sector are required to provide some form of retirement benefits which are usually paid in one lump sum when service is discontinued.

Political Environment

The Republic is a one party state. Legislative power rests with the unicameral National Assembly, with 172 members (158 elected by universal suffrage, the Attorney-General and Speaker, and 12 members nominated by the President) serving a term of five years, subject to dissolution. Executive power is held by the President, who is directly elected for five years and who is assisted by an appointed Vice-President and Cabinet.

Socio-Economic Environment

Kenya lies astride the equator on the east coast of Africa, with an area of 580,000 square kilometres and a population of 18.9 million, the overwhelming majority of whom are Africans (World Bank 1985).

Population and Growth. The success of the health system, coupled with a very high population growth rate (estimated at an annual rate of four per cent), will bring strain to the already stretched Kenyan economy. By the year 2000, it is estimated that the population will be 36.8 million, of which those under 15 years of age will be more than 50 per cent (see Table 1). This will substantially increase the burden for educational and health services.

TABLE 1: AGE STRUCTURE OF KENYA'S POPULATION: 1978, 1983 AND PROJECTED FOR 2000

Age	Number ('000s)			Percentage		
	1978	1983	2000	1978	1983	2000
Under 15	7,500	9,000	20,700	49.7	51.2	53.7
15 - 59	7,100	8,600	16,800	46.4	45.1	43.5
60 & over	600	700	1,100	3.9	3.7	2.8
Total	15,300	19,100	38,600	100.0	100.0	100.0

SOURCE: Roushdi & Mott 1979.

Kenya

How Kenya will cope with the increased pressure of more children of primary school age, more schools, more teachers and few working adults to pay the necessary taxes is unknown. Already the country carries a heavy international debt and has been forced by the International Monetary Fund to devalue at least once.

Though Kenya was the first African nation to establish a National Family Planning Programme in 1967, few of its women use the services, partly because of lack of information, and partly because of unconscious self-interest (Kaplan 1982, p.83). Children are a form of old-age security, especially for women who are discriminated against in property rights. Kenyan men may practice polygamy but widows often have no rights to property or inheritance and therefore expect their children will take care of them.

Agriculture. Kenya's population is predominantly rural, which is an important cushion to the unusually high unemployment of about 30 per cent of the work force. (The government is quite aware of the value of increasing dependence on the rural area and allocates as large a percentage of the Development Plan budget to agricultural projects for irrigation, new crop development, new markets and some resettlement.) The agricultural sector provides alternative employment, income, kinship, friendship, housing and other supports.

In 1981 (latest available data) 78 per cent of the workforce was in the agricultural sector, which produced about one third of Gross Domestic Product (GDP).

Cooperatives. The most important are the coffee and tea cooperatives representing the two major foreign exchange earners. Expenses for fertilisers, storage and marketing of products are deducted before any distribution to the farmer. In most cases school fees are also paid directly to the appropriate authorities.

The Continuing Land Struggle. Pre and post colonial Kenya is still one of land struggle, land hunger, and relentless territoriality: a struggle for prime land for agriculture, grazing and bequeathing with very few welfare benefits expected from the state.

The country continues to create what has been called a patchwork society: 'a human mosaic of

Kenya

forty African ethnic groups plus Asian, Arab, and European sub-cultures' (Miller 1984, p.1) each responsible for its own welfare with relative minor involvement of the goverment.

Economic Development. The high rate of economic growth achieved in the decade after independence, which produced a 27 per cent increase in GDP per capita, has not been maintained. The problems of unemployment and inflation (10.8 per cent average annual rate between 1973 and 1983) and the unequal distribution of wealth remain unsolved.

THE WELFARE SYSTEM: AN OVERVIEW

Kenyans have been responsible for their own governance since winning their independence from the British in 1963. Objectives of the government have been directed toward achieving high and growing per capita incomes, with equitable distribution, in an effort to protect the population from poverty, illnesses, diseases and exploitation. Social justice, the equality of opportunity, the worth and dignity of the people, and political equality must be guaranteed and in keeping with tribal traditions and the mutual social responsibility of the extended family (Burrows 1975, p.14).

Kenya continues to be a land in transition. The remnants of colonisation are obvious. The cost of education, health care problems, scarcity of doctors, location of health facilities, lack of modern technology, lack of adequate social services, negligible social security benefits and rural problems in agriculture continue to plague the population.

Social Security Administration

National Social Security Fund. Social security was adopted with a two-fold purpose: so that workers would have greater security in their old age and so that a fund would be accumulated that could be paid out to retired people. (Old age insurance was not introduced because of the inaccuracies of statistical data on Kenyans regarding their age.) The national provident fund was erected to allow each contributor or his or her heirs to draw out the amount accredited to the account.

Kenya

The Ministry of Labour. This administers a workmen's compensation scheme which covers all employed persons earning less than 2,000 shillings a month.

The National Hospital Insurance Fund and the National (Voluntary) Hospital Insurance Fund. These jointly administer Kenya's limited national health scheme, under the supervision of the Ministry of Health.

Public Service Commission (PSC). Employment in the various Ministries of the government is processed through the Public Service Commission (PSC). Workers who qualify for permanent and pensionable employment are covered with a non-contributory retirement scheme which provides them with a lump sum payment at retirement (age 55) and a monthly stipend.

Teachers Service Commission (TSC). The hiring and welfare of all teachers in public schools is under the Teachers Service Commission which is parallel to PSC in service and retirement practices.

Personal Social Service Administration

The Ministry of Health. The government provides free medical services for all children and all out patients at central government hospitals and health centres through this department. Health centres tend to be more prevalent in urban areas. In addition to the government health centres there are a number of private and mission health centres.
 The limited statutory personal social services available in Kenya are a part of the Ministry of Cooperatives and Social Services. Most of the human services have been concentrated in the area of education.

Education Services. Education is the single largest budget item in government expenditure, averaging some 25 per cent in most years (Five Year Plans 1974-78 and 1979-84). Education is seen as the most direct avenue to the good life. Primary education, while not universal, is free. The community participation in the building of Harambee schools increases the demand for teachers and the government strives to fulfil its commitment.

Kenya

The Harambee (Self-Help) Movement. This has mobilised local resources and encouraged local people to participate in the development of projects (Burrows 1975, p.205). Harambee funds are allocated according to the initiation and persistence of local sponsors of projects. These programmes are directed toward increasing agricultural outputs and employment and reducing land hunger among Kenyans.

The Voluntary Sector. The Kenyan government launched a programme of nation-building through community development. The Department of Community Development seeks sound, self-generating, economic and social growth of people at all levels. The intensity of the services provided by these voluntary community agencies and self-help programmes have resulted in thousands of community facilities throughout Kenya. These facilities include schools, nursery centres, health care clinics and dispensaries, fish ponds, access roads, small bridges, pipelines, dams, rock catchments and protected springs to provide water. Some areas lack the technical personnel to plan and implement needed projects. Political influences have often been a detriment to many of these services. The voluntary sector has proved invaluable in mobilising local resources and motivating people to assist in programme development. These efforts are integrated peripherally into the overall design and planning of the government. Funding of these services by the government is directly influenced by the initiative and persistence of local politicians and sponsors of the agencies and projects.

The Department of Social Services. The personal social services are coordinated by the Kenya National Council of Social Services which is an advisory board designed to make recommendations to voluntary agencies on the planning and implementation of welfare services. Representation is drawn from voluntary agencies, government ministries, local authorities and co-opted members. Experimental programmes, voluntary financial contributions and work, planning for youth, restoration of children from institutions to the programme for vagrant children, rehabilitation of the disabled, programmes for the aged and infirm and education

Kenya

for social workers are among the critical needs of the personal social services.

Family and Clan. Reserve funds operate in many clans. In this system families deposit part of their herds with relatives and friends who live at a distance. This is a protection against prolonged droughts or disease outbreaks. This social protection also includes cost of medical care, which may be an in-kind transaction, such as poultry, food and cattle (Musiga 1974, p.481). Fiscal planning and programmes directed toward protection of Kenyans are changing many of the traditional interactions in families and the clan system.

The clan system served as a type of social security. It was a form of insurance. The government plans to replace the security of the clan with old-age pensions from employers, free education and medical care. The clan functions like a labour union in that they both discriminate by taking care of their members and keeping others out (Clark 1969, pp.35-42). This creates ethnic loyalty.

Social Security Finance

The National Social Security Fund. This is financed by equal contributions from the employee and employer at a rate of five per cent of the wages each. A contribution ceiling of 1,600 shillings a month earnings is specified (Burrows 1975, pp.180; US Social Security Administration 1985).

Limited National Health Scheme. This is financed by flat-rate contributions from employees earning more than 1,000 shillings a month.

Workmen's Compensation. This is entirely financed by employers through the direct provision of benefits or insurance premiums paid to private insurance companies.

Personal Social Services Finance

Statutory Personal Social Services. The Department for Social Services is responsible for social development and housing facilities. Programmes financed under this Department include social welfare, community development, adult

Kenya

education, training, vocational rehabilitation, national libraries, museums and sports. Housing construction is the most capital-intensive programme in this Department. There is an extreme urgency for both rural and urban housing development.

Municipal or Urban Councils and Country or Rural Councils. There are eleven municipal or urban councils and thirty-eight county or rural councils. Both council groups are financed by the central government, fees for services, and taxes levied by local authorities. The services include housing, water supplies and sewage, fire protection, welfare services, public libraries, markets and inspection for grading and storing produce. Municipal councils provide primary education, health clinics, dispensaries and other medical services (Burrows 1975, p.174). Municipal councils operate principally in rural areas to provide services for the poor.

Local councils rely on property taxes, agricultural levies, market stalls and licence fees for funds.

Health Services. Expenditures on rural health care are increasing. Field training of rural health teams, expanded rural health service programmes, building of rural health centres and family planning programmes are among the growing needs. Hospitals and some health care clinics and dispensaries are financed by the government. A number of health care institutions are supported by large-scale commercial and agricultural interests and various religious and missionary groups.

The Voluntary Sector. The government assumes the responsibility of ensuring that people have basic services of primary schools, health care centres and roads. These services are of major concern to local authorities and voluntary agencies. The urgency of these needs require government funds for personnel, resources, management and formulation of projects. These projects also include rural water programmes.

THE AGED

Kenya has a young popoulation, 50 per cent is 15 years of age or younger. The urban population and

Kenya

well educated women have fewer children. This is related, in part, to the availability of family-planning facilities in rural areas. There is an increase in the number of live births because of improved standards of hygiene, nutrition and health care. It is estimated that only four per cent of the population is 65 years of age or older. The life expectancy was 55 years of age in the early 1980s but is now 60 years of age.

The extended family shares the responsibility for caring for the aged. Respect for age is a paramount value among Kenyan tribes. Aged parents expect their children to care for them when they are no longer capable of providing for themselves (Tiemey 1986).

Social Security

Provident Fund Benefit
Upon substantial retirement for regular work (after age 60 for both men and women) a lump-sum benefit equal to the latest employee and employer contribution, plus interest, are paid to provident fund members. (This may be taken as an annuity or in instalments.) It is payable at age 55 if the member has been out of covered employment for three months.

Personal Social Services
Traditional mutual aid of the family, clan and organised groups, especially in rural areas where most of the population lives, continues to be the major source of services provided for the aged. Funeral grants are sometimes made. Older Kenyans are being separated from the able-bodied poor. The aged and the unemployed are the major causes of dependency and poverty in Kenya.

Evaluation
Responsibility for the welfare of the aged rests predominantly with the extended family. The range of statutory social services available to this group is quite limited and focused on the urban areas.

Social security protection is provided by a provident fund.

Kenya

NEEDY FAMILIES

The local community assumes some responsibility for both the social and economic needs of its members. People live in close groups and do give communal and mutual support to those in need. These services include returning individuals to their particular tribes or kinship groups. Social needs are met by the natural means related to usage and custom. Provisions are often made and paid for in kind. These standards of exchange are established by each tribal group. Community kitchens for orphans and poor families, funeral grants, care of widows, help during droughts and famine, sickness and disease are among the services provided in these communcal services to the needy.

Women in Kenya. Women produce much of the country's food, but do not own the farms. Most of them, along with their children, farm while the husband is employed in another village or town. They carry water from long distances, transport their goods to market, farm the land, tend the children, gather fuel and at times respond to community or church demands. Dowries, polygamy and female circumcision are ancient controversial issues. Dowries are valued in some areas not only as a tradition to link families, but also as a market deal for financial gain (Kaplan 1982, p.341).

Agriculture and services employ the greatest number of women in the private sector. The services sector requires a school certificate and includes labour such as nurses, midwives, teachers and typists. The majority of Kenyan women do not work in wage employment and monetary market systems. Maternal and child care, malnutrition, diseases, environmental sanitation, clean water and location of health care facilities are major social problems confronting Kenyan women.

The government has a family planning programme through most of the rural health facilities.

Social Security

Survivors' Benefits. Survivors of provident fund contributors receive the balance in the deceased's account in the form of either a lump-sum payment, an annuity or in instalments.

Under the workmen's compensation scheme

Kenya

dependent survivors receive a lump-sum of 41 months' earnings, less any disability benefits paid, up to a maximum of 29,000 shillings. A lump-sum funeral grant covering the cost of a funeral is also paid.

Personal Social Services
The personal social services are provided by the Department of Housing and include community development, adult education, social welfare training, sports, vocational rehabilitation, national libraries, culture and museums. The Department of Social Services, through adult education, provides literacy classes and formal education; nursery school teachers, club leaders, local authority councillors and farmers are trained under this project. Priority has been given to areas of education, health care, housing and water.

Evaluation
Responsibility for the welfare of needy families is shared by the central government and the local community.

CHILDREN AND YOUTH

Children under 15 years of age make up 50 per cent of the population (Burrows 1975). At one time there was an ordinance prohibiting the employment of children. Recent surveys, mostly in the rural areas, show children aged between 8 and 14 years to be part of the active work-force. In rural areas, children work along with the total family to secure the family income. This is often in line with the cultural tradition of many of the families.

Personal Social Services
Youth development programmes are among the projects of social welfare. Youth programmes are responsible for taking care of problems of school leavers and preparation of youth aged between 16 and 30 years for employment. This programme is financed by grant-in-aid from the Ministries and local authorities.

Voluntary and international agencies operate family and child welfare services. The orientation is toward prevention rather than remedial treatment. Foster care and institutional care are also provided by these agencies. The

Kenya

government provides consultation and supervision for those agencies from the Council of Social Services. Adoption is not widely accepted in Kenya. Day-care and nursery centres continue to grow. Nursery school teachers and supervisors are trained through the government's district training centres.

Infant mortality rate is high. Children under the ages of 16 pay little, if any, fees for public health care.

Adoption and foster care is the responsibility of the Department of Social Services, which administers and monitors child placements.

Orphanages are available in some urban areas, sponsored by voluntary agencies.

Evaluation
A modest range of services are available predominantly to children in urban areas. No social security programmes are aimed at this target group.

THE UNEMPLOYED

Unemployment among Kenyans continues to be a problem. There are three types of unemployment: rural migrants to urban areas, rural unemployed and under-employed (unskilled) and the educated unemployed. School leavers pose a problem for employment. The majority of the population in both the urban and rural areas have low incomes and a lack of services.

The flow of eligible labourers from one district to another in search of work has affected the productivity of many areas, especially small land owners where many times women and children are left to farm. There is a shortage of men to provide labour on many of their own farms. Their migration has caused problems of unemployment in other towns. The unemployed, including the labouring poor, sell mostly to tourists. They are the wood carvers, weavers, basket makers, jewellers, goldsmiths and artists. Herbalists, diviners, doctors or healers are among this group. This is a day-to-day existence, with fierce competition and limited goods and without permanent returns (Sandbrook 1982, p.162).

Casual labourers are among the labouring poor and are under-employed. These are day labourers, auto mechanics, tailors, unemployed desperate youth, and small scale manufacturers.

Kenya

Social drop-outs or rejects comprise a minor portion of the unemployed economy. Alms giving from the more able population helps this group to survive. In some areas there are associations to protect themselves and promote their common interests (Sandbrook 1982). The intellectuals and the educated unemployed represent many university students; some exist on very small incomes. Some of these are experiencing political discontent.

The government exercises strict control over trade unions in Kenya. All trade unions must be registered, avoid striking, be supervised by state-supervised centres and have membership in the federation of unions. However, various organised groups become involved and strike for the mutual concerns of the participants for their economic and political welfare.

Personal Social Services

The Kenyan government finances training institutions to develop skills in five major areas: foundry and mill operating, electric components and machines, tailoring and dress making, furniture making and joinery and the assembly of small equipment and machines.

Migrant labour systems provide large numbers of unskilled labourers from which employers may choose employees. This relieves the employer of many social security obligations to workers. Tribal groups also provide direct security for their members.

The National Youth Services, the tripartite agreement between employers, labour and government, road construction and unemployment relief programmes are direct actions to reduce unemployment and problems arising from unemployment. The government regulates conditions of wage employment to ensure reasonable remuneration, reasonable treatment of employees and a decent working environment. Programmes are designed for upgrading knowledge and skills in order to improve the labour force.

Evaluation

Chronic unemployment is an on-going problem in Kenya. Vocational training is available. Responsibility for the welfare of the unemployed falls largely on families and tribal groups. No social security protection is available.

Kenya

THE SICK

Kenya has a national health service which in theory assures adequate health care for all. However, the majority of the people still depend on traditonal healers as the first line of defence against illness (UNICEF 1981, p.20). The system uses an upward referral system with dispensaries in the most rural areas, clinics in small townships and hospitals in major urban centres.

Health Care Services. The health care system is classified as: public health care, missionary health care which has some orientation toward hospitals and curative care, mostly in rural areas, and the private services where there is a fee for health care.
   The responsibility for public health care is under the auspices of the Ministry of Health.
   Central government trains health care service providers.

Rural Health Care. Approximately 85-90 per cent of Kenya's population is rural. There are mobile clinics, dispensaries, sub-health care centres and health centres provided by the government through the Ministry of Health. Out patient services are free. Patients must often walk miles in rural areas for care.
   Water related childhood diseases and intestinal infections cause illness and death in children. Many skin conditions exist because of contaminated water supplies. Water is often taken from springs, dams, boreholes and rivers.
   Low level of literacy is problematic for dispensing literature related to specific instructions or preventative health care.

Social Security

Temporary Disability Benefits. An allowance of 50 per cent of earnings is provided as part of the workmen's compensation scheme to covered workers, which is payable after a three-day waiting period (which is waived if the disability exceeds three days) up to a maximum of 540 shillings.

Evaluation
Kenya has sought to provide an adequate health system but it has, however, been only moderately successful. Social welfare support for the sick and injured is virtually non-existent.

Kenya

ASSESSMENT OF THE KENYAN WELFARE SYSTEM

There is a paucity of social services for the needy in Kenya, which is a land in transition. It is a young country that has been responsible for its own governance since winning independence from Britain in 1963. Many natural problems plague the country.

Cultural factors influence the trends of the country. There are four major tribes and several other smaller tribes in Kenya. The diversity in belief systems and the basic needs, values, traditions and customs affect use and distribution of the limited resources of Kenya. Change in Kenya is swift and dramatic.

Governmental services, are extremely limited, and decentralised. Availability, accessibility and acceptability are the major sources of concern. Basic needs of food, shelter, clothing and housing are unmet. There is regional inequality in distribution of resources from the government. The extended family, clan and/or tribe interact and share to meet many of the basic needs. Most of the population lives in rural areas and is involved in agricultural production.

Unemployment is a major problem. There are three major categories of unemployed: rural migrants to urban areas, rural unemployed and unskilled and the educated unemployed. The increasing migration of the population has a direct influence on the availability of jobs in certain localities. The school-leavers, the inequality of women (Kenya is a male dominated society where women do most of the agricultural work), poor working conditions; high youth unemployment and the lack of employment benefits contribute to the rampant poverty in much of Kenya, especially in the rural areas.

There are self-help groups and moves toward community cohesion in decision making and provision of resources. Many social problems are, however, still prevalent.

Health care, especially in the rural areas, is inadequate. There are problems of immunisation, maternal care, child care, environmental hygiene, contaminated water, high infant mortality, short life expectancy, malnutrition, lack of modern technology and a shortage of trained medical professionals to meet the basic health care needs of most of Kenya. There is an inequality of distribution of services between the rural and urban areas. Urban areas which, according to Kimani (1981, p.336), 'comprise only about ten per cent of Kenya's population are overcrowded with health care facilities'. Under utilization of existing resources is also a problem in many of the rural areas. This phenomenon has a relationship to cultural values, the distance one has to travel to get to the services, economic conditions and knowledge about the services.

Geographic diversity, seasonal changes and seasonal conditions affect the economy and the welfare of the Kenyans. Farming and agriculture are the major areas of the economy. The farm is in transition and is moving from family subsistence to the fast growing market place.

More and more emphasis is being placed on educating the masses. Education has been one of the fastest growing expenditures of the government. There is a pressing need for an expansion of social services for the maximum benefits to the people (Burrows 1975, p.37).

Research and statistical data are becoming more prevalent as interested scholars identify objectives and goals to accommodate or meet the needs of the Kenyan population.

The basic human needs continue to go unmet among the majority of the population in Kenya. The social welfare system is not yet adequately meeting the needs of the people. The conditions that impoverish or contribute to the debilitation of people affect many communities of Kenyans. Solutions could be found, but only with money and technology that Kenya does not have at this time.

REFERENCES AND FURTHER READING

Ake, Claude (1981), <u>A Political Economy of Africa</u>, London: Longman.

Bates, Robert H. (1983), <u>Essays on the Political Economy of Rural Africa</u>, New York: Cambridge University Press.

Burrows, John (1975), <u>Kenya in the Second Decade</u>, Baltimore: John Hopkins University Press.

Clark, Leon E. (1969), <u>Through African Eyes: Cultures in Change</u>, New York: Frederick A. Praeger.

Kenya

Dumonga, John (1969), Africa between East and West, Pennsylvania: Dufour Editions.

Fosbrooke, H. A. (1960), 'Social Security As a Felt Want in East and Central Africa', International Social Security Association Bulletin, 13(6), 279-89.

Hartwig, Charles W. (1979), 'Church-State Relations in Kenya: Health Issues', Social Science and Medicine, 136, 121-7.

Hazlewood, Arthur (1978), 'Kenya: Income Distribution and Poverty - An Unfashionable View', The Journal of Modern African Studies, 16, 81-95.

Hopkins, John (1963), The Economic Development of Kenya, Baltimore: John Hopkins Press.

Kamarck, Andrew (1967), The Economics of African Development, New York: Praeger.

Kaplan, Marion (1982), Focus Africa, New York: Doubleday.

Kenyatta, Jomo, Facing Mount Kenya, Nairobi: Heinemann Educational Books.

Kimani, Violet Nyambura (1981), 'The Unsystematic Alternative: Towards Plural Health Care Among the Kikuyu of Central Kenya', Social Science Medicine, 15B, 333-40.

Legum, Colin (ed) (1980-81), African Contemporary Record: Annual Survey and Documents, New York: Africana Publishing.

MacPhee, Marshall A. (1968), Kenya, New York: Frederick A. Praeger.

Mburu, F.M. (1981), 'Implications of the Ideology and Implementation of Health Policy in a Developing Country', Social Medicine, 15A, 17-24.

Miller, Norman N. (1984), Kenya: The Quest for Prosperity, Boulder, Colorado: Westview Press.

Kenya

Musiga, L. O. (1974), 'Problems of Social Protection in Kenya', International Social Security Association Bulletin, 27(4), 479-98.

Mwahi, Germano M. (1986), 'Health Care Decisions At the Household Level: Results of a Rural Health Survey In Kenya', Social Science Medicine, 22, 315-19.

Nelson, Harold D. (ed.) (1984), Kenya, A Country Study (3rd edition), Washington DC: US Government Printer.

Nielsen, Waldemar A. (1966), Africa, New York: Atheneum.

Olorunsola, Victor A. (1972), The Politics of Cultural Sub-nationalism in Africa, New York: Doubleday.

Oser, Jacob (1967), Promoting Economic Development, Evanston: Northwestern University Press.

Roushdi, H. and Mott, S. (1979), 'The Impact of Current and Future Population Growth Rates on the Short Term Social and Economic Development in Kenya', Population Studies and Research Institute, University of Nairobi, September (mimeo).

Rweyemamu, J.F. (ed) (1980), Industrialization and Income Distribution in Africa, Senegal: CODESRIA.

Sandbrook, Richard (1982), The Politics of Basic Needs, Toronto: University of Toronto Press.

Tiemey, John (1986), 'Fanisi Choice', Science, 7, (1), January, pp.26-42.

Ungar, Sandford J. (1978-1985), Africa, The People and Politics of An Emerging Continent, New York: Simon and Schuster.

UNICEF (1981), Country Profile: Kenya, Geneva.

US Social Security Administration (1985), Social Security Programs Throughout the World, Washington, D.C.: Department of Health and Human Services.

Kenya

Wasow, Bernard (1981), 'The Working Age Sex Ratio and Job Search Migration in Kenya', The Journal of Developing Areas, 15, pp.435-44.

World Bank (1985), World Development Report 1985, New York: Oxford University Press.

MAURITIUS
Mohipnarain Joynathsing

THE WELFARE SYSTEM ENVIRONMENT

The Socio-Economic Environment
The state of Mauritius, with a population of one million people, has about 2,000 square kilometres of land but within its 200 mile limit of economic sovereignty it has 1.6 million kilometres of territory.

Human settlement only started in Mauritius in the seventeenth century with the Dutch. When the Dutch left in the eighteenth century the French came in. Nearly a century later, during the Napoleonic war, the French were to give way to the British, who ruled for more than 150 years before granting Mauritius her independence in 1968. With the Dutch, the French and the British came influxes of people from many localities in Africa, the Indian sub-continent and China. Around three per cent of Mauritians are of Chinese origin, while some 68 per cent originate from the Indian sub-continent; the remainder are labelled 'general population' and follow mainly the Roman Catholic faith.

Mauritius is a meeting place of great ancient cultures. The population is also multilingual - the official language is English, but many prefer to speak French. Indeed, the lingua franca is Creole and Bhojpuri - a dialect from Bihar in India - is the second most popular language.

Mauritius has no mineral resources, although its zone of economic sovereignty is not lacking in renewable and non-renewable resources.

Mauritius has always had a highly open economy. Although it is no longer quite the one-crop economy it was in the 1960s, the sugar industry is still the dominant foreign exchange earner. Mauritius has a small population which

Mauritius

provides only relatively small domestic markets, often insufficient for modern large-scale activities in commerce and industry. Moreover, the country is geographically isolated. Nevertheless, Mauritius had a per capita Gross National Product of $US1,160 in 1983 (World Bank 1985).

Despite such handicaps, strenuous efforts have been made and are continuing to be made, in the setting up of manufacturing industries (especially within the Export Processing Zone); in the intensification and diversification of agriculture; in the development of tourism; in the setting up of an Export Services Zone; and to promote regional economic cooperation.

Mauritius has, since the late 1970s, adopted a series of austerity measures taken in conformity with guidelines from the International Monetary Fund and the World Bank. She is under severe pressure to reduce the deficits on both her recurrent government budget and her balance of payments. This accelerated the rate of inflation quite markedly.

The country experienced a very high population growth rate in the 1950s and 1960s - so much so that the population of 600,000 at the end of 1950 was expected to reach three million by the year 2000. Considerable efforts were made, and continue to be made, to curb population growth rate. The population is now expected to reach 1.2 to 1.3 million by 2000. The labour force, which was estimated at 273,000 in 1975, is expected to reach about 485,000 by the turn of the century.

THE POLITICAL ENVIRONMENT

Mauritius is a democracy with regular elections, universal suffrage, a written constitution and an independent and well-established judiciary. As a parliamentary democracy it has been operating along the pattern of Westminster but with marked differences: there is only one chamber, namely the Legislative Assembly; the Head of State is, to all intents and purposes, the Governor-General, appointed by the British Monarch; and the Head of Government is the Prime Minister.

The past 25 years have seen a major expansion in public spending on the social services. The actual proportion of recurrent budget devoted to health, education, social security and food subsidies remains unchanged at about 42 per cent, but the level of spending rose 15 times in current prices from 1958 to 1980.

This expansion of social welfare activities reflects a long standing commitment of the Mauritius Labour Party (in power up to 1982) to social welfare spending. As far back as 1949, Sir Seewoosagur Ramgoolam, the last Labour Party Prime Minister, was arguing in favour of food subsidies, old age pensions, health insurance and improved educational services. At the same time, he proposed the levying of a sugar export tax in order to pay for social expenditures. The Mauritius Labour Party's commitment to social welfare derived more from British Fabian thinking than from any general development strategy.

IDEOLOGICAL ENVIRONMENT

The foundation stone of the Welfare State in Mauritius was laid by the Labour Party, founded in February 1936 by Dr Maurice Cure and led by Dr (later Sir) Seewoosagur Ramgoolam from the 1950s onwards, which waged a relentless struggle for the setting up of an egalitarian society.

Prior to 1936, the oligarchy of French planters and merchants, with the connivance of the British Governor of the Crown Colony of Mauritius, held both economic and political power. The workers had to toil very hard for starvation wages and in their old age they were left to beg for a living. There was no provision for old age pension and even medical care was almost non-existent for the poor. Primary education was the preserve of a privileged few, while the majority of working-class children had to work in the fields to supplement the meagre wages of their parents.

The Mauritius Labour Party brought the masses into the mainstream of Mauritian politics by organising them into trade unions under the party's umbrella. In its early days the party was led by firebrands and left wing revolutionary politicians whose aim was to overthrow the old non-egalitarian and unjust order. General strikes were organised to paralyse the economy, but these strikes were severely crushed by the British Government in league with the French planters. In 1950 Dr Ramgoolam became the leader of the Labour Party. Deeply imbued with a sense of justice and fairness, Sir Seewoosagur was inspired by Fabianism, and more particularly by the Webbs,

George Bernard Shaw and Harold Laski, all of whom he met in his student days in England. He came to the conclusion that socialism, that is, a greater sense of social justice via a redistribution of wealth, can be achieved peacefully by gradual, evolutionary changes. He was, therefore, more acceptable to the British Government and the British colonial authorities.

The advent of the Labour Government in England in 1946 and the publication and eventual implementation of the Beveridge Report had an impact on the colonial authorities in Mauritius. They became less insensitive to the plight of the suffering masses. The lonely and yet forceful voice of Dr Ramgoolam, as a nominee from the 1940s, awakened the colonial powers to the stark reality of our unjust social system.

However, Dr Ramgoolam was quick to realise that the key to any improvement in the living and working conditions of the workers lay with political power. The Labour Party, under his leadership, militated for one man one vote, self-government and finally independence. The right to vote, hitherto the preserve of the propertied class, was extended in 1948 and in the subsequent elections the Labour Party won a majority in the legislature.

Under pressure from the Labour Party, social legislation was passed in the 1950s to institute old age pensions and widow and orphan reliefs. A vast school-building programme was undertaken to ensure that all the children of school-going age could receive primary education. Furthermore fully-equipped hospitals were built to attend to the sick.

Adult universal suffrage became a reality in 1959 and was followed by a partial transfer of power to the majority party - the Labour Party. More welfare legislation was passed, financed by imposing a progressive income tax on the propertied classes. When in 1968 Mauritius became independent, under the leadership of Dr Ramgoolam, the socialist-oriented Labour Party consolidated and further strengthened the Welfare State. Sir Seewoosagur Ramgoolam, the grand old man of Mauritian politics, passed away in 1982. His greatest legacy is the Welfare State of Mauritius. He has succeeded in instituting a new social order, amidst fierce opposition by the landowning classes, through gradual and evolutionary changes.

Mauritius

HISTORICAL ORIGINS

When Mauritius became independent in 1968, the main constituents of the welfare system were the following:

- the social services provided by the state and the provisions for social security and fiscal welfare;
- provisions made on an occupational basis for civil servants and other employees;
- charitable provisions assisted by the State; and
- the activities of trade unions and friendly societies.

State Provisions. In addition to free and universal health and educational services there was also a system of relief. The government's channel for the distribution of relief to needy people was the Public Assistance Department. Since 1950 the Department has also administered non-contributory old age and blind pensions. Orginally these pensions were subject to a means test, but this was abolished in 1957. Until 1960 pensions were not considered as a taxable income.

Workmen's Compensation. A system of compensation for industrial injuries and diseases was provided for by the Workmen's Compensation Ordinance in 1931.

War Disability Pensions. War disability pensions were paid to Mauritian ex-service men after the Second World War at half the rates applicable to United Kingdom war pensioners.

Outdoor Relief. A means tested outdoor relief system has long been administered by the Public Assistance Department, which inherited this function from the Old Poor Law, dating back to the 1830s. There were Public Assistance Officers in all the towns and larger villages to receive new applications or to examine renewed applications. Each new application was considered by the Public Assistance Advisory Committee composed of prominent members of the local community. Outdoor relief was not granted to the able-bodied unemployed except in extreme cases of destitution. In the great majority of cases the granting of relief was dependent on the applicant

Mauritius

obtaining a medical certificate from a Government Medical Office.

Outdoor relief was a system of part-maintenance and calculated on the basis of a scale rate which took into account the composition of the household and the circumstances of its members. Additional allowances were given in cases of one-person households and sickness such as tuberculosis and other wasting diseases. A wage stop could be applied and if there was a child in the household earning in excess of a prescribed amount, part of the excess was deducted from the relief proposed.

Fiscal Welfare. Persons whose income was large enough to be subject to income tax had additional provisions made for their needs by a system of income tax concessions; allowances were allowed in respect of all children under 16 or attending full-time instruction. More generous allowances were granted for children studying abroad. Life assurance premiums were also tax deductible.

Occupational Social Security. The oldest occupational retirement scheme dates back to 1859 and it gives a pension on the retirement of clerical and higher civil servants at age 60 (or earlier on compulsory retirement) and a gratuity at death before retirement.

Compassionate Allowances. Originally, no comparable scheme existed for non-pensionable manual workers in the civil service. Since 1905, less generous provisions have been made for them. A pension became payable to non-pensionable civil servants at the discretion of the Governor and for this reason was called 'compassionate allowances'. In practice, however, they were granted automatically except in cases of dismissal on grounds of misconduct.

Widows and Orphans Pensions. The contributory Widows and Orphans Pension Fund has existed since 1886 to enable pensionable civil servants to provide for their dependants in the event of their death. Membership of the Fund was compulsory.

Local Bodies Pension Schemes. Pension schemes for certain employees of Town Boards and the Municipality of Port Louis were set up in 1925 and

Mauritius

1929 respectively. They were modelled on the civil service scheme.

Sugar Industry Pension Fund. This scheme was set up in 1956 and covered all sugar industry workers paid monthly. Both employers and employees contributed to the Fund. A retirement pension was provided.

Charitable Funds. Additional arrangements have existed since the Second World War to supplement the statutory provisions for ex-servicemen and for the blind. The Ex-servicemen's Welfare Fund was set up in 1946 to provide temporary assistance for ex-servicemen. The Fund derived its revenue from the Lotteries Fund and partly from a government grant.
   In addition to the old age pension for blind persons over the age of 40, an additional allowance has been paid by the Welfare of the Blind and Prevention of Blindness Society. The Society also provided blind men with an opportunity of earning a small income by basket-making at the Lois Lagesse Residential and Training Centre.

Friendly Societies and Trade Unions. There are a number of associations in Mauritius which carry on friendly society activities. Among the earliest is the Civil Service Mutual Aid Association which was incorporated in 1894 to make loans to civil servants. Other 'Mutual Aid Societies' existed whose main function was the payment of funeral benefits. Some of the trade unions also had burial funds.

Informal Arrangements. In Mauritius where family ties are still strong when normal sources of income are interrupted the individual can usually rely for some degree of assistance from the family. Otherwise there is also a system of credit which enables daily needs to be met. A very important person in this system is the village shop keeper from whom most of the necessities of life are purchased. If the customer is unemployed or is short of cash the shop keeper will give credit. Payments or part-payments are normally effected on a weekly basis or when the person goes back to work.
   Another source of credit is the employer. In the villages this usually means the job

Mauritius

contractor or the sirdar, but the practice of making loans to employees on the security of their accrued or future earnings is found in most types of employment. Although these arrangements may sometimes result in the job contractor acquiring an undesirable hold over his debtors they are sometimes beneficial in the absence of social security provisions and they certainly help the worker and his family to weather some of the contingencies of sickness and unemployment.

THE WELFARE SYSTEM: AN OVERVIEW

It is a mark of every civilised society that it shows compassion for the least fortunate of its members. This compassion manifests itself through the setting up of social services catering for the needs of vulnerable groups. The expansion of social services in recent years bears testimony to government's determination to eradicate the problem of want, disease and ignorance. There is now a comprehensive system of social security and the services of health, education and family planning are mostly free and universal. There is also a Ministry of Youth and Sports which promotes healthy activities for the youth without any form of discrimination.

Social Security Programmes

A dominant feature of the Mauritius welfare system is, undoubtedly, its social security system (see Table 1). The use of the term 'social security' in Mauritius is limited to what many countries describe as income maintenance programmes. It thus excludes the provision of medical care, but embraces both social insurance and social assistance programmes. Historically, social assistance dates back to legislation at the start of the twentieth century, whereas social insurance as a state concern is essentially a product of the 1970s.

The social security system comprises:

- a Social Aid Scheme which derives from the Old Poor Law,
- a National Pension Scheme,
- a Family Allowance Scheme, and
- an Unemployment Hardship Relief Scheme.

Mauritius

TABLE 1 : THE MAURITIUS SOCIAL SECURITY SYSTEM

Programmes[1]	1981-2	1982-3	1983-4[2]	1984-5[3]
1. Outdoor Relief				
. No. of beneficiaries (regular)	13,659	12,354	12,122	9,640
. Total amount paid (Rs Mn)	18.4	19.5	20.9	20.5
2. Indoor Relief				
. No. of persons in infirmaries	639	611	623	627
. No. of persons in orphanages	166	162	138	114
. Total per capita grants paid (Rs Mn)	2.44	2.45	2.46	2.59
3. Family Allowance				
. No. of beneficiaries	28,858	25,173	21,637	18,972
. Total amount paid (Rs Mn)	19.10	16.70	14.40	12.50
4. Retirement Pension				
. No. of beneficiaries:				
Basic Pension	67,477	68,677	71,515[3]	74,168
Contributory Pension	3,604	4,588	6,399	7,856
. Amount paid (Rs Mn):				
Basic Pension	112.70	133.40	151.80	168.90
Contributory Pension	2.58	3.93	5.65	7.88
5. Widow's Pension & Child's Allowance				
. No. of beneficiaries:				
Basic Pension	17,074	17,262	17,194	17,090
Contributory Pension	683	993	1,264	1,524
. Amount paid (Rs Mn):				
Basic Pension	35.50	40.30	44.10	45.60
Contributory Pension	0.65	1.02	1.46	1.84
6. Orphans' Pension & Guardian's Allowance				
. No. of orphans:				
Basic Pension	1,030	1,012	981	964
Contributory Pension	105	125	133	135
. No. of guardians:	690	705	693	680
. Amount paid (Rs Mn):				
Basic Pension	1.04	1.22	1.25	1.29
Contributory Pension	0.02	0.04	0.04	0.05

Mauritius

7. Invalidity Pension & Child's Allowance				
. No. of beneficiaries:				
Basic Pension	8,541	10,173	11,179	12,094
Contributory Pension	427	574	780	926
. Amount paid (Rs Mn)				
Basic Pension	15.70	21.70	26.40	30.50
Contributory Pension	0.30	0.48	0.72	1.00
8. Inmates Allowance[4]				
. No. of beneficiaries	558	544	530	525
. Total amount paid (Rs Mn)	0.16	0.18	0.19	0.20
9. Industrial Injury Benefit[5]				
. Total amount paid (Rs Mn)	1.81	2.22	2.81	3.02
10. Lump Sum Payment to ex SIPF Members				
. Total amount paid (Rs Mn)	3.42	3.21	3.72	3.85
11. Unemployment Hardship Relief[6]				
. No. of beneficiaries	-	5,837	8,203	8,428
. Total amount paid (Rs Mn)	-	1.71	12.24	17.31

Notes:

1. Payment of contributory benefits under the National Pension Scheme has been effective as from July 1978. Beneficiaries of basic and contributory pension are shown separately. But since beneficiaries of contributory pension are also eligible for the corresponding basic pension, the number of beneficiaries of the basic pension also includes those receiving contributory pension.
2. Revised.
3. Provisional.
4. An allowance payable to a person who is otherwise qualified to receive a basic pension but is disqualified to receive that pension because he is an inmate of a charitable institution.
5. Effective as from August 1979.
6. Effective as from February 1983.

SOURCE: Mauritius, CSO 1985.

Mauritius

Social Aid. The Social Aid Act 1983, which superseded previous public assistance legislation, defines the categories of persons entitled to social aid: any person who, as a result of (a) any physical or mental disability, (b) any sickness or accident certified by an approved medical practitioner, (c) abandonment by her spouse, (d) any sudden loss of employment which has lasted continuously for not less than six months, and (e) being temporarily or permanently incapable of earning adequately his livelihood and having insufficient means to support himself and his dependants, shall be qualified to claim social aid. This scheme thus covers the various vulnerable groups in society, such as children, the elderly, the disabled, deserted wives and the unemployed.

The computation of social aid requires a comparison of a claimant's resources with his or her requirements. Eighty per cent of the monthly income of all children, after deduction of a sum of Rs. 100 from that income, is disregarded in the means test. To encourage claimants certified fit for light work and their spouses to work, an amount representing 50 per cent of their total monthly income is also disregarded. When computing the resources of an applicant for social aid, only his apparent income is taken into account such as rent, financial assistance from relatives, income from cane and tea cultivation, proceeds from sale of vegetables and wages from part-time work. Immovable property, furniture and electrical appliances are completely disregarded if they do not generate income.

The Social Aid Act also provides for the following benefits:

- Fisherman's Allowance: an allowance is paid to a registered fisherman whenever bad weather prevents him from engaging in his normal occupation for three consecutive days (excluding public holidays).

- Funeral Grant: a funeral grant is paid in respect to the burial of a social aid claimant or a destitute retirement pensioner.

- Allowance to Cyclone Refugee: a daily allowance is paid to each adult and child belonging to the afflicted family for a period not exceeding three days.

Mauritius

- <u>Allowance to Fire Victims</u>: cash and in-kind assistance is extended to the victims of a fire.

- <u>Cash Assistance to Discharged Destitute Prisoners</u>.

- <u>Refund of Travelling Expenses Incurred by the Sick Seeking Medical Treatment</u>.

- <u>Assistance in Kind</u>.

<u>The National Pension Scheme</u>. The National Pension Scheme is based on a report to the government in April 1976 by Professor Brian Abel-Smith and Mr Tony Lynes. The proposals were enacted in the National Pensions Act 1976, which has since been amended by the National Pensions (Amendments) Acts of 1979, 1980 and 1981.

The Scheme provides for payment of three different classes of pensions:

- 'Basic Pensions' for which everyone in Mauritius is eligible, subject to certain conditions such as residence;
- 'Contributory Pensions' for which only those who have paid contributions to the scheme are eligible; and
- 'Industrial Injury Pensions' for which only those contributors who are employed are eligible.

Basic pensions are non-contributory and are payable at a flat rate and this cost is borne wholly by government. Contributory pensions, on the other hand, are earnings-related, the size of the pension depending on the amount of the earnings-related contributions that have been paid in respect of the individual. Industrial injury pensions are earnings-related and depend on the size of the employee's earnings during the 12 months before the injury occurs.

- <u>Basic Pensions</u>: there are five main components of basic non-contributory pensions:

    - <u>Basic Retirement Pensions</u>: these are payable to everyone over the age of 60 who has satisfied certain residence qualifications.

Mauritius

- Widow's Pensions: these are payable to widows under the age of 60 who have not contracted a subsequent civil or religious marriage. However, upon remarriage a lump sum equal to 12 times the monthly pension is payable and upon reaching the age of 60 basic retirement pension becomes payable. A child's allowance is payable for up to three children where there are dependent children.

- Invalidity Pensions: these are payable to those between the ages of 15 and 60 who have been certified by a medical board as being substantially disabled either permanently or for a period of at least 12 months. Child's allowance is payable for up to three children where there are dependent children.

- Orphan's Pensions and Guardian's Allowances: Orphan's pensions are payable for orphans under the age of 15 (or under 18 if still in full-time education) and guardian's allowance is payable to the person looking after the orphan.

- Inmate's Allowances: these benefits are payable to those inmates of charitable institutions who would otherwise be eligible for retirement or invalidity benefit.

The basic pensions are flat rate with the following monthly benefit rates as from 1 July 1985:

```
Retirement            -  Rs 201  (higher pensions
                                  are payable to
                                  persons over the
                                  age of 75 or who
                                  are handicapped)
Widow's Pension       -  Rs 201
Invalidity Pension    -  Rs 201
Orphan's Pension      -  Rs  50  per orphan
Guardian's Pension    -  Rs  81  per guardian
Child's Allowance
  under age of 10     -  Rs  40
  age 10-15           -  Rs  61
  (18 if at school)
Inmate's Allowance    -  Rs  29
```

Mauritius

Increases in the benefit rates for basic pensions are at the government's discretion.

- Contributory Pensions: where everyone in Mauritius is potentially eligible to receive basic pensions, only those people who have actually paid contributions to the National Pension Scheme (or their dependents) are eligible to receive contributory pensions. The amount of contributory pension payable depends on the number of pension points accrued which in turn depends on the amount of contribution paid. The cost of a pension point and its 'value' are in the ratio of 10.8:1; pension points acquired each year are added to those accrued in earlier years so that, with annual revaluations of the cost and value of pension points in line with the movement of earnings, the pension rights acquired each year do not lose their value over the years before pension becomes payable. Increases in contributory pensions in payment are at the government's discretion.

  - Retirement Pensions: a contributory retirement pension becomes payable from age 60, although it is open to anyone to defer receipt of his pension until after age 60. The ratio of the cost of a pension point to its value is such that someone with constant earnings (in real terms) paying contributions for 40 years can expect a contributory pension of one-third of his earnings (for the standard contribution of nine per cent) or one half of his or her earnings if he or she is contributing at the higher rate of 13.5 per cent. However, to enhance the level of pension payable to those unable to pay contributions to the scheme for 40 years, those aged 40 or over at the start of the scheme have had their number of pension points doubled when assessing the level of their contributory retirement pension; those aged between 20 and 40 at the start of the scheme have had their pension points adjusted as though they had accrued at their average annual rate for 40 years. There is a guaranteed minimum level of contributory retirement pension payable and the

Mauritius

government meets the cost of the excess of this guaranteed minimum over the amount that would otherwise have been payable.

- Widows Pensions: a contributory widow's pension is payable to widows of all ages, the amount payable depending on the number of pension points that her husband has acquired. To enhance the level of pension payable in cases where the husband was able to pay contributions for only a few years because, for example, of death occurring shortly after the introduction of the scheme or at an early age, the pension points accrued are enhanced as though they had accrued at their average annual rate for 20 years or until age 60 if this is less. The aim is to achieve for widows under age 60 a widow's pension of one-sixth of the husband's average earnings for the standard rate contribution or one-quarter of the husband's average earnings for the higher rate contributor.

  For a widow under age 60 with dependent children or where widowhood occurred within the past year, the level of contributory widow's pension is calculated as described above; in other cases where she is below age 60 the pension is payable at two-thirds of this amount. For a widow over age 60 the level of contributory widow's pension is based on the full amount of contributory retirement pension that her husband was, or would have been, entitled to receive at the time of his death.

- Invalidity Pensions: the amount of invalidity pension payable is calculated in a way very similar to that described above for widows, with enhancement just as for widow's pension and a two-thirds rate of benefit payable where there are no dependent children. The pension points accrued though are based on the invalidity pensioner's own contributions record rather than the spouse's.

Mauritius

- <u>Orphans Pensions</u>: the amount of pension payable is 15 per cent of the contributory pension that was, or would have been, in payment to either parent, whichever is higher.

- <u>Industrial Injury Pensions</u>: an industrial injury benefit may be payable where an employee who is a member of the scheme suffers from an accident or a prescribed disease resulting from his employment. An Industrial Injury Allowance is paid during any time of temporary total incapacity for work except for the first two weeks when the employer must pay normal earnings; the level of benefit is equal to 80 per cent of the employee's monthly earnings averaged over the 12 months before the injury occurs. A disablement pension is paid where the employee is disabled as a result of the accident, the size of the pension depending on the employee's earning and the percentage disablement. However, in the majority of cases the pension is commuted and a lump-sum payable instead. If death results from the accident any surviving widow would be eligible for a survivor's pension payable at the rate of half the deceased's monthly earnings; where there is no widow, benefits may be payable to any orphans or other dependants.

- <u>A Housing Loan Scheme</u>: the National Pension Scheme also provides for a Housing Loan Scheme for the benefit of insured persons.

<u>Family Allowance</u>. By the Family Allowance Ordinance 1961, as subsequently amended, all families having three children under the age of 15 and whose income does not exceed Rs 10,000 annually are entitled to a monthly family allowance of Rs 50. There is no doubt that this small amount, however insignificant it might seem, proves valuable for the purchase of food essential to children. This scheme was in line with government's population policy to encourage the three child family. However, with government's revised policy to reduce gross reproduction rate from 1.34 in 1981 to 1.12 by 1987 the relevance of this scheme, in its present form, is being questioned.

Mauritius

Unemployment Hardship Relief. This scheme was implemented in 1983 in accordance with the Unemployment Hardship Relief Act 1983.

The relief is payable to heads of households below the age of 60 who have family responsibilities and whose resources fall short of their minimum needs. The computation of the relief takes into account the minimum individual requirements of the head of family, his wife, unmarried dependants under the age of 20, and provides for an allowance for the payment of house rent. A woman who has no husband and is not entitled to social aid but has a family to look after is considered as the head of the family and is entitled to claim relief. Dependants include step and adopted children but do not comprise any collaterals.

Family income, if any, is considered when assessing the quantum of the relief payable. In order to encourage the working members of the family to remain in employment and stay within the household, part of the family income is disregarded. No account is taken of (a) the first Rs 100, (b) 50 per cent of the remaining family income, and (c) 80 per cent of the children's income, if any. Any National Pensions benefit or family allowance is deductible when determining the quantum of relief.

The main conditions for entitlement are that the claimant should be capable of and be available for work and have signed on regularly at the Employment Exchange and renewed his claim monthly at the Social Security Office of his locality.

Workmen's Compensation. In case of temporary but total incapacity it provides for an amount not exceeding 80 per cent of the worker's average weekly wages before the accident - where the incapacity is partial a weekly payment during incapacity of an amount not exceeding one half the difference between the worker's average weekly wages from the employer before the accident and the average weekly wages he is earning or able to earn after the accident.

Payment in either case is made for a maximum period of 36 months.

For permanent incapacity the amount of compensation under the act is:

- where the incapacity is total, a lump sum not exceeding eight years' wages; and where the incapacity is partial and depending on the nature of the injury either a percentage of the compensation that would have been payable in the case of permanent total incapacity or such percentage of the compensation that would have been payable in the case of permanent total incapacity as is proportionate to the loss of earning capacity permanently caused by the injury. However, the amount of compensation should not exceed 70 per cent of eight years' wages.

When the workman dies from injury caused by accident the act provides for compensation of up to six years' wages to his dependants. If he does not leave such dependents but leaves dependants in part dependent on his wages an amount, not exceeding six times the sum or value of the benefits received by such dependants from the workman during the 12 months immediately preceding the accident, is payable.

Social Security Finance

Social Assistance. The cost of the Social Aid Scheme, the Family Allowance Scheme and the Unemployment Hardship Scheme is wholly financed by government out of general revenue (see Table 2).

The National Pension Scheme. This is by far the most challenging social security programme that has been attempted in Mauritius for many years, and covers all employees aged between 18 and 60. Self employed and non-employed persons may join voluntarily. Contracting out is allowed only in respect of those who are covered adequately by other existing occupational schemes namely civil servants, employees of local authorities and parastatal bodies and all those who were members of the Sugar Industry Pension Fund prior to 1 January 1974.

The scheme is financed by contributions from employers and employees. However, government makes a substantial grant to the National Pension Fund to enable it to meet the cost of non-contributory basic pensions. Contributions are earnings-related and collected on a pay-as-you-go basis. Most employees contribute at the standard rate of three per cent of basic earnings and their employers contribute six per cent. Most employees on sugar estates contribute

Mauritius

TABLE 2 : GOVERNMENT EXPENDITURE ON SOCIAL WELFARE
1981-2 to 1984-5

	Rs Million			
	1981-2	1982-3	1983-4	1984-5
Education	474.9	532.6	531.9	542.5
Health	235.2	275.6	290.8	312.0
Social Security and Welfare	377.0	443.5	500.6	548.2
Housing and Community Amenities	43.8	20.2	25.0	28.5
Other Community and Social Services	19.4	21.5	22.0	18.0
Food Subsidies (Rice & Flour)	230.0	190.0	100.0	113.8
1. Total Social Welfare Expenditure	1,380.3	1,483.4	1,470.3	1,563.0
2. Total social welfare expenditure as a percentage of total current expenditure	47.7	46.0	43.3	42.3

SOURCE: Mauritius, CSO 1985.

five per cent of basic earnings and their employers 8.5 per cent. Other employers and their employees may opt to pay this higher rate of contribution.

Self-employed and unemployed persons may contribute voluntarily by multiples of Rs 5 up to a maximum of Rs 50 a month.

There are upper and lower limits of earnings for contribution liability; those earning below the earnings floor pay no contributions and those with higher earnings pay contributions only on earnings up to that ceiling. The level of the contribution floor and ceilings is adjusted periodically in accordance with the movement in earnings. With effect from 1 July 1985 the

Mauritius

maximum salary on which contributions are paid is Rs 2,500. The minimum monthly salary is:

- for domestic servants: Rs 156
- for others   Rs 247

Employers are responsible for the payment of the total contributions but are empowered to deduct the employee's share of contributions from his remuneration at the time of payment. Employees contributing at the higher rate are entitled to a pension, on retirement, representing half of average earnings after 40 years of contribution. Those contributing at the standard rate are entitled to a pension representing one third of average wage after 40 years of contribution.

All contributions from employers and employees are paid into a National Pension Fund into which government pays from general revenue the cost of all non-contributory benefits. The Fund is administered by the Minister for Finance. Accumulated funds are invested mainly in long term government stocks and Treasury bills thus meeting one of the many objectives of the scheme which is to build up a fund for national development.

Social Security Administration

The overall responsibility for the administration of social security rests with the Ministry of Labour and Social Security, Women's Rights and Family Welfare (henceforth the Ministry).

The Ministry is headed by a Permanent Secretary who is responsible for all policy matters. He is assisted by two Principal Assistant Secretaries and a number of administrative officers.

The Social Security Division of the Ministry is sub-divided into Social Aid and National Pensions. The Social Aid division is responsible for the administration of both outdoor and indoor relief and the family allowance scheme. The National Pension branch is responsible for the National Pension Scheme and the Unemployment Hardship Relief Scheme.

For the purpose of administering the social security schemes the island has a network of 39 local offices and a total of 142 other pay-points at which payments are made. Claims for social aid benefits are handled locally. With the exception of Family Allowance which is awarded by Higher

Mauritius

Social Security Officers posted at Head Office, assessment and payment of outdoor relief is effected at local level. Application for indoor relief is also processed at local level.

With the exception of retirement and industrial injury benefits which are paid by postal orders and cheques respectively all other benefits paid under the National Pensions Act are paid in cash by mobile pay clerks.

Unlike the case with Social Aid and the Unemployment Hardship Relief Scheme, the National Pensions Act provides for the setting up of appeal tribunals. A person not satisfied with the decision of a medical officer or a medical board may appeal to the Medical Tribunal. Where the appeal is against the decision of the awarding officer and not related to a medical issue, it goes to an appeal tribunal. Each tribunal is presided over by a member of the legal profession and assisted by two assessors.

Claims to any National Pension Scheme or Unemployment Hardship Relief Scheme benefits are determined centrally by Higher Social Security Officers. However, in order to avoid or reduce delay in cases of industrial injury, claims are handled by the Industrial Injury Branch, within the National Pensions Division.

The National Pensions Division is also responsible for the collection of contributions by the self-employed, keeping records of contributions credited to the account of each individual, processing, adjudicating on and assessing claims for pensions and arranging for regular payment of pensions.

Officers of the Visiting Branch are posted at local offices throughout the island. Their main task is to make employers aware of their obligations to pay and deduct contributions, to ensure that they complete correctly the returns showing the contributions which should be credited to the account of each member and make the necessary returns and payments regularly as the law requires.

For the purposes of the National Pension Scheme a National Pensions Board, operating in an advisory capacity to the Ministry executing the scheme, has been set up. The Board is a forum for consultations with representatives of employees and members of the scheme. The Board is also available for consultation on the administrative arrangements and, at the initial stage, on the

Mauritius

phasing-in of the scheme. At the implementation stage of the scheme the views of the Board were sought in draft regulations concerning entitlements to benefits and on how discretion should be exercised in such matters as the payment of widow's pensions and on any extra allowances for disabled pensioners. The Board may also advise on any matter relating to the National Penson Scheme referred to it by the Minister. It may also, of its own accord, advise on any matter relating to the Scheme.

The Administration and Financing of Personal Services

In the context of Mauritius the personal social services are referred to those services provided by government, to give help, other than medical and financial, to those needing such help because of old age or physical and mental infirmity. The people falling within the ambit of this definition include the elderly, the disabled, the blind, deaf, dumb, mentally handicapped and so on.

The aim of the personal social services is to combat the limiting effects of the disability on the personal and social life of the afflicted.

Ministry of Social Security. The major part of the expenditure on personal social services is derived from general revenue and channelled through the Ministry (see Table 2). Most of the services are administered at local level via a network of social security offices, social welfare centres, community centres and health centres.

Indoor Relief. Indoor relief is available in institutions run by charitable and voluntary organisations for orphans, elderly persons, unmarried mothers or deserted wives. At present there are 19 such institutions with a total number of inmates ranging from 700 to 800. These institutions are run on a purely voluntary basis by religious and cultural organisations from donations made by the public and the wages of religious brothers and sisters in Christian institutions. On rare occasions individuals and groups offer food to the inmates.

Government in conformity with the Social Aid Act provides some measure of assistance to these institutions through the Ministry. This assistance includes a per capita grant, a grant for the maintenance of building, a grant for the

Mauritius

employment of such staff as may be approved by the Minister and a yearly contribution in respect of every inmate.

THE AGED

The needs to which old age is likely to give rise do not stem solely from diminished physical or mental powers but from fundamental, and often sudden, changes in the social situtation caused by retirement, widowhood or isolation, accompanied generally by a substantial reduction of income. In Mauritius the family is still the primary caretaker of its elderly members and attempts to provide for these needs. As in many parts of the developing world elderly parents usually live with their married children from whom they get economic support while being a valuable help with child care and household tasks. However, whether supported by children or not elderly people are in need of a measure of financial independence. In Mauritius this financial independence is derived as occupational pensions in respect of past employment, from social security provisions or both.

Social Security

Retirement Pensions. A significant proportion of employees in Mauritius are covered by pension schemes related to their occupations and some of those schemes offer generous benefits. The Civil Service Pension Scheme and the scheme for employees of parastatal and local goverment bodies are among the schemes offering the most generous benefits. They guarantee a pension representing two-thirds of the retiree's last salary after the completion of 33.33 years' service. The size of the pension is, by and large, determined by the length of service.

The other major group of employees covered by an occupational pension scheme are monthly-employed workers in the sugar industry who are members of the Sugar Industry Pension Fund. Membership is limited to employees of estates of 100 arpents or more. Until 1973 the Fund had about 9,000 members, of whom about 3,300 were labourers, the remainder being artisans or staff. On 1 January 1974, as a result of Wages Order No. 134 of 1973, 28,000 workers formerly employed on a daily basis became monthly paid and were therefore admitted as members of the Fund which in 1976 comprised about 36,000 members.

Sugar estate workers on estates of between 25 and 100 arpents and some older workers on larger estates were covered by the provisions of the Sugar Industry Retiring Benefits Act 1973 under which, on retirement at the age of 60 or over after three years' service with the same employer, they were entitled to a gratuity and a small monthly pension.

Employees in the civil service and similar public sector schemes are in a special position in that pensions in payment can be and are revised when the cost of living increases though in the past the pension increases awarded have not fully matched the increase in prices. The government has been able to give this protection to ex-employees of the public sector because it can cover the additional cost through taxation. While the private employers can and sometimes do increase pensions in payment, they cannot guarantee to do so, as they have to consider the competitiveness of the prices of what they produce and the profitability of their enterprises.

However, with the advent of the National Pension Scheme in 1976 the entire pension scene has changed. This scheme provides for both a non-contributory basic pension for which everyone in Mauritius is potentially eligible, subject to satisfying age and residency qualifications; and a contributory pension of one-third of average earnings after 40 years of contribution. Employees who work to make additional provision through supplementary occupational schemes are encouraged to do so by generous tax concessions.

The scheme covers all employees aged between 18 and 60. Contracting out is allowed only in respect of employees of the public sector and persons who were members of the Sugar Pension Fund before 1 January 1974.

The basic pension is deemed to be sufficient in itself to provide for a reasonable standard of living and the earnings-related pension is intended to reflect the fact that pensions are deferred pay. The scheme also incorporates an element of both pre-retirement and post-retirement dynamism.

Rent Allowances. Elderly people living alone and who are liable to pay rents are, subject to a means test, entitled to a supplementary allowance under the Social Aid Scheme.

Mauritius

Personal Social Services
The government has spared no effort to promote the well-being of the elderly through care in and by the community. The government's strategy is to provide a range of community services which will enable old people to live, in dignity, in the community for as long as possible. For those who for health or other reasons can no longer live with their families or on their own, residential institutional facilities are provided. Finally, government, in close collaboration with voluntary organisations, endeavours to promote a better understanding of the process of ageing so that old age can become a more positive and productive period, not only for the elderly themselves but also for the community at large.

In keeping with government objectives social welfare centres, community centres and social clubs provide a series of activities aimed at promoting the well-being of the elderly living outside residential institutions. Activities such as group outings and community education (such as health talks, volunteering and so on) feature regularly. Elderly people can also travel in buses at half rate off peak hours.

Elderly people requiring hospital or outpatient treatment are treated free of charge in hospitals, dispensaries or health centres. There is also a community nursing service which extends its services to geriatric patients.

Elderly people, subject to a means test, are issued with free dentures, crutches, hernia trusses, spectacles and inhalers when prescribed by a doctor. A blanket is issued every other year to elderly people above the age of 70.

Evaluation
The elderly (those aged 60 and over) constitute less than seven per cent of the total population of Mauritius (Mauritius, CSO 1985), or some 65,000 people. Under the National Pension Scheme they all receive the non-contributory basic retirement pension. Unfortunately not all of them qualify for an occupational pension, principally because either they have never had a job (mainly applies to women) or they were in uncovered employment.

Those who have to depend solely on the basic pension have either to turn to social aid for supplementary assistance, especially where they pay rent, or have to look to family support in their old age. When such support is not forthcoming elderly persons rely heavily on

Mauritius

community support. This helps to keep the elderly out of poverty.

Unfortunately, because of the limited financial, manpower and other resources support, shortfalls of various services are great, despite the fact that the government uses the lowest projection of need. Such shortfalls have a direct impact on the welfare and the well-being of the elderly.

In spite of what is being done to promote the welfare and well-being of the elderly there is no doubt that both the intra-mural and the extra-mural care should be upgraded and consolidated. The needs of the elderly mostly concern: finance, loneliness as a result of loss of husband or wife, problems with children, advice in choosing the right solution to the existing situation, meals, recreation, domestic help, and so forth. These needs are not met adequately not because of unfavourable attitudes toward the elderly but because of lack of resources.

THE DISABLED AND THE HANDICAPPED

The disabled and the handicapped have the same need as others for friendship, a satisfying job, an adequate income, recreation, a choice of reasonably comfortable housing and personal independence. Unfortunately their efforts to meet these needs are often frustrated by the physical obstacles they encounter in trying to use the environment in which they live. The extent to which society discharges its responsibility towards the disabled and the handicapped reflects the prevailing social attitude towards them.

As in other parts of the world the welfare philosophy is dominated by the work ethic. It is therefore not surprising that adequate provision is made for workers who sustain an injury at work leading to disability. On the other hand those who are born handicapped usually resign themselves to a low income and a way of life that offers an extremely limited range of activities and have, sometimes, to seek refuge in public institutions which very often deny them the opportunity to develop their capabilities and skills to the maximum.

Social Security
Social security provision for the disabled and the handicapped is characterised by the elements of

Mauritius

compensation and long term support. A worker who is disabled at work is compensated for loss of earning capacity while those who are congenitally handicapped or emotionally disturbed receive continuing income support under social security legislation whether they live on their own or with a family.

Industrial Injury Pensions. Industrial injury pensions are earnings-related and depend on the size of the employee's earnings during the 12 months before the injury.

Industrial injury benefits are payable where an employee who is a member of the National Pension Scheme suffers injury or death caused by an accident arising out of and in the course of the employment or by a prescribed occupational disease. Injury benefits are also payable to an employee who is incapacitated for work or disabled in an accident while travelling as a passenger to and from his place of work in a vehicle provided by his employer for this purpose. The industrial injury scheme covers all employees aged between 18 and 60 in respect of whom contributions are payable and all employees aged between 15 and 18 without any contributions. The scheme supersedes the former Workmen's Compensation Ordinance in respect of insured persons who, however, retain their right to common damages. Self-employed and non-employed persons who have become members of the National Pension Scheme are not covered for industrial injury benefits.

- Temporary Incapacity: during the first two weeks of incapacity for work the employee is entitled to his full basic pay from his employer. In case his employer refuses to pay, the employee may register a complaint at the social security office of his locality. From the third week of incapacity the employee is entitled to an industrial injury allowance equal to 80 per cent of his basic salary on production of satisfactory medical evidence. In case of partial temporary incapacity or where the employee is recommended for light work the provisions of Workmen's Compensation Ordinance still apply. The employee must contact his employer in the first instance in such a case.

- Disablement: an employee who is 100 per cent disabled is entitled to a monthly pension at the rate of 80 per cent of his monthly basic salary. Where the employee is aged between 52 and 60 a lump sum equal to eight years' basic salary is payable. For disablement which is less than 100 per cent, the pension payable is equivalent to the product of 65 per cent of the employee's basic salary and the degree of disablement. Where the disablement is less than 20 per cent, however, the employee may opt to receive a lump sum equal to the product of eight years' basic salary and the degree of disablement. The degree of disablement is assessed by a medical board.

- Survivors: the widow of an employee who dies as a result of an industrial accident is entitled to a monthly pension equal to half the basic salary which her husband was drawing. Where there is no widow, dependants other than an orphan, may claim a dependant's pension which is payable at a flat rate. An orphan is entitled to a monthly pension equal to 7.5 per cent of the basic salary of the deceased parent.

Contributory Invalidity Pensions. These are payable, on medical certification, for disability of at least 60 per cent lasting for a minimum period of 12 months. The amount of pension payable depends on the pensioner's own contribution record. However, if a person has been able to pay contributions for only a few years, the pension points accrued are enhanced as though they had accrued for 20 years or until age 60 if this is less.

Basic Invalidity Pensions. These are payable to those between the ages of 15 and 60 who have been certified as disabled to a degree of at least 60 per cent and for a period of at least 12 months until the pensioner reaches the age of 60 when the retirement pension becomes payable.

Therefore, the existing provisions are such that the disabled and the handicapped fall into two broad categories. Those who have a contribution record are eligible for both the contributory and non-contributory benefits while those with no contribution record have to rely on basic non-contributory benefits.

Personal Social Services
A wide range of services provided by government

and voluntary agencies are available to families with handicapped and disabled members. This includes nursing and day-care facilities, provision of crutches, wheelchairs, and so forth. The object is to relieve the pressure on the family to combat the limiting effects of the disability on the personal and social life of the afflicted, to make the disabled person, as far as possible, a 'normal' person and to put him on an equal footing with the rest of the population, especially by integrating him into working life whenever possible.

Institutional Care. For disabled persons who cannot look after themselves or whose social and medical needs cannot be met at home residential care is provided in the form of long stay houses, commonly known as convents. These institutions are financed by a per capita grant from the Ministry of Social Security and are available free of charge. A few of the institutions cater exclusively for a particular handicap or disability as in the case of the deaf and dumb and the blind, while others tend to accommodate the aged, the physically handicapped, the convalescent and homeless children, all under one roof. However, the tendency now is to have separate institutions for each group. Most of the institutions are administered by religious bodies or voluntary associations which sometimes claim a nominal fee from the resident on the basis of his income. On top of the government grant these institutions also rely on donations, the proceeds of public collections and from profits of sales, as in the case of the Centre for the Blind which relies heavily on profits derived from sales of baskets made at the Centre.

For children who are mentally handicapped there are boarding schools which are suitably equipped to cater for their educational needs. These schools are run jointly by government and voluntary organisations.

Rehabilitation. To integrate the disabled in the community, a variety of social rehabilitation services are provided by government and the voluntary sector. These include counselling, residential care, sports and recreation. The main hospitals have medical social workers who extend counselling services to the disabled. Adult disabled who can live independently are being

Mauritius

encouraged to do so within the community. Those who are in accommodation which is not suitable may be eligible for accommodation under the low cost housing programme.

Transport is available free of charge to disabled persons who have to attend hospitals or sheltered workshops.

Sports and recreation services are essential to a balanced life and are of particular importance to the disabled. Government provides assistance to suitable voluntary agencies which provide services for the disabled. The emphasis is to integrate the disabled and the able-bodied through participation in leisure activities.

The importance of vocational rehabilitation as a process that leads to the economic independence of the disabled and his integration into the productive labour force of society is also stressed in government's policy.

The responsibility for vocational training of the disabled is at present entrusted to the Ministry of Education, Arts and Culture. The objective is to provide vocational training centres for those who are severely disabled and cannot integrate within ordinary institutions and training schemes.

Evaluation

The number of disabled persons in the Mauritius community is unknown, but it is estimated that some 10-15 per cent of the population could be classified as handicapped or disabled.

Although government is sparing no effort to promote the welfare of the disabled, prejudice towards this group is a serious handicap. This prejudice becomes evident in education, employment, transport, housing and so on.

Moreover, shortfalls are most serious in the provision of pre-school care and training for the severely disabled, the education of mentally handicapped and sheltered work. The expansion of these services will depend on the primary awareness to further help all vulnerable groups in the community and on our continued economic growth which will support a better life for each one of our disabled people.

NEEDY FAMILIES

At any one time a large number of people in the population are not economically active and are,

Mauritius

therefore, dependent. There is no work income for people who are sick or disabled, who cannot find jobs, or are forbidden to work (children) or not expected to work for gain if they prefer not to (such as housewives and the retired). There is also the case of the breadwinner whose work income falls short of the socially acceptable minimum. Then there are other major dependency situations when work income fails altogether. The breadwinner may die leaving dependants or he may desert the family.

An extensive network of social services has developed in Mauritius over the years to help needy families. These are predominantly statutory services but there are also services provided on a voluntary and denominational basis.

Welfare Support During Pregnancy
The Family Planning, Maternal and Child Health Services of the Ministry of Health offers a wide range of services: ante-natal and post-natal care, domiciliary midwifery, child health clinics, immunisation, family planning and family health education, through a network of health centres, community centres and social welfare centres. These centres are attended by doctors, nurses and midwives and the services are available to all free of charge.

Social Security. Workers in government, parastatal and local authority services are entitled to 28 days paid sick leave in any one year; thereafter the worker is entitled to sick leave on full pay for a period of up to six months on producton of a medical certificate. Sick leave on half pay may be granted in respect of absence exceeding six months in any period of 12 months.

Agricultural and non-agricultural workers employed on a monthly basis are entitled to 21 days sick leave on full pay and a further 21 days on half pay in any one year (Remuneration Orders GN 214/83 and GN 129/85).

Female employees in the public sector are granted two months paid leave in connection with each pregnancy as maternity leave. Maternity leave is limited to three pregnancies. Miscarriages are not counted as pregnancies and are, therefore, reckoned as sick leave.

Female agricultural workers, after working for 150 days, are entitled to maternity leave of 12 weeks on half pay which may be taken before or

Mauritius

after a delivery. In addition, the female worker is entitled to a maternity allowance of Rs 75 and the issue of one bottle of milk per day for three months following delivery or a cash equivalent instead.

The wife of a non-agricultrual worker employed on a monthly basis is entitled to a maternity allowance of Rs 40.

Welfare Support for Low Income Families

There is no deliberate policy to supplement the income of low-income families except for provisions which exist under Social Aid legislation and the Unemployment Hardship Scheme.

Social Security. The Social Aid Division of the Ministry of Social Security provides assistance for persons who are without resources to meet their requirements or whose resources (including benefits receivable under the National Pensions Act) must be supplemented in order to meet their requirements. The only circumstances normally excluding persons from such entitlements are in respect of:

- persons who are in full time employment or their dependants;
- persons below the age of 15 whose requirements are to be considered in relation to adults on whom they are dependent; and
- persons on strike (although assistance may be payable to their dependants).

Assistance is sometimes granted in urgent cases, over-ruling these qualifications. This system is non-contributory and financed from general revenue.

In essence the act lays down a level of 'subsistence requirements'. The assistance allowance payable is normally the amount by which the subsistence requirements exceed the applicant's resources. A 'wage-stop' ruling provides that the family income after receipt of assistance should not exceed the normal average earnings of the applicant. The applicant who claims assistance under the Unemployment Hardship Relief Scheme while unemployed is normally required to register with the local employment exchange as 'available for work'. This ruling does not apply to mothers with dependent children.

Mauritius

The level of benefit under social aid is closely paralleled to those payable to unemployed heads of households under the Unemployment Hardship Relief Scheme. Dependent child allowances are graded according to the child's age and they vary according to the child's position in the family. An allowance for rent is also allowed under these schemes.

Welfare Support for Families Without a Breadwinner

Provision exists for the payment of survivors' benefits upon the death of a breadwinner. The nature and amount of benefit is related to the scheme under which the breadwinner as an employee was covered.

Social Security. In return for a compulsory contribution of two per cent of salary all male permanent employees of the Public Sector are covered by the Widows and Orphans Pension Scheme. Upon the death of a male member his widow is entitled to a widow's pension representing one-third of the full pension accruing to her husband. If there are orphans they are entitled to one-sixth of the father's pension. In case there is no widow the orphans are entitled to half of their father's full pension. By and large the Scheme aims at providing a combined survivors' pension of about 33 per cent of the member's salary after 400 months service.

Employees of parastatal bodies and local authorities are covered by a Family Protection Scheme provided by the State Insurance Corporation of Mauritius (SICOM) and unlike the Widows and Orphans Pension Scheme the scheme covers both male and female employees. Against a contribution of four per cent of salary the scheme provides for a lump sum benefit to a widow or widower on the death of a member. However, the survivor may exercise the option of converting the lump sum into a monthly pension. Both the lump sum and the pension are related to the age of the member when joining the scheme and his monthly salary.

Agricultural and non-agricultural workers and the senior staff of the sugar industry not covered by the National Pension Fund are covered by the Sugar Industry Pension Fund. The Fund provides for a lump sum payment of 120 months salary to survivors when death occurs in service. When death occurs after retirement the widow is entitled to a percentage of the pension of her

Mauritius

husband which is itself based on his salary in 1977 plus one-thirty-sixth of his contributions.

Under the National Pension Scheme a contributory widows pension is payable to widows of all ages, the amount payable depending on the number of pension points that her husband had accrued. The aim of the scheme is to achieve for widows under 60 a widow's pension of one-sixth of the husband's average earnings (for the standard rate contributor). The scheme also provides for the payment of an orphan's pension representing 15 per cent of the contributory pension that was, or would have been, in payment to either parent (whichever is higher).

The widow of an employee who dies as a result of an industrial accident is entitled to a monthly pension equal to half the basic salary which her husband was drawing. Where there is no widow, dependants, other than an orphan, may claim a dependant's pension. An orphan is entitled to a monthly pension equal to 7.5 per cent of the salary of the deceased parent.

Evaluation
An extensive welfare safety net has been created in Mauritius to protect the needy families.

CHILDREN AND YOUTHS

The incidence of poverty is more pronounced among the larger families in the lower income groups. Earnings which are adequate for a man and his wife become increasingly inadequate as children are born. However, when older children start earning and contribute to the family income the cycle is reversed and the family reaches a peak of prosperity which lasts until the children are married and have families of their own. In recognition of this cycle of deprivation government's social policy is geared towards redistribution in favour of families with dependent children.

Social Security
An obvious answer to the problem of families with many dependent children is the provision of family allowances. In Mauritius there is a scheme of helping dependent children which gives no encouragement to parents to have more than three children. A modest family allowance is granted to families with three or more children below the age

Mauritius

of 15 subject to the family not having an income of more than Rs 10,000 a year. There is no payment in cases where there are less than three dependent children and no increase of benefit if there are more than three children. This scheme was originally designed to popularise the three child family and the spacing of children. The qualifications for a claimant's eligibility are:

- that he is normally resident in Mauritius and has a family of three or more children under the age of 15;
- that he should have resided in Mauritius for a period of at least two years immediately before the month in respect of which the allowance is claimed;
- that he is not in receipt of a child's allowance or orphan's pension under the National Pension Scheme; and
- that his yearly income does not exceed the prescribed threshold.

There are also provisions for child allowances in the income tax system for up to three children. The allowance varies according to the age of the child. There is an additional allowance for children studying abroad.

The payment of family allowance and the provision of both fiscal and occupational welfare are all linked to the government's policy on population. Families who have more than three children under the age of 15 are disadvantaged since family allowance is paid in respect of only three children. The income tax system allows for deductibles in respect of three children only.

Personal Social Services

Welfare Food. Children attending primary schools receive milk and bread and also cheese and dried fruits depending on availability free of charge. The policy of distributing free milk has been developed after careful investigation. It has been found that the issue of milk is the cheapest way of ameliorating the dietary deficiencies of childhood.

Residential Care. Residential care facilities are available to all vulnerable children and young persons who cannot adequately be looked after by their families and for whom no better alternatives are available.

Mauritius

Residential care is provided in three types of institutions:

- residential creches and nurseries for very young children and children's homes for older children and young persons who cannot adequately be cared for by their parents or guardians due to neglect or unforeseen circumstances such as illness, desertion, imprisonment, and so forth;
- hostels for boys who have behaviour problems and are committed by a court of law to the care of a probation officer; and
- homes for unmarried mothers which provide necessary support for unmarried expectant mothers who need temporary shelter pending confinement.

Non-Institutional Care. Non-institutional care has a long history in Mauritius. It is provided in the form of foster care for children whose parents, because of illness, death or other causes, cannot look after them. Originally, this was done on an informal basis; today government extends financial support to fostering in a normal home.

Day-Care Service. Day-care facilities are provided either by the welfare department of local authorities or by voluntary organisations subsidised by government in the form of day creches for infants and day nurseries for young children. The purpose of this service is to provide day-care services for children who cannot satisfactorily be looked after by their own families for one reason or another.

Welfare Support for Children Affected by Marriage Breakdown. In approximately 90 per cent of divorce cases the mother receives custody of the child. When deciding about the custody of a child the court is guided by the welfare of the child, which includes not only material welfare but also the psychological and emotional development of the child. Unless there are compelling reasons which dictate otherwise the father of the child is usually allowed to visit the child. The father is also liable in law to provide for the upkeep of a child; the maintenance grant depends on his income, the number of children and his other commitments. When the husband is for one reason

Mauritius

or another unable to provide for the maintenance of his child/children, then the mother may apply for Social Aid.

Illegitimate Children. In accordance with Mauritian law illegitimate children have the same right as legitimate children. Income support is available to unmarried mothers under social aid legislation. However, after a child attains the age of one year the mother is expected to work and assistance is then discontinued or decreased. In practice social security officers show a fairly lenient attitude towards mothers with young children and allow the assistance to continue until the mother actually finds a remunerative job.

Institutional Care for Orphans. In Mauritius where the family tie is still strong it is only in isolated cases that orphans are sent to institutions. The Ministry of Social Security makes a per capita grant to the institution. Those who are not in institutions receive an orphan's allowance from the Ministry of Social Security.

Foster Care. Before resorting to institutionalisation, social security officers endeavour to foster out orphans either to relatives, friends or neighbours. Orphans who are fostered out are also eligible for an orphan's pension. They are visited on a regular basis by social security officers who have to report on their welfare. Children who are not properly cared for may be removed and placed in an institution.

Adoption. One of the ways of providing the security of a good alternative home for a child permanently deprived of a normal home life with his own parents is by adoption.

In spite of government having no declared policy on adoption there are many couples who are anxious to adopt a child. Yet, the number of children so available is limited.

Recently government has tightened adoptive procedures, giving the courts the power of transferring parental rights and duties irrevocably from the natural parents to the adopting parents; the legislation, at the same time, has sought to ensure that the adoption is for the welfare of the child, given precedence to

Mauritius

this above all other consideration. The adoptive parents take over all rights from the natural parents, and the adopted child has the same rights as a born child. The adoption regulations also seek to ensure that adequate inquiry is made as to the suitability of the adoption, that supervision is undertaken, and that the risk of third party adoption is minimised.

<u>Youth Services</u>. In order to meet the social, recreational and development needs of young people, the government, through its Ministry of Youth and Sports, provides a wide variety of programmes to cater for the majority of young people. These programmes are extended to both urban and rural youths. The youth services have been dominated until recently by traditional youth work. However, the pressure of the youth population and the right to vote being brought down to 18 warranted a major overhaul of the youth services. Today emphasis is placed on the recreational and sport activities in order to attract the participation of very large numbers of young people. However, despite the expansion of youth programmes, there remains a fairly large number of young people who are not attracted to youth clubs and other organised activities and these unattached young people are much more in need of the service than those who are presently served.

<u>Evaluation</u>
A protective net of services is provided in respect of children and youths in Mauritius.

THE UNEMPLOYED

Unemployment had been growing every year since 1960, from about 12 per cent of the labour force in 1960 to 16 per cent in 1972 and 20 per cent in the mid-1980s. Since the sugar industry already uses highly labour-intensive methods, and since land for sugar cultivation could not be significantly increased, additional employment opportunities could only be identified outside the sugar industry.
    As early as 1963, the government had attempted to deal with the unemployment problem by launching a Relief Worker's Scheme to do simple maintenance work for a number of Ministries and agencies. The initial size was 1,000 relief workers which

Mauritius

increased to 30,000 by 1967, and decreased to 12,000 by 1973 partly because of shortage of funds and partly because of the difficulty of managing a large workforce by numerous Ministries and agencies.

In an effort to convert the relief work programme into a more productive programme, the government launched what it called 'Travail Pour Tous' (TPT) in 1970. The TPT programme aimed at providing employment and incomes to the unemployed and underemployed, eliminating much of the sub-marginal employment and capitalising the existing abundance of labour for creating productive investment. To manage the programme and to execute various development activities, the government created that same year a special parastatal called Development Works Corporation (DWC).

The project concept was based on a World Bank mission that visited Mauritius in 1971 and in its report noted that 'an opportunity exists for designing a social development project suitable for IDA financing which would help strengthen and expand the TPT programme' (Mauritius Rural Development Project Reconnaissance, Special Projects Department (IBRD), March 22, 1972). The project was designed to support an important objective of the Mauritian four-year plan for the period 1971-1975, viz. to eliminate unemployment by 1980.

In addition to alleviating unemployment, the project also aimed at generating benefits that would accrue to the poorest 20 per cent of villages. This objective was especially crucial because of the uneven distribution of land holdings in Mauritius.

A Rural Development Unit was established within the Ministry of Economic Planning and Development with one of its functions being to liaise with planning units in the Minisries, public authorities and district and village councils in the preparation of labour intensive rural development projects. This programme has helped to ease the problem of unemployment in Mauritius.

However, being an island economy with extreme population pressure, great dependence on one crop - sugar - and high unemployment among the educated youth there was a prima-facie case for diversifying the economy. Hence, government's present commitment to agricultural diversification

Mauritius

and the expansion of export-oriented industries. A major package of incentives has been given to motivate people to invest and to create jobs. Business interests, both local and overseas, have responded positively to the government's call. This year for the first time in our history the gross export earnings from the sugar sector has been overtaken by the industrial sector.

However, in spite of government efforts to create more jobs the problem of unemployment still presents a formidable challenge to the nation. In an attempt to democratise the economy a small entrepreneur scheme has been successfully launched. Recently the University of Mauritius has been commissioned to mount a series of courses of short duration in entrepreneurship for unemployed graduates and diplomates. The objective of this training programme is to provide insights and training in business and entrepreneurship to unemployed graduates and diplomates so as to increase their opportunities for self employment both in small scale industries and in agriculture.

Social Security
There is no contributory unemployment benefit in Mauritius. However, an Unemployment Hardship Relief Scheme was introduced in 1983 to ease the hardship of the unemployed. Eligibility of applicants for the benefit is determined according to a means test similar to that applying to Social Aid. Part of the income of children and wife is disregarded in order to encourage the family to stay together. Single persons with no family responsibilities are not entitled to benefits.

Personal Social Services

Employment Counselling. In order to provide career information for as large a number of job seekers as possible, the Employment Service of the Ministry of Employment, beside providing a network of offices where the unemployed are registered for work, provides employment counselling and career guidance. This programme is intended to help young people in their career choices and vocational plans and also to enable them to adjust to the world of work.

Evaluation
There is no denying that substantial progress has

been made, and continues to be made, on the employment front. Most sectors of the economy have registered increases in employment. The Export Processing Zone (EPZ) alone accounted for the creation of more than 18,000 new jobs in 1984-5. Indications are that in 1986-7 investment prospects would continue to improve. The public sector has embarked on major infrastructure projects. Private sector investment continues to increase. The EPZ leads the way and the level of investment is expected to be maintained. Similarly the hotel and agricultural sectors are recording substantial increased investment.

By and large, in the absence of some major disruptions in the export market, we can expect a continuing increase in employment in the manufacturing sector, in particular. Hence, there is a need to improve the level of education so as to facilitate the adaptation of new job seekers to the factory environment. In labour-intensive manufacturing industries, survival in a competitive environment depends, to a large extent, on productivity and labour costs.

AN ASSESSMENT OF THE MAURITIAN WELFARE SYSTEM

The government has declared its commitment to protect the weaker sections of our society. This commitment has translated into the following:

- income tax exemptions and increases in personal allowances to low income households. Households with an annual income of Rs 30,000 per year are exempted from payment of income tax;
- a National Solidarity Fund has been set up to further assist the lower income groups;
- compensation in respect of increase in cost of living has been extended to cover all recipients of social benefits such as old age pensioners, widows, |orphans and the handicapped;
- the budget of the Ministry of Social Security has been expanded much faster than that of any other Ministry, experiencing an increase of over Rs 100 m in the last three years; and
- the policy of providing subsidies for simple food commodities has been maintained. This includes subsidies on rice, flour, potatoes and subsidies given to small holders and metayers of the tea industry affected by a fall in the price of tea on the world market.

Mauritius

However, extension of welfare activities can be seen qualitatively as well as quantitatively. There is now free primary and secondary education. Following a report by Abel-Smith (1976) a contributory national pension scheme was established, operating side by side with existing non-contributory benefits. The government has been heavily involved in promoting co-operatives. There is now a substantial government housing programme. Health services are now accessible to all citizens.

However, if we look at the welfare elements in Mauritian policy, it is at least arguable that some parts of this policy have been regressive in their impact. Almost certainly, rich families benefit more than poor families from educational spending, merely because the children of rich families are likely to stay longer at school and to be more than proportionately represented in higher education, which is far more costly per head than primary education. Again, subsidies on water and housing are erratic in their incidence, but since the poorest people are those most likely to be without a piped water supply and better off people obtain income tax concessions on mortgage interest payments it is possible that these programmes too have their regressive elements. Benefits from the National Pensions Scheme must be judged in the context of the overall structure of contributions and outgoings.

This is not to argue that the Mauritian welfare programmes have not helped the poor. However, there are certain issues which have not been examined in Mauritius. What is the purpose of such programmes and who are their intended beneficiaries? Who actually benefits? What are the total benefits of the programme? What is the distribution of benefit and, in particular, what is the distribution of benefit between actual beneficiaries and intended or potential beneficiaries?

REFERENCES AND FURTHER READING

Abel-Smith, B. (1976), A National Pension Scheme for Mauritius, Port Louis: Government Printer.

Joynathsing, M. (1979), 'The Future Shape of Retirement Pensions in Mauritius', Journal of the University of Mauritius, (2 & 3), 95-106.

Mauritius

_____ 'Social Security Protection Schemes for the Unemployed: The Case of Mauritius', *Journal of the University of Mauritius*, (14 & 15), 145-90.

_____ (1984), 'Report of the Study Group on Poverty', unpublished paper, University of Mauritius, Port Louis.

Manrakhan, J. et al (1983), *Mauritius 2000: A Generalised Framework for Academic Activities*, Port Louis: University of Mauritius.

Mauritius (1971), *Four Year Plan 1971-75 for Social and Economic Development*, Port Louis: Government Printer.

_____ (1982), *International Fund for Agricultural Development - Mauritius - Small-Scale Agricultural Development Project - Appraisal Report*, Port Louis: Government Printer.

_____ Central Statistical Office (CSO) (1985), *Annual Digests of Statistics*, Port Louis: Government Printer.

_____ Ministry of Employment (1985), *Employment Service Statistical Review*, Port Louis: Government Printer.

May, M. D. (1981), *An Actuarial Review of the National Pensions Scheme*, Port Louis: Ministry of Social Security.

Selwyn, P. (1984), *Mauritius: The Meade Report Twenty Years After*, unpublished mimeograph.

Titmuss, R. M. & Abel-Smith, B. (1960), *Social Policies and Population Growth in Mauritius*, Port Louis: Legislative Assembly, Sessional Paper No. 6 of 1960.

World Bank (1985), *World Development Report 1985*, New York: Oxford University Press.

NIGERIA
A.O. Sanda

THE WELFARE SYSTEM ENVIRONMENT

Ideological Environment

Nigerian society currently manifests a welfare philosophy and an ideology which represent an amalgam of several strands and heritages. On the one hand there is the unstated or latent adherence to elements of its heterogeneous ethnic traditions, particularly with respect to communal orientation, extended family or lineage concern for the predicament of its members, and the widely accepted principle of sharing both happiness and sadness among relations. On the other hand, however, there is the diffusion of the Western capitalist ideology injected into the Nigerian social system through colonialism and perpetuated by the new business and intellectual elites, whose leadership in society is dependent upon their astute manipulation of the core values of the capitalist society - profit maximisation, efficient competition, survival of the fittest, initial pursuit of accumulation, growth and development before ultimate redistribution of rewards according to differential contributions.

These values and ideological preferences are however mostly at the latent unwritten level. At the manifest, documentation level, the Nigerian society openly adheres to the mixed economy ideology, a middle-of-the-road option.

One of the most recent public statements which reflect the ideological and value preferences of many Nigerians has been made by a former Head of State, General Obasanjo, in his famous Jaji address (1981). In that address, he perceived the frequent attempts to choose between capitalism and socialism as futile and diversionary. He praised

Nigeria

the value choice in the traditional society's respect for age, experience, and authority, 'or the norm that everybody is his brother's keeper' (p.144). He categorised Nigeria as being developed and aspiring to become 'a disciplined, fair, just and humane society' (p.144).

Such a society extols the value of each citizen seeking the welfare and happiness of others, sharing reciprocal duties and obligations, with government extolling the virtue in equal opportunities and equality before the law. He further asserted that:

> ... a man pursuing happiness exclusively may never find it, and he may die frustrated; but a man who is concerned with the happiness of the society in which he lives has greater chances of finding happiness because it will be contradictory and absurd to be unhappy in a happy society (p.145).

It is, nevertheless, important to underscore the fluid and dynamic content of the ideological background to the welfare policy and administration in Nigeria. What is certain is the public avowal of government pursuit of the mixed economy ideology. This is reflected in both the Nigerian development plan document and the partly suspended 1979 Nigerian constitution. The attempt to integrate both socialist and capitalist ideology in Nigeria's brand of the mixed economy has resulted in several inevitable contradictions, which influence directly the form and content of social welfare in the society.

According to the 1979 Constitution Section 16, 1(a) the state shall:

> Control the national economy in such manner as to secure the maximum welfare, freedom and happiness of every citizen on the basis of social justice and equality of status and opportunity.

Section 16, 1(b) and (c) provide for the participation of individual citizens in all sectors of the economy, while at the same time conceding the right or responsibililty of the state to manage the economy. Section 16, subsection 2(b), (c) and (d) further elaborated on the welfare objectives of the state within the ideological framework of the mixed economy.

Nigeria

According to those sections:

> The state shall direct its policy toward ensuring ...
>
> (b) that the material resources of the community are harnessed and distributed as best as possible to serve the common good;
> (c) that the economic system is not operated in such a manner as to permit the contraction of wealth and the means of production and exchange in the hands of few individuals or a group; and
> (d) that suitable and adequate shelter, suitable and adequate food, reasonable national minimum wage, old age care and pensions, and unemployment and sick benefits are provided for all citizens.

Historical Origins

Prior to the end of the Second World War, there was very little formal state promotion of welfare in Nigeria. This was partly because of the informal assumption at this time of welfare responsibilities by individual extended families, ethnic associations and mutual aid societies. Indeed, there were variations in the extent of significance attached to the care of the aged, disabled, handicapped, children and youth; unemployment was unknown in the form in which it now plagues the new Nigerian society, since everyone was integrated with the work environment and the youth always had farm land to till, or a trade to learn, or a guild in which he was an apprentice.

Nevertheless, collective concern for the needy family, or the sick and disabled individuals, or for community wants like bridges and access roads, all generated community or collective responses, mostly palliative or ameliorative. With the advent of the missionaries, many new voluntary organisations became committed to the formal provision of welfare services through the schools, the churches and the voluntary associations (like the Discharged Prisoners Aid Society, the Red Cross Society, the Nigerian Leprosy Relief Association, the YMCA and the YWCA, Child Welfare, St John's Ambulance Association and the Ex-Service Men's Welfare Association).

The colonial government's welfare efforts were

Nigeria

selective and discriminatory, and frequently they were reactions to problems which the changes in society had brought about.

It is probably instructive to identify the major changes which rendered the extended family ineffective in its traditional roles of providing welfare for its members (Sanda 1981). First, the advent of the missionaries led to the introduction of mission schools and hospitals, both of which contributed in no small way to the urban drift of young literate or educated men and women. The eventual congestion in the cities created social problems like epidemics, mass youth unemployment, housing or accommodation shortages and great dispersal of initially sedentary members of the family. The separation of youths from their aged parents made the traditional care of the aged by the young ones more difficult and irregular. The children who were also away from the traditional supervision and discipline by the family also became more involved in deviant behaviour than before the inception of these social changes. And the introduction of a new industrial work environment also occasioned new problems arising from conditions of work, the rewards of work and social services for workers. Finally the introduction of new colonial laws also created a new body of offenders and resulted in prison congestion and after service needs for parole and re-integration into the society.

Consequently, the colonial government responded to the specific social problems which arose. One of the earliest of such British colonial government responses was the Public Health Ordinance No. 5 of October 1899, which was enacted in Lagos, and on the basis of which a Sanitation Board was established. By 1904 however, the Board had stopped functioning and it was later replaced by another in 1910.

The bubonic plague of 1924 compelled the British to enact another law for the enhancement of the health service of colonial subjects. Such initial reforms were, however, restricted in scope, as they were limited to areas in which British subjects were living, especially in the capitals (Faniran, Odekunle). By this time there had not evolved any comprehensive approach to the welfare need of the whole country. From 1870 to 1910 therefore, the health care of the nation was largely in the hands of the missionaries, even though the state coped with the health needs of

167

the British soldiers through the military hospitals in Zungeru, Lokoja and Zaria. Nevertheless, the great fire which consumed Lagos in 1877 induced the state to pay greater attention to environmental health and hence the public ordinance of that year which required buildings with thatched roofs to be at least seven feet apart.

The First World War created the need for the bush hospitals particularly in areas close to the war zones. It was not until after the Second World War however that the missionary initiatives began to be superseded by the direct efforts of the Colonial State to plan for the development of the nation and to cope with the health, education and welfare needs of the society. The great depression of the 1930s, the discontent among the ex-service men, and the nationalist agitations all combined to direct the attention of the colonial government to the society's welfare needs. The social problems of the times included unemployment, displaced children and needy families, hence the 1940 laws which were designed to cope with the labour and children welfare needs and the 1945 ordinances which were directed at solving the problems of disabled soldiers. Similarly the 1948 laws were directed at enforcing the duties or obligations of families to children under fourteen years in every household, empowering the Courts to put delinquent children under the care of surrogate parents and providing also for the care of lunatics.

With respect to the regulation of labour matters, the Workmen's Compensation Ordinance of 1941 and the 1945 and 1958 laws of the Federation of Nigeria all tried to protect workers on matters of contracts, injuries at work, compensation, forced labour, employment of young persons, wages, maternity leave, and so forth. For example, the factory ordinance of 1955 tried to promote the safety of workers through the provision of guidelines on conditions that should prevail in factories with respect to machines, protective clothing, report of accidents, and so forth. And the 1957 Wage Board Ordinance provided for appropriate wages, hours of work, holidays, and rudiments of collective bargaining.

The emergent structure of the Nigerian welfare system therefore became a combination of the traditional pre-colonial and colonial heritages with an equal dependence upon the efforts of the

Nigeria

voluntary associations and the government as well as the extreme regionalisation before the advent of the military.

Political and Socio-Economic Environments
Nigeria is a Federal Republic in which 19 states differentiated into 301 local government units subsist under a federal government. The federal arrangements as well as the political differentiation are partly a consequence of the nation's ethnic hetrogeneity (Sanda 1974a) and the need to ensure a compromise political system which can integrate the over 250 ethnic groups into a federal union (see Tables 1 and 2).

TABLE 1 : ETHNIC PLURALISM IN NIGERIA

Ethnic Group	1952-53 Census	Percentage of Total Population	1963 Census	Percentage of Total Population
Hausa	5,544,000	18.5	11,653,000	21.2
Ibo	5,458,000	18.2	9,246,000	16.8
Yoruba	5,045,000	16.8	11,321,000	20.6
Fulani	3,030,000	10.1	4,784,000	8.7
Kanuri	1,302,000	4.3	2,259,000	4.1
Tiv	788,000	2.6	1,394,000	2.5
Ibibio	762,000	2.5	2,006,000	3.6
Edo	435,000	1.4	675,000	1.2
Ijaw	343,000	1.1	1,089,000	1.9
Others	7,245,000	24.1	10,318,000	18.8
TOTAL	29,951,000	99.6[1]	54,745,000	99.4[1]

NOTE: 1. The balances are non-Nigerians.

SOURCE: Sanda 1979, p.55.

The current estimate of the population is put at around 130 million (Sanda 1986, p.20) with a currently stable annual rate of growth of 2.5 per cent. The economic fortune of the society has fluctuated over the last two decades, from an agriculturally-based economy, largely dependent upon cash crops for export and foreign exchange earning, to an oil-based economy, largely

Nigeria

dependent upon the export of crude petroleum, and hence upon the vicissitudes of the international oil market. The glut in the latter has recently heralded a period of economic recession and depression with their attendant retrenchment in both the public and private sectors and large scale youth unemployment among graduate school leavers.

TABLE 2 : NUMBER OF NEW STATES CONTROLLED BY MAJOR ETHNIC GROUPS

Ethnic Groups	Number	Total Population[1]	Percentage of Nigeria
Hausa-Fulani	4	16,843,231	30.25
Yoruba	5	12,645,577	22.72
Ibo	2	7,277,892	13.07
Others	8	18,903,352	33.96
TOTAL	19	55,670,052	100.00

NOTE: 1. Based on 1963 Census figures.

SOURCE: Sanda 1974a

Perhaps the single most significant economic policy choice in Nigeria's history of economic management is the government decision to sell several unproductive or inefficient public enterprises - the so-called policy of privatisation. In addition the recent debates on whether or not the nation should take the International Monetary Bank loan in order to revive the ailing economy, the high rate of inflation, and the decision to operate a Second-Tier Foreign Exchange Market in an attempt to avoid direct devaluation of the nation's currency all attest to the fact that all is not well with the Nigerian economy.

The social and economic misfortunes of the Nigerian society are not unconnected with her problems of political instability. Nigeria has experienced seven coups d'etat in 15 years and yet there does not seem to be an end in sight for military interventions. The politicians were discredited for their electoral malpractices,

Nigeria

corruption and economic mismanagement. But the soldiers who have been publicly probed have also been revealed to be as guilty as the politicians. This is the context within which Nigeria's welfare system may be understood.

THE WELFARE SYSTEM: AN OVERVIEW

The Structure and Administration of the Welfare System

It is necessary to differentiate between the welfare system available to the public servants in Nigeria and that which is available to the private sector or commercial enterprises in the society. Even within these two broad categories the welfare systems manifest internal differentiations in the types, extent and level of benefits which are enjoyed by workers. In addition, there are different organisations which are usually responsible for the administration of different aspects of the welfare system in Nigeria.

The Public Sector. The Ministries of Health, Education, Social Development; Youths, Sports and Culture; Employment, Labour & Productivity are responsible for one type of welfare service or another (Olowu 1981). For example, the Ministry of Health through its various hospitals, as well as through the enforcement of government policies in private hospitals, provides various forms of medical and health care services for the citizens. Similarly, the Ministry of Social Development, through its relevant unit, provides specifically for the care of old people, while the Ministry of Employment, Labour and Productivity administers the workmen's compensation, although the Courts usually adjudicate claims and settle disputes. This Ministry also coordinates government efforts to reduce unemployment and administers the National Provident Fund. All these Ministries which are at the federal level often have counterpart Ministries in the various states.

It is significant to note also that prior to the introduction of the pension decree No. 102 of 1979, which was to take effect retrospectively as from 1 April 1974, the federal government had a conditions of service and pensions scheme which was fairly different from the conditions and scheme which were operative at the states level. The Udoji Review Commission which heralded the

Nigeria

unification of the public services and the subsequent decrees eliminated most of the differences even though a different scheme exists for the armed forces (through Pensions Decree No. 103 of 1979).

It is necessary to underscore the fact, however, that the most significant social security scheme in Nigeria is the National Provident Fund, which has been established since 1961. The scheme provides for five main categories of benefits: old age; invalidity; withdrawal; survivors and emigration.

The Private Sector. A majority of companies operate a variety of cash payment schemes, some of which may be insured. The payments may be made on a quarterly or yearly basis. The schemes are often non-contributory and the benefits related to both length of service and final salary of the employee. (The Nigerian Breweries, the United Africa Company and Shell are good examples of companies operating this kind of scheme.)

The main organisational structure which is responsible for the approval of the retirement benefit schemes which are established for the private sector (such as limited liability companies) and charitable organisations is the Joint Tax Board. This Board has a member representing each state of the federation who is nominated by the Commissioner in charge; and the Director of Inland Revenue, who represents the federal government on the Board is the Chairman. It is this Board which is empowered to approve either a pure pension fund or a provident fund for the private sector. The law allows only a maximum contribution of 25 per cent of the employee's annual salary or less to the latter fund. Although differentiations may be further made between approved schemes for an indigenous company or for a subsidiary of a foreign company as different from non-approvable schemes (that is, those whose funds are established outside the country), all contributions to a scheme are either insured with an Insurance Company or are invested by the Trustees of the fund, in accordance with the Insurance Act of 1976 or the provisions on investments in section 17(1)(f) of the Income Tax Management Act of 1961.

Financing Social Welfare
In the public sector the welfare system is largely

Nigeria

financed or subsidised by the government, both directly and indirectly. In spite of the workers tax contributions, and the concept of pension and gratuity as deferred payments that should have been earned by the worker, the state finances the health, education and employment of the citizens, all of which are forms of social security, most heavily. Nevertheless, the workers and their employers are supposed to make equal contributions into the National Provident Fund at the rate of six per cent of wages or payroll respectively, subject to a contribution ceiling of 95 naira a month.

In the private sector both workers and their employers, provided they employ 10 or more workers, also contribute to the National Provident Fund, which is subsequently used to pay the cash benefits plus interest upon retirement or death. In other words, workers' and employers' contributions and accruing interest feature in the financing of cash payments of benefits in both the public and private sectors, while the public sector indirect social security programmes are heavily financed by the state. The costs of occupational sickness, injury and maternity are borne by the employer in both the public and the private sectors, but through different systems. Sometimes the provisions are made as part of the general entitlements; at other times, specific hospitals and clinics are provided for workers. There is, however, considerable variation from one private sector organisation to another, while the situation in the public sector is much more uniform.

THE AGED

Old age in Nigeria is still considered to be deserving of the care of the young and the attention of government. However, the pressures of urbanisation, the demands of other responsibilities of government, and the increasing disintegration of the extended family, which previously provided such social security for the aged, all have made the welfare of the aged very precarious.

The age at which a worker may voluntarily retire from government service in Nigeria is 45 years. However, the statutory retirement age for the public sector workers is 55 years. For university staff the mandatory retirement age is

Nigeria

60 years, while for judges it is 65 years. In general, therefore, anyone who has reached the mandatory retirement age is regarded as old and classified as the aged in Nigerian society. And for this category of citizens there are two main avenues for their care; one is the traditional and informal avenue while the other is institutional and formal.

Social Security
The extended family system in many respects still continues, and is still encouraged to provide care for its old people. And in spite of the numerous constraints of urban and modern living, this traditional approach has not disappeared altogether. At the same time, however, the National Provident Fund allows total lump-sum withdrawal of the balance in members' accounts upon attaining age 50 years for covered workers who retire from regular employment. Such payments and government retirement gratuity benefits are meant to provide old age security. However, it is now common to find retired workers unable to collect their entitlement because many die during the process of attempting to collect the benefits.

Personal Social Services
There are a few old people's homes in Ibadan, Oyo State, Benin City, Bendel State and Lagos in Lagos State. Old people who are unable to find relations to provide them with care are referred to such old people's homes, either by the Courts, by the doctors, or by the old people applying themselves.
    It is worthwhile to note that the old people's homes in Lagos were started by both the Salvation Army and the Roman Catholic Missions, which administered the homes until 1938, when they were handed over to the Lagos City Council. The Lagos Local Government Ordinance (Cap. 93) of the Laws of Nigeria 1958, Section 142 (Subsection 17) formally instituted the early government sponsored old people's home in Nigeria. The minimum age of admission in the home is 50 years.

Evaluation
Welfare support for the elderly is predominantly a family responsibility. Only limited public support is available.

Nigeria

THE DISABLED AND THE HANDICAPPED

Before the 1967-70 Civil Wars in Nigeria, the majority of the disabled and handicapped people were beggars; mainly the lame, the blind, the dumb, lunatics, epileptics and lepers. While the number of disabled and physically handicapped people increased during both World Wars, it was the 1967-70 Civil War that was the most important single factor responsible for the aggravation of destitutes amongst the disabled and handicapped in Nigeria. Moreover, this has been exacerbated by the droughts experienced by Nigeria's northern neighbours, causing periodic migration into Nigeria which has resulted in street begging. This is not to overlook the religious and cultural motivation for begging among some segments of the society, particularly in the Moslem north.

The response of the government to the condition of the disabled and the handicapped was initially sporadic and demonstrative, rather than comprehensive. On the occasion of Nigeria's 10th independence anniversary, for example, about 700 beggars were collected and camped on the outskirts of Lagos, in order to prevent their begging and roaming the streets from constituting sources of embarrassment during the celebration. A similar attempt was made during the Second All Africa Games, when another 465 beggars and destitutes were camped on the outskirts of Lagos and Bariga. On both occasions many of the beggars escaped in order to engage in street begging during the festivals or celebrations.

The colonial laws which derived from Section 4 of the English Vagrancy Act of 1924 and Section 241 of the same criminal code made begging (which is engaged in by the destitutes, handicapped and disabled) illegal, and punishable by one month imprisonment. However the application of the Law has not been strict, or even effective, since it is not usually invoked by the police (except on some wandering able-bodied beggars). Some of the initial efforts of the federal government included the setting up of the Ordia Committee in 1965, through the Ministry of Labour, to study the problem of beggars and destitutes, including the disabled and handicapped. In 1966, an ILO expert was invited to study the problem and make recommendations to the federal government. By 1967 the federal government attempted to implement the Ordia Committee's recommendation by

Nigeria

repatriating beggars to their states of origin. However, most of the beggars returned to Lagos, and the other state capitals, within a short time. As a consequence another Ordia Committee was asked to survey the problem all over the nation. And in 1971 on invitation by the federal government, the Chief of the United Nations Rehabilitation Unit visited the country to study the problems and advise the government. The government engaged in much more positive responses to the problem following the Civil Wars and during the second and third National Development Plans.

Personal Social Services
During the 1970s four rehabilitation centres have been established in Lagos, Oyo, Kaduna and Anambra initially, with two others subsequently created in Kano and Sokoto states during the fourth National Development Plan (1981-85). The objectives of these centres were to provide facilities that would enable the handicapped and the disabled to adjust to their physical and mental states and to acquire adaptive skills that would enable them to secure employment and be re-integrated into the society.

Social Security
Social security protection is available to workers covered by the National Provident Fund or the workmen's compensation scheme.

National Provident Fund. Covered workers who are unemployable as a result of an incapacity are able to withdraw the balance standing in their account.

Workmen's Compensation. Manual workers and non-manual workers earning 1,600 naira or less a year are covered by the workmen's compensation scheme. The permanent disability benefit provided in the event of an occupational disability is a lump-sum payment of 54 months' earnings (if totally disabled), with the maximum payment set at 3,200 naira and the minimum payment at 600 naira. A 25 per cent additional payment is payable as a constant attendance supplement.

A proportional payment is payable in the event of a partial disability. Medical benefits, including hospitalisation, medical care, medicines, appliances and transportation, is also provided.

Nigeria

Evaluation

The success of the state in meeting its objectives with regard to the disabled and the handicapped is still very limited. Indeed, the fourth National Development Plan acknowledged the newness of the social development and welfare sector as recently conceived. It noted that:

> The process of social transformation has brought in its wake the weakening of the system of informal social security based on kinship obligations and extended family ties particularly among the educated youth in the urban centres. This has led to an increasing number of destitutes and the handicapped all over the country roaming the towns and cities. It is the objective of policy not only to arrest this trend, but also to formulate a programme of action aimed at improving human welfare and quality of life (1981, p.312).

The Plan envisages the concentration of state policy on the most vulnerable groups in society – defined as the children and women, the beggars, destitutes and the handicapped and youths. However, state policies directed at all these target groups are handled by different Ministries at the federal level, and are in need of greater coordination.

CHILDREN AND YOUTH

It must be recognised that the dominant perspective on children and youth in Nigeria is that primary socialisation is the responsibility of parents. Governments provide a variety of institutions for secondary socialisation through the primary schools, the secondary schools and the universities and technical colleges. It is only recently that more and more public concern is becoming expressed on the moral content of education (that is the quality of education) and on the need of the less fortunate children and youth. At the same time however, government comes to the aid of brilliant but disadvantaged children and youth through the provision of scholarships for their education beyond the levels at which provisions are made for free education.

Nigeria

Personal Social Services

A variety of arrangements are made by different States for fostering children and, in a few cases, for their adoption. In the main, however, it is the voluntary associations that provide the greatest support for the deprived or the disadvantaged children (such as motherless babies by means of the motherless babies homes). The Red Cross Save Our Soul Children's Village Association, the Business and Professional Women's Club of Nigeria, the Association of University Women, Young Men's and Young Women's Christian Associations provide abandoned children and other neglected children with care. These associations are numerous and they exist in virtually all cities and States in Nigeria.

The federal government sponsors a National Youth Service Scheme, which provides opportunities for at least one year's support by government for youths who would otherwise be either unemployed or in search of further education. In addition, each State's formal social welfare institutions (such as Remand Homes, Approved Schools and Rehabilitation Centres at Akure and Ado Ekiti respectively) provide reformatory services for delinquent youths. Operational Centres also exist for the care of abandoned children and for monitoring the work of voluntary youth and charitable organisations which provide some services for youths.

The experiment in the provision of free medical services for all has been handicapped by the crisis in the available financial resources of the government, which has also adversely affected the health care of youth and children.

Evaluation

The government's role with respect to the welfare of youths and children is restricted to that of protecting those at risk. The voluntary sector, however, does provide a range of services to support this population group. Resource limitations have seriously limited the extent of support available to children and youths.

NEEDY FAMILIES

The problem of poverty which is common to the great majority is yet to receive the state's sympathetic understanding and response.

Nigeria

Personal Social Services
Counselling of families exists for those who approach social workers with a variety of problems, ranging from simple marital problems between spouses, to problems with their children and with government agencies. For even estranged partners that are reconciled need to eat, drink, wear some clothes, and live in simple but decent accommodation. These considerations of the basic needs for the majority have not yielded much result. The Ministry of Labour, Employment and Productivity has sponsored studies and encouraged the registration of the unemployed; but the impact on the majority of citizens is yet to be felt.

Social Security
Survivors of deceased covered workers do receive lump-sum payments from the National Provident Fund or under the auspices of the workmen's compensation scheme.

National Provident Fund.
Surviving spouses (or other dependent relatives) are able to withdraw the balance standing in a deceased member's account.

Workmen's Compensation.
A lump-sum of 46 months' earnings of a deceased worker whose death was work-related is apportioned by the Courts among dependent survivors. The minimum amount is set at 400 naira, while the upper limit is 1,600 naira.

THE UNEMPLOYED

Until 1985 the unemployed merely registered with a State or the federal Ministry of Labour and hoped for a job placement, which, in most cases, never materialised. Over the last year, however, the new military regime has introduced a more aggressive policy of assisting the unemployed to become self-employed through state loans for small scale industries and for agriculture. Beyond this modest effort, there is no special unemployment benefit to be enjoyed by those who lose their jobs or who have never been employed. Covered workers participating in the National Provident Fund could, however, withdraw half their entitlements after one year's unemployment.

The burden of the care of the unemployed therefore lies heavily on the extended family. The family endeavours to feed, house and clothe

Nigeria

the unemployed relations and to assist in locating relevant jobs with time.

THE SICK AND INJURED

The sick have access to the state clinics and hospitals, where the cost of their care is supplemented by the state. Those covered by a group sickness insurance scheme for workers receive additional benefits (which do not accrue to the unemployed) which are provided for the employed worker in both the public and private sectors.

Social Security
The injured worker may however have recourse to state supplementation of care, as well as insurance entitlements in cases where the individual has taken private insurance cover. Benefits are usually classified as those due to death, permanent disablement, or temporary disability. In addition, medical expenses are provided (in the absence of the preceding) to cover the medical cost of the injury. Benefits in the latter circumstances range from lump-sum payments to the payment of salaries to cover days or weeks lost to the employer up to, for example, 100 weeks at times. Some public and private companies as well as government companies and parastatals take out group sick insurance on behalf of their workers.

Workmen's Compensation. The benefits accruing to covered workers who are injured while working include a temporary disability benefit equal to two-thirds of their wages up to a maximum of 40 naira a month. This is payable after the first day, if the incapacity lasts more than four weeks, otherwise after a three-day waiting period, and is payable until recovery or certification of a permanent disability after 96 months.

Evaluation
The sick and injured worker has modest social security protection under the workmen's compensation scheme. Group sickness and sickness insurance schemes, where they exist, provide additional protection. The government's contribution is in the form of subsidised health care.

Nigeria

AN ASSESSMENT OF THE NIGERIAN WELFARE SYSTEM

By default, rather than by design, both traditional extended family centred welfare values and the post-colonial state's concern for the welfare of its citizens have combined to influence the level and types of welfare available to Nigerians. The partly suspended 1979 Nigerian Constitution states that:

> The security and welfare of the people shall be the primary purpose of government (Section 14(2b)).

> The state shall direct its policy toward ensuring that ... suitable and adequate shelter, suitable and adequate food, reasonable national minimum living wage, old age care and pensions and unemployment and sick benefits are provided for all citizens ... (Section 16 (2b)).

However, government conception of the social welfare sector is still very restricted for it excludes education, health and housing aspects. This relative ambiguity in the government's conception of social welfare and the recent financial downturn in government agencies have both limited the amount of services available to Nigerian citizens. Such services as are available are still limited in their extent and coverage. For example, most States are still without old people's homes. Moreover, social security protection is limited to that provided by the National Provident Fund and by the workmen's compensation scheme. Long term contingencies (old age, invalidity, death and permanent disability) give rise only to an entitlement to a lump-sum payment, which has little to recommend it as a means of providing social security protection.

The financial constraints notwithstanding, the government has pledged to implement a welfare system that would enhance the quality of life of its citizens and, in particular, to focus attention on the most vulnerable group - the aged, youths, women, expectant and nursing mothers, beggars, destitutes and the handicapped.

REFERENCES AND FURTHER READING

Adebagbo, S.A. (1978), 'Institutional Care of the Aged: A Study of the Lagos City Institution for the Aged', Nigerian Behavioral Sciences Journal, 1(3), 150-61.

Adebo, E.A. (1974), Social Welfare Services in Lagos, Lagos: Lagos City Council.

Faniran-Odekunle, O. (1978), 'Nigeria's Social Welfare Services: Past, Present and Future', Nigerian Behavioral Sciences Journal, 1(3), 174-94.

Federal Republic of Nigeria (1970), Second National Development Plan 1970-75, Lagos: Federal Ministry of Information Printing Division.

_____ (1975), Third National Development Plan 1975-80, Lagos: Federal Ministry of Information Printing Division.

_____ (1981), Fourth National Development Plan 1980-85, Lagos: Federal Ministry of Information Printing Division.

Government of the Midwestern State (nd), Social Welfare in Midwestern State, Benin-City: Government Publication.

Obasanjo, O. (1981), 'The Jaji Address', in Oyediran, O. (ed.), Survey of Nigerian Affairs 1976-77, Ibadan: Macmillan.

Ojesina, J.O. (1983), 'The Problem of Begging and Destitution in The Urban City of Ibadan', Nigerian Journal of Social Work, 1983, (pp).

Okediji, F.O. (1972), 'The Rehabilitation of Beggars in Nigeria', in Proceedings of a National Conference National Council of Social Work, Ibadan: University of Ibadan Press.

Olowu, D. (ed.) (1981), The Administration of Social Services in Nigeria: A Challenge to Local Governments, Ile-Ife: Local Government Training Programme, University of Ife.

Nigeria

Sanda, A.O. (1974a), 'A Comparative Analysis of Political Leadership and Ethnicity in Nigeria and Zaire', Journal of Eastern African Research and Development, 4(1), 27-47.

_____ (1974b), Ethnic Relations in Nigeria, Ibadan: Caxton.

_____ (1976), 'The Influence of Culture on Family Health in Africa', The Journal of the Society of Health, Nigeria, XI, 100-6.

_____ (1979), 'Ethnic Interests and Political Fragmentation in Nigeria', Nigerian Behavioural Sciences Journal, 2, 53-68.

_____ (1980a), Problems and Prospects of the National Youth Service Scheme in Nigeria, Ibadan & Lagos: NISER/Academic Press.

_____ (1980b), Social Science and Social Policy in Nigeria, Ibadan: NISER.

_____ (1981), 'The Nature of Social Services and the Evolution of Social Policy in Nigeria', in D. Olowu (ed), The Administration of Social Services in Nigeria: A Challenge to Local Governments, Ile-Ife: Local Government Training Programme, University of Ife.

_____ (1982), The Challenges of Nigeria's Indigenization, Ibadan: NESIR/INTEC.

_____ (1986), 'Minimum Government and the Sociology of Nigeria's Public Administration: Inaugural Lecture', Ile-Ife: University of Ife.

Sofoluwe, G.O. and Bennet, F.T. (1985), Principle and Practice of Community Health in Africa, Ibadan: University Press.

SOUTH AFRICA
Brian McKendrick and Erzsebet Dudas

THE WELFARE SYSTEM ENVIRONMENT

Ideological Environment

The Republic of South Africa extends over 1,220,000 square kilometres of the southernmost part of the African continent. It is a developing country that contains patches of high industrialised development, so that a prosperous, urban, Westernised society exists side by side with extensive rural poverty. Its total population in 1984 was estimated as 32,614,458 people (see Table 1).

TABLE 1 : THE SOUTH AFRICAN POPULATION, 1984

	Number	Percentage
Africans (including those in the 'independent' states)	24,103,458	73.9
'Coloured'	2,817,000	8.6
Indian	887,000	2.7
White	4,807,000	14.8
TOTAL	32,614,458	100.0

SOURCE: Survey of Race Relations 1984

South Africa

The pervasive ideological environment of South Africa is one of emphasis upon racial and cultural differences, and the separate development of ethnic groups. The prevailing political philosophy thus divides the population into 13 nations: whites, coloured persons (that is, of mixed race), Indians, and ten different black nations, if the independent African states are included. A contradiction in terms, 'plural society', is used to describe the people who live within South Africa's borders, since the concept provides for both the division and the coexistence of the racially fragmented population. Separate development, and the laws by which it has been applied, has resulted in white persons becoming established as a privileged elite: they occupy the most skilled jobs, have the highest incomes, generally live in urban areas and are the country's political power group. They also enjoy the most sophisticated welfare provision, in terms of both quality and quantity. African people are the reverse: they are least likely to have skilled jobs, high income or urban residence, and they have access to a narrower range of welfare facilities. Between the polar groups of whites and Africans fall the other two groups, 'coloured' people and Indians.

The South African preoccupation with ethnicity, multi-national development and separate facilities for different race groups colours all aspects of the country's life, and is also the predominant characteristic of the Republic's welfare system. Within this broad context, three key principles mark welfare philosophy and practice:

An Abhorrence of Socialism. While the state accepts a duty to take measures to prevent social suffering on the part of its citizens and for making a selective contribution to relieving and combating social distress, this is viewed as a supplementary responsibility. The major onus lies on the person himself, his family and the community. The stance taken by the state is that,

> The Government in the Republic of South Africa does not accept full responsibility for its citizens' welfare. Furthermore, not one of the principles of a welfare state is accepted or applied (Department of Constitutional Development and Planning 1985b, p.6).

South Africa

Partnership Between State and Community. Flowing logically from the preceding principle, the community has traditionally been viewed as having an important role in welfare provision, one recognised in practice through the inclusion of voluntary sector and church representatives in welfare decision-making structures at all levels, and through a comprehensive system of state financial support for the service activities of community-sponsored welfare organisations.

Movement from Residential and Therapeutic Services to Community-based and Preventive Services. Until the 1980s, the bulk of the Republic's social services were therapeutic in nature, with a strong reliance on residential care. Since this orientation has led to a heavy dependency on state funding and subsidisation, the state has begun to make strenuous efforts to encourage the growth of preventive services and community-based care facilities.

South Africa's welfare system is thus founded on a complex and often paradoxical value base. On the one hand, it has characteristics that can be found in the welfare systems of many modern, Western, capitalistic countries, such as the growing accent on prevention and community care, and partnership in human welfare provision between state and community. On the other hand, the system is characterised by traits that are the very opposite of modern social welfare philosophy, principally as the result of discrimination on racial grounds.

Historical Origins

1652   First Dutch settlement. Agricultural economy, with the family and kinship group the keystones of welfare for Africans and whites.

1795   First British occupation of the Cape of Good Hope, and exodus inland of Dutch farmers ('Boers').

1814   First orphanage established at the Cape by the Dutch Reformed Church. Subsequently, Cape Providence enacts first legislation regarding care of children and the physically disabled, relief of indigency.

South Africa

1870	Diamonds discovered at Kimberley, and gold 15 years later on the Witwatersrand. Move of whites, Africans and foreign migrants to new urban areas.
1899-1902	Anglo-Boer War. Beginning of 'Poor White Problem'. Voluntary organisations established to help poor whites.
1910	Union of Cape, Natal, Transvaal and Orange Free State.
1924	Depression. State work schemes for poor whites. Department of Labour established. Black poverty grows in congested reserves; migrant work in towns leads to breakdown of family and kin helping systems. First nationally-organised welfare organisation established.
1928	First Old Age Pension Act (non-contributory pensions).
1932	Publication of report by Carnegie Commission of Inquiry into the Poor White Problem. Training and employment of social workers recommended.
1936	First Blind Persons Act and pensions for the blind.
1937	State Department of Social Welfare established. State subsidy scheme for voluntary organisations employing social workers. First Unemployment Insurance Act.
1939-1945	Second World War. Parliament rejects national contributory social security system, but promulgates first Workmen's Compensation Act.
1946	First Disability Grants Act.
1948	Present government comes to power. Separate development enforced by law in all spheres of life.
1949	First legislation to regulate voluntary welfare organisations.

South Africa

1960   Creation of separate state departments to address welfare needs of different race groups began.

1965   New National Welfare Act. Regional Welfare Boards and a National Welfare Board created.

1966   State policy introduced that separate voluntary welfare organisations should be established for different races.

1978   Revised welfare legislation to encourage the planning of welfare on racial lines, to regulate fund-raising from the public, and to provide for the control of the social work profession.

1983   New constitution and tricameral Parliament. Welfare becomes an 'own affair' for each racial group.

Political and Socio-economic Environments

Over the past 10 years the political debate in South Africa has swung from examining the pros and cons of apartheid, to an almost universal concern about how racial discrimination can be removed, and the pace at which this change should take place. Until 1983, only white persons were enfranchised, and the legislature comprised an all-white Parliament. The Republic of South Africa Constitution Act, 1983, enfranchised 'coloured' and Indian citizens. It created an Executive State President, a President's Council; and three Houses of Parliament: the House of Assembly (whites), House of Representatives ('coloureds') and the House of Delegates (Indians). Each House is required to approve legislation that relates to 'common affairs' (such as the budget or defence matters), but every House is individually empowered to enact legislation restricted to the 'own affairs' of its group. 'Own affairs' is defined in section 14(1) of the Republic of South Africa Constitution Act as:

> Matters which specifically or differentially affect a population group in relation to the maintenance of its identity and the upholding and furtherance of its way of life, culture, traditions and customs.

South Africa

'Own affairs' include education, health and welfare.

Africans are excluded from direct participation in the new dispensation, and, in terms of the Act, the control and administration of 'black affairs' is vested in the State President, although in practice white Cabinet Ministers manage the portfolios concerned with African administration, development and education. At the time of writing, the future way in which Africans will be directly involved in government remains a matter of conjecture and debate.

The 1983 constitutional dispensation has not resulted in increased racial harmony in the Republic, and has been rejected by most Africans. Opponents to it also include substantial numbers of whites, 'coloureds' and Indian people. Proponents of the dispensation view it as the first step in a process of enfranchising all South Africans, while simultaneously protecting the rights of minority groups.

Concurrently with the introduction of the tricameral Parliament, South African agricultural production was severely affected by the worst drought in living memory, an economic recession occurred, and the price of gold, South Africa's major foreign exchange earner, fell on the world market.

Widespread African unrest in 1985 led to the declaration of a temporary state of emergency in parts of the country, which in turn led to a rapid drop in the foreign exchange value of the rand, and the refusal of foreign banks to extend the repayment period of loans to South Africa. These circumstances combined to give the country a zero economic growth rate in 1985 and an annual inflation rate of 20 per cent.

The Department of Statistics provided the following figures for the economically active population (EAP) per race group for 1982 and 1983, excluding Transkei, Bophuthatswana, Venda, and the Ciskei, which are 'independent' states.

South Africa

TABLE 2 : SOUTH AFRICAN EMPLOYMENT, 1982 and 1983

	1982 Number	Percent	1983 Number	Percent
African	5,516,000	63.2	5,665,000	63.2
Indian	270,000	3.1	285,000	3.2
'Coloured'	952,000	10.9	987,000	11.0
White	1,986,000	22.8	2,026,000	22.6
TOTAL	8,724,000	100.0	8,963,000	100.0

SOURCE: Survey of Race Relations 1983

THE WELFARE SYSTEM: AN OVERVIEW

Structure and Administration of the Welfare System
In pursuance of the principle that the state and community share responsibility for the provision of welfare services, there is a definite division of responsibility between the two sectors. The state's task is overall planning, social security provision and statutory social service programmes, while the private sector, comprising community- and church-sponsored welfare organisations, has primary responsibility for non-statutory personal social services.

State Welfare Services. These are delivered through regional and local offices of state departments. Because welfare (including social assistance) is considered an 'own affair' four state departments are involved: the Departments of Health Services and Welfare of the Houses of Assembly (whites), Representatives ('coloureds') and Delegates (Indians), and the Department of Constitutional Development and Planning (Africans). The eight self-governing or 'independent' African states each have their own departments of health and welfare.
The workmen's compensation scheme is administered by the Workmen's Compensation Commission. (Black workers are assisted by the Department of Plural Relations and Development.) The Department of Labour has a general supervisory function.
The compulsory unemployment insurance scheme

South Africa

is administered by the Unemployment Insurance Fund, managed by a bipartite board, with local unemployment benefit committees and claim officers, under the supervision of the Department of Labour.

Community-Sponsored Services. These are rendered by 1,600 local welfare organisations, most of which are affiliated to one of 18 nationally- or provincially-organised bodies (for example, the SA National Council for Child and Family Welfare, or the Jewish Family, and Community Council of the Transvaal). These national and provincial bodies attempt to co-ordinate services within their functional fields.

Co-ordination and co-operation between the state and private sector is facilitated through four structures. Firstly, nationally- and provincially-organised bodies each liaise with the state on issues concerning the field in which they function, while on matters of common interest they combine together into an ad hoc committee for dealings with the state. Secondly, the National Welfare Act (1978) provides for 24 regional welfare boards representing state and community interests, which have the duty of regulating, co-ordinating, promoting and planning welfare activity within their regions. These boards are uniracial. At the national level, the multiracial South African Welfare Council advises the state on social welfare needs and issues. Thirdly, the country is divided into eight development regions, each with a multiracial Regional Development Advisory Committee, charged with the task of identifying priorities for co-ordinated social, physical, economic and constitutional development within the region. Each regional committee is represented on the National Development Advisory Committee, which advises the Cabinet on development needs. Fourthly, a national Population Development Programme, launched in 1984, has the aim of stimulating community development activities at the local level in order to accelerate improvement in the quality of life of all communities. Local community development committees are represented on sub-regional development associations, which, in turn, are represented on the regional development advisory committees discussed earlier. Within each region, state and community activities to promote the Population Development Programme are co-ordinated

South Africa

through an inter-departmental committee on which the private sector is represented.

Financing Social Welfare
Finance for South African social welfare services is predominantly provided by the state from income tax revenue. Income tax sources reflect the unequal distribution of the country's wealth, since it is estimated that the top 10 per cent of taxpayers contribute 50 per cent of individual income tax revenue, while the bottom 50 per cent contribute only 5 per cent of the total (Hansard 1984, cols.6,533-6,534).

The allocation of tax monies to government expenditure accounts is an attempt to redistribute the country's wealth. In 1984-5, a total sum of R1,155,358,000 was allocated to expenditure on welfare services (see Table 3):

TABLE 3 : GOVERNMENT WELFARE EXPENDITURE

	1983-4 Budget ('000R)	Per- centage	1984-5 Budget ('000R)	Per- centage
Africans	228,432	21.0	241,227	20.9
'Coloureds'	287,019	26.3	303,427	26.2
Indians	76,992	7.1	81,460	7.1
Whites	497,828	45.6	529,244	45.8
TOTAL	1,090,271	100.0	1,155,358	100.0

SOURCE: Estimates of Expenditure 1984

Most of the amount reflected above was disbursed on non-contributory social security benefits, but a portion was used to contribute to capital expenditure on the creation of new residential facilities, while a further portion was used to subsidise welfare activities undertaken by the voluntary sector, through grants towards the cost of residential care, community services and the salary and administration expenses of social workers. The total expenditure on these latter grants in respect of all population groups was R81,725,000 in 1982-3 (Department of Constitutional Development and Planning 1985b).

South Africa

Work-related social security provision involves funding from other sources in addition to the state. Unemployment insurance (including sickness and maternity benefits for workers) is jointly funded by contributions from employees (0.5 per cent of wages), employers (0.3 per cent of wage bill) and the state (25 per cent of total contributions); while work injury benefits (workmen's compensation) are financed entirely by employers through insurance premiums which vary with risk. Employers must normally insure their social security liability with the Public Accident Fund, but in some instances this can be done through licensed employer mutual associations.

The private sector is a significant source of funding for community welfare organisations, despite state grants and subsidies. Although no recent figure exists of the total income of the Republic's 1,600 community-sponsored welfare organisations, the van Rooyen Commission estimated their 1976 income as R130 million per annum (Report of the Commission of Inquiry into the Collection of Voluntary Financial Contributions from the Public 1976). Allowing for inflation, such income can be projected to exceed R250 million in 1986.

THE AGED

Philosophy. While the state and community accept a responsibility to promote the care of the aged, the onus for making provision for old age is upon the individual and his family. Only when the individual is unable to help himself will the state provide financial assistance (Department of Social Welfare and Pensions 1976). This assistance is given on the principle of 'exclusion', via a means test, rather than 'inclusion' as a citizen right. It has also become accepted policy over the last decade to maintain old people in the community wherever possible, and to regard institutional care as a last, rather than a first, resort.

Need. Although the South African population is predominantly a young one, increasing numbers of people are living to pensionable age (60 years for women, and 65 years for men). Presently an estimated 4.9 per cent of South Africans are in this category, but the proportion differs by race: 4.16 per cent of Africans; 3.75 per cent of

South Africa

'coloured' people; 2.95 per cent of Indians; and 9.14 per cent of whites (Eales 1980).
Services for the aged of all varieties are more often available in urban than rural areas, and the cumulative impact of South Africa's separate development policy has resulted in white old people having the best range and quality of services. At the other extreme, both in the city and the country, Africans have the least adequate resources. For urban Africans this is largely the result of neglect, since until 1978 government policy was not to regard them as permanent city dwellers; while for rural residents, the lack of facilities reflects the general underdevelopment of their homelands, and an official, albeit questionable, belief that '[old] persons are cared for in the extended family system' (<u>Hansard</u> 1984 col.1,237).

Personal Social Services
The state facilitates the work of the non-government sector in three ways: through financial aid to voluntary organisations (low-interest loans and subsidies for community services for the aged); through subsidies of up to 75 per cent of the running costs of welfare organisations; and through 100 per cent building loans to local authorities for special housing units for old people (Department of Foreign Affairs 1985). Community-sponsored welfare organisations serving the aged are affiliated to one of a number of National Councils, the most important of which is the SA National Council for the Aged, which provides a co-ordinating, standard-building and developmental function in respect of its 160 affiliated but autonomous societies, most of which are situated in urban areas and do not serve African people. In addition to registered welfare organisations, supplementary services to old people are provided in local communities by church and civic groups.

Services Delivered by the Non-government Sector.
In earlier years, old age homes were frequently viewed as a first-line resource for meeting the needs of the aged, a legacy of which is the unusually high proportion (7.0 per cent) of white aged who live in residential institutions (Joseph 1977). In recent times, a thrust from the voluntary sector, complemented by a shift in state policy, has resulted in focus being redirected to

maintaining the aged in the community. Thus, in addition to developing and running old age homes, voluntary organisations increasingly emphasise services such as pre-retirement preparation, home help, social clubs, service centres, home visiting, holiday schemes, luncheon clubs and individual- and group-oriented professional social work services for the aged in the community. Under the auspices of the SA National Council for the Aged, a major service/research project has been established in the densely urbanised Southern Transvaal to pioneer community development approaches to the provision of local services for African aged people. The aim is to evolve service models that can be adapted to all urban areas, thus stimulating the rapid growth of facilities for the African aged.

State Services. The state manages a handful of old age homes and subsidises others (see Table 4).

TABLE 4: STATE SUBSIDISED OLD AGE HOMES, 1984

	No. of Homes
Africans (in 'white' areas)	19
'Coloureds'	30
Indians	2
Whites	350
TOTAL	401

SOURCE: Hansard 1984 cols.1,577, 1988-89; Department of Foreign Affairs 1985

State subsidies to old age homes are a major item in state financial provision for the aged. The per capita subsidy takes into reckoning the proportion of frail aged: for example, in Category A (where up to 40 per cent of residents are infirm) the monthly per capita subsidy is R32.33 for Africans, R123.84 for 'coloured' people, R131.89 for Indians and R111.84 for whites (Survey of Race Relations 1984). Reducing the backlog of subsidised residential accommodation for African old people is a current priority.

South Africa

Social Security

Pensions. In 1984-5, a total of R559,740,000 was set aside by the state for the provision of means-tested old age pensions (see Table 5).

TABLE 5 : SOUTH AFRICAN OLD AGE PENSION

	Allocation to Old Age Pensions 1984-5(R)	As a Percentage of Total Expenditure on the Aged	Number of Pensioners 1984
African (in 'white' areas)	154,369,000	99.1	248,839
'Coloured'	106,356,000	89.4	97,488
Indian	24,523,000	99.2	22,786
White	274,492,000	75.4	144,000
Total	559,740,000		513,113

SOURCE: Estimates of Expenditure 1984; Hansard 1984, cols.638, 105, 157; Department of Health and Welfare 1984.

The retirement age for men is 65 years and for women 60 years. Non-citizens must satisfy a three-year residency test.

Pension payments differ by race, as the above data suggest. In October, 1984, the maximum monthly old age pension was R65 for Africans, R103 for 'coloured' people and Indians, and R116 for whites (Department of Health and Welfare 1984). (This reflects a ratio of 1:1.6:2.5 which is a narrowing of the ratio 1:2:4 which pertained before the government announced a policy decision to progressively reduce the pension discrepancy between whites and other races.) Pension increments, differentiated by race, are paid for the deferral of retirement. A constant attendance allowance, again differentiated by race, is also provided. All pensioners are entitled to free medical care.

As only one in 10 South Africans of pensionable age is financially independent, there

South Africa

has been a growing dependence on non-contributory state pensions, so that despite relatively stringent means tests, the number of state old age pensioners has increased by 50 per cent from 1973 to 1983, while expenditure on this item, not taking inflation into account, has increased by 545 per cent (Press Release - Select Committee on Pension Benefits 1984).

Occupation Pensions. Less than half of the economically-active population, and in particular black people, have access to occupational pension funds (Eales 1980). For those persons who do have such access, pension fund contributions are not transferable from one fund to another.

A select committee of Parliament was appointed in 1984 to investigate occupational pension funds, and particularly 'the compulsory preservation of pension rights by means of transferability or otherwise' (Financial Mail, April 5, 1985). The committee has not yet reported.

Evaluation

While white urban aged people undoubtedly have the nearest to adequate resources available to them, even this group do not enjoy the facilities necessary for dignified life in the community. The need is therefore for services and resources for all existing pensioners to be up-graded to a level that enables a minimally acceptable standard of community living. Nowhere is this need more pressing than in the case of urban and rural African people. For future pensioners, the heart of the matter lies in having the ability to provide, at least to some extent, for their financial security in old age. A prerequisite of this is for more of the economically active group to have access to occupational pension schemes, and for contributions to such schemes to be safeguarded when people change jobs.

THE DISABLED AND HANDICAPPED

Philosophy. The guiding concept regarding the welfare of the disabled is that everything possible should be done to assist the severely handicapped adult in his social functioning as a member of the community, with institutionalised care being a final resort (Department of Foreign Affairs 1985).

South Africa

Need. No reliable figures exist of the Republic's total handicapped population, although exact data are available concerning disabled people who receive social pensions. Since this latter group has been sifted through a means test, however, it is likely that they will constitute but a fraction of the total population.

Personal Social Services
The state provides a small amount of personal social services, but plays its major role in policy formulation and the allocation of loans and subsidies for services offered under private sector auspices.

Voluntary organisations in the private sector are affiliated to one of five multiracial national councils, which promote and co-ordinate private sector activity within functional fields: they are the SA National Councils for the Blind, Cripple Care, the Deaf and Mental Health, and the SA National Epilepsy League. These five independent councils come together to act jointly on matters of common concern through an SA Federal Council on the Rehabilitation of the Disabled. Each of the councils has affiliates at the local level which provide direct service in their field of concern.

Services Delivered by the Non-government Sector.
Space does not permit a review of services delivered in all of the five functional fields that constitute the care of the disabled in South Africa, but the field of services to the blind may serve as an example. The SA National Council for the Blind's Optima Centre in Pretoria offers a range of services on a multiracial, national basis, including an aids depot, library, bureau for the prevention of blindness (screening over 25,000 people, mainly rural Africans, each year), a pre-vocational training and rehabilitation unit, and a vocational training college. Its 40 affiliated local societies render professional social work, eye care services, elementary pre-vocational rehabilitation including orientation and mobility instruction, workshops and work projects, open labour market placement and provision of aids. One affiliate, the SA Guide-Dogs Association for the Blind, trains 'seeing eye' dogs, while another, the SA Blind Workers' Association, is the major source of braille translation and literature production. Most of the Republic's 23 hostels and apartment

South Africa

complexes for the blind are operated by Council affiliates, as are most of the 28 workshops and work projects (SA National Council for the Blind 1985).

Through the SA National Council for the Rehabilitation of the Disabled, the SA National Council for the Blind and its sister councils have sponsored a service/research project in KwaZulu to test the feasibility of innovative income-generating projects for disabled rural people (McKendrick 1985).

State Services. Personal social services rendered by the state include the provision of professional social work services in mental hospitals, and the direct administration of a number of agricultural settlements for the disabled and their families. The state also provides subsidies for the non-government sector for the provision of services. Table 6 shows the state budget for services for disabled people, excluding pensions and grants in 1984-5.

TABLE 6 : STATE EXPENDITURE ON THE DISABLED 1984-5

	State Budget for Services (R)
Africans in 'white' areas	845,000
'Coloured'	557,000
Indian	118,000
White	8,617,000
TOTAL	10,137,000

SOURCE: Estimates of Expenditure 1984.

Social Security
The Blind Persons Act (1968) provides for the payment of pensions and allowances to registered blind people aged 19 and over and subsidies for sheltered workshops.

The Disability Grants Act (1968) provides for the payment of disability grants to severely physically and mentally handicapped people over the age of 16 years.

Provision for the setting of eligibility criteria in respect of these pensions and grants

South Africa

is contained in the Social Pensions Act (1973). Applicants are required to satisfy a residency test and a means test.

Blind pensions and disability pensions, constant attendance allowances and medical care benefits are the same as those given to old age pensioners. The total sum set aside for these items in 1984-5 is reflected in Table 7.

TABLE 7 : EXPENDITURE OF DISABILITY PENSIONS, 1984-5

	Blind Persons Pensions	Disability Pensions
Africans in 'white' areas	2,939,000	64,701,000
'Coloured'	1,549,000	71,313,000
Indian	300,000	19,834,000
White	1,450,000	50,336,000

SOURCE: Estimates of Expenditure 1984

The distribution of recipients of blind and disability pensions in 1984 is given in Table 8.

TABLE 8 : THE DISTRIBUTION OF BLIND AND DISABILITY PENSIONS, 1984

	Blind Pensioners	Disability Grantees
Africans in 'white' areas	4,452	98,765
'Coloured'	1,581	62,882
Indian	256	17,976
White	750	29,000

SOURCE: Hansard 1984, col. 1,831; Department of Internal Affairs 1984; Department of Health and Welfare 1984.

The Workmen's Compensation. This applies to employees in factories and offices whose average annual earnings do not exceed R18,000 per annum. It provides for compensation to be paid to a worker in respect of temporary or permanent disability to work resultant from injuries

South Africa

suffered or disease contracted in the course of his employment, or to his dependants in the event of his death. It does not apply to persons employed in certain capacities as, for example, persons in military service undergoing training, casual employees and domestic servants in private households (Department of Foreign Affairs 1985).

The permanent disability pension is 75 per cent of the beneficiary's previous monthly earnings, up to a maximum of R600 a month if totally disabled. Partial disability attracts a pro rata permanent disability pension, depending on degree of disability. For 30 per cent or less disability a lump sum compensation (up to R600) is paid. Free medical care is also provided for up to two years (longer if special need established).

It is evident that the upper income group, comprised of professional and business men, and the lower income group, comprised of unskilled workers (for example approximately two million agricultural workers and 800,000 domestic workers) are excluded from benefits in terms of the above schemes.

Evaluation

In urban areas, services have swung strongly to aim at keeping the disabled within the community, although this goal is hard to achieve in respect of disabled people in the sub-economic category whose primary or only source of income is a state pension or grant.

Although the pattern of white privilege recurs in services to the disabled, more attention has perhaps been paid to African needs than in some other welfare fields. For example, in the field of the blind, 13 of the 17 schools for the blind are for African children, and Africans have access to 19 of the country's 28 sheltered workshops and work projects (SA National Council for the Blind 1985). Despite this, large regions, more especially rural areas with predominantly African populations, remain

> deprived of the social and economic infrastructure that is essential for service delivery where it is required, and in a form that would be meaningful in a specific environment (SA National Council for the Blind 1985).

South Africa

Tertiary services to meet the needs of physically and mentally handicapped people are relatively well developed, particularly in the urban areas, although an acute need exists to prevent disability, when it is preventable. In some fields, such as the prevention of blindness and national programmes to reduce drinking and driving, keen attention is being given to prevention, but in others it is markedly lacking. An example is the poor quality and spread of primary health care facilities in rural South Africa.

A major innovation, the full effect of which is yet to be felt, is the inception during the early 1980s of an active, multiracial disability rights movement, Disabled People South Africa. This movement, through its assertive promotion of the disabled persons' point of view and human rights, is already challenging complacent, long-established attitudes held within some welfare organisations and the wider community, and seems likely to be a force that will accelerate the development of facilities and resources for the disabled (McKendrick 1985).

CHILDREN, YOUTH AND NEEDY FAMILIES

Philosophy. Sound family life and the care of children within a family setting are traditional values in South Africa. At the same time, it is acknowledged that the responsibility for the child is primarily that of the parents. Thus, the country's approach has been to view children, youth and families as part of a common system, and a single field of service, 'child and family welfare', has evolved. It is widely agreed that services to promote the quality of family living are the ideal, although in reality these are lacking since resources are inevitably being devoted to emergency and individual case-oriented services.

Needs. The country's population is a young one, with 50 per cent being under the age of 15 years. Despite increasing longevity, it is estimated that by the year 2000, 60 per cent of a projected population of 45 million will be in this age category (Survey of Race Relations 1984). A sound family life for these young people is seriously impaired by rural poverty, exacerbated by years of drought; rural-urban migration; high unemployment;

South Africa

low family income, especially for Africans; the physical division of families as a consequence of influx control legislation; a shortage of housing for urban families other than whites; and political turmoil.

Personal Social Services
Uniracial state departments deal with statutory social work, while voluntary welfare organisations provide services in areas not covered by the state. Community- and church-sponsored welfare organisations operating at the local level are affiliated to, or are branches of, one of ten national councils concerned with children and families, the largest of which is the SA National Council for Child and Family Welfare. While most of the larger societies have a multiracial clientele, many are uniracial.

Parallel with state and community welfare services is a network of non-welfare organisations which provide promotive services to youth, such as the Scouting and Voortrekker movements.

Services Delivered by the Non-government Sector.
The bulk of personal social services are given by community-sponsored but state-subsidised welfare organisations, and their primary focus is therapeutic. For example, during 1984 the main areas of direct service concern of organisations affiliated to the SA National Council for Child and Family Welfare were foster care, where the daily average number of children under their auspices was 12,797, and where reconstruction services were concurrently being undertaken with the children's own families; day care services; child neglect, of which 5,794 instances were dealt with; marital problems, where 5,174 couples were aided; and unmarried mothers, of whom 3,895 approached the societies for help, often requiring associated adoption work. Affiliated societies were concurrently involved in 456 developmental community projects, all but 73 of them in black communities. In the same year, organisations affiliated to the Family and Marriage Council of South Africa reported two main service thrusts: marriage counselling to 9,058 persons of all races, and a total of 2,124 educational/preventive group sessions with young people, engaged couples and others (FAMSA 1985).

South Africa

State Services. The state departments charged with direct welfare functions all provide personal social services for children and families, both statutory and pre-statutory. An example is the Department of Health and Welfare, where in 1982, 4,025 or 32 per cent of the total statutory workload concerned children in need of care, and 6,467 or 54 per cent of the total pre-statutory load involved 'uncontrollable' children, child battering, marital problems, divorces and unmarried motherhood (Department of Constitutional Development and Planning 1985a).

The overall state budget and its racial distribution in 1983-4 for services associated with child and family welfare is given in Table 9.

TABLE 9 : EXPENDITURE ON CHILD AND FAMILY WELFARE SERVICES 1983-4

White	R73,244,900	(37.4)
Indian	R27,671,000	(14.1)
'Coloured'	R86,182,200	(44.0)
African (in 'white' areas)	R 8,914,000	(4.5)
TOTAL	R196,012,100	(100.0)

SOURCE: Survey of Race Relations 1983.

Adoption. In 1983, a total of 3,701 children were placed in adoption. The majority (2,618) were white children, and, of the balance, 573 were 'coloured', 179 Indian, and 331 African (Hansard 1984 cols.795, 1,098, 1,238).

Foster Care. This has increasingly become the favoured alternative for children who temporarily cannot remain in their own homes. Data relating to the total number of children in foster care and the allowances paid is not available, but it is known that in 1983-4, 15,518 'coloured' children were being fostered at a cost of R13,907,119 (Department of Internal Affairs 1984), while the comparable figures for white children were 5,360 and R9,600,000 (Department of Health and Welfare 1984). Foster care grants vary by race. In 1984, monthly rates were R114 for whites, R77.50 for Indians and 'coloureds', and R40 for Africans

(Hansard 1984 cols.1,577-8). The low payment to African foster parents impairs the extent and quality of fostering. In the African community it is generally old age pensioners who become foster parents, and the grant paid makes impossible adequate nutrition and an acceptable standard of care (Foster Care Action Group 1985).

Residential Care. Facilities for the residential care of children depend upon race. In 1983 there were for white children 891 places of care (763 are privately owned, and 128 are run by welfare organisations) accommodating 53,992 children (Department of Health and Welfare 1984); for 'coloureds', six places of safety, 26 children's homes and three schools of industry for 4,117 children; for Indians six children's homes, two schools of industry and a place of safety (Department of Internal Affairs 1984); and for Africans in white areas six children's homes and six places of safety for 1,088 children (Department of Co-operation and Development 1984a). State subsidies to children's homes in 1983-84 were R12,376,758 for whites (Department of Health and Welfare 1984), R457,040 for Indians (Department of Internal Affairs 1984), R1,983,575 for 'coloureds' (Department of Foreign Affairs 1985), and at the monthly rate of R60 per child for Africans (Department of Co-operation and Development 1984b). The extent to which residential care is used, as opposed to foster care, is not known for the whole population. In respect of whites, however, there were 749 residential placements in 1984, compared with 1,260 in foster care (Department of Health and Welfare 1984).

Creches. Details of state-subsidised creches available for the children of working mothers, and the subsidies paid are given in Table 10.

TABLE 10 : STATE-SUBSIDISED CRECHES, 1982

	No of Creches	Subsidy per child per day (R)
White	45	0.80
'Coloured' and Indian	91	0.50
African (in 'white' areas)	4	0.075

SOURCE: Survey of Race Relations 1983

South Africa

Social Security

Maintenance Grants. These are paid in respect of children where one breadwinner or parent is absent, and family income is inadequate for satisfactory child care. The means-tested per capita monthly grants in 1983-4 were R178.98 for whites, R118.00 for Indians and 'coloureds', and R60.00 for Africans (Hansard 1983 cols.935-6, 1,085-6). Full information regarding payments is not available, but it is known that in 1984 there were 16,679 Indian beneficiaries at a cost of R27,245,231 (Department of Internal Affairs 1984), and 15,707 whites at a cost of R50,240,000 (Department of Health and Welfare 1984).

Family Allowances. Only resident employed whites with three or more children and with an earned income below R2,808 a year qualify for family allowance of up to R111 a month for the first three children, plus R37 for each additional child with a supplement of R8 for each additional child at school. In 1984, an average of 70 to 90 such allowances were paid each month (Department of Health and Welfare 1984).

Maternity Benefits. The Unemployment Insurance Fund, a contributory scheme, makes provision for maternity benefits on the same basis as unemployment benefits (see below). These are payable for four weeks before confinement and eight weeks after. Free medical care is also provided.

Survivors Pensions (Work Injury). Under the workmen's compensation scheme survivors receive a pension equal to 40 per cent of the deceased's pension plus a lump sum payment of R300 or two months' earnings, which ever is less. Orphans receive 20 per cent of the deceased's pension. The maximum survivor pension is 100 per cent of the deceased's pension. A funeral grant of up to R400 may also be paid.

Evaluation
Existing social services are relatively adequate in addressing the needs of families within the skilled, urban, industrialised sector of the population that develop problems. Restorative and therapeutic social services, as well as social security provision, are strongest for white family

South Africa

members, then Indians and 'coloureds'. Facilities for Africans in white areas are rudimentary, while for Africans in rural areas and homelands they are often absent. Hence, major gaps at present are the lack of comprehensive, preventive and promotive child and family welfare services for the population as a whole, and an acute need for developmental programmes to improve the basic quality of living for the unskilled, urban and rural poor, who are predominantly African people.

In 1982 a Committee was formed at the request of the Cabinet to formulate a national family programme. The report, published in 1985, proposes a programme aimed at safeguarding the family as the fundamental unit in society, and suggests measures which are designed to promote the quality of marriage and family life, as well as to encourage stable communities in which families can function effectively. An emphasis is upon primary and secondary prevention, while a feature of the report is the recommendation that discriminatory policies and practices that affect the quality of black family life be removed (Department of Constitutional Development and Planning 1985a).

THE UNEMPLOYED

Philosophy. Every individual is entitled to a basic minimum standard of living. If people are unable to provide for themselves and their families by means of income from gainful employment, the state and certain sectors of the community, notably sectarian welfare organisations, assume this responsibility.

Registered unemployment by race group for 30 June 1983 and 31 August 1984 is given in Table 11.

TABLE 11 : REGISTERED UNEMPLOYMENT IN SOUTH AFRICA 1983 AND 1984[a]

	African	Indian	'Coloured'	White	Total
1983[b]	..	7,591	18,132	13,846	..
1984	34,114	3,980	12,406	13,089	65,589

South Africa

NOTES: a   Unemployed people do not have to register, therefore registered unemployment data may not reflect the actual level of unemployed.

b   Figures for Africans not available for 1983.

SOURCE: <u>Survey of Race Relations</u> 1983.

As it is not compulsory for unemployed people to register, these statistics cannot be viewed as comprehensive.

It has been estimated that, if the present trends continue, only half the potential African economically active people will be formally employed by the year 2000, while some 13 per cent would make a living in the informal sector, and more than 36 per cent would be unemployed (<u>Rand Daily Mail</u>, 18 July 1985).

The University of Stellenbosch's Institute for Future Research has estimated that South Africa's jobless pool could swell to more than 5.0 million by the year 2000 from 1980's estimated 3.4 million. It is said that the increase would be caused by an additional 350,000 work-seekers becoming available every year for the next 16 years (<u>Sunday Times</u>, 22 July 1985).

In the light of the alarming figures reflected above it is evident that social security will have to be extended or alternate solutions to the country's unemployment problems will have to be found.

<u>Social Security</u>
The major legislation concerned is the Unemployment Insurance Act (1966), the Social Pensions Act (1973) and the Children's Act (1960).

<u>The Unemployment Insurance Fund (UIF)</u>. This makes provision for unemployment, illness and maternity benefits as well as payment to dependants of deceased contributors.

Membership is compulsory for all persons who work under a contract of service, apprenticeship or learnership, whether expressed or implied, except those whose incomes exceed R21,600 per annum, domestic servants, persons employed in agriculture (excluding forestry), officers of the public service, provincial administration employees who contribute to a government service

South Africa

pension fund, employees of the SA Railways and Harbours and seasonal, casual and contract workers (excluding those from the Transkei, Bophuthatswana, Venda and Ciskei).

Eligibility for unemployment relief requires that 13 weeks' contributions during the last 52 weeks be paid; that the applicant be capable of and available for work; and that the unemployment not be voluntary. The benefit provided is 45 per cent of previous weekly earnings payable after a seven-day waiting period, for up to 26 weeks in any 52 week period, or for one sixth of the period during which contributions were paid if less. (Some administrative discretion applies in the event of prolonged unemployment.)

During 1983, payments from the state's UIF continued to rise as a result of the continuing high level of unemployment (see Table 12).

TABLE 12 : UNEMPLOYMENT PAYOUTS, 1981-3

	1981	1982	1983
No. of contributors:			
- employers	117,513	120,210	123,520
- employees	4,141,000	5,084,228	4,734,934
Total contributions (Rm)	110.1	126.1	140.1
Benefits paid out (Rm)	88.6	120.7	189.0
- unemployment	34.5	52.8	104.2
- illness	23.1	28.4	36.0
- maternity	22.2	29.0	35.5
- dependants of deceased contributors	8.8	10.5	13.3
Amount in fund at December (Rm)	253.2	272.8	246.6

SOURCE: Hansard 1984 col.1,359.

In 1983, benefits were paid to 320,475 unemployed contributors, compared with 268,000 in 1982 (Hansard 1984 col.1,359).

South Africa

Social Relief. Voluntary welfare organisations are increasingly providing social relief in the form of food, clothing and financial assistance for unemployed people and their families.

The state has traditionally made provision for social relief in the form of vouchers for food and minimal financial assistance for indigent persons. In September 1985 a system of special social relief was introduced, as an emergency measure, in order to provide financial aid for those persons who have been retrenched. This entirely state-funded system was introduced for a period of six months. The payment in respect of whites and 'coloureds' is R164 per adult and R49 per child, per month. The applications are reviewed monthly. A similar scheme in respect of Indians has been approved but not yet been implemented.

No similar scheme for Africans has yet been made known. The state does however subsidise registered welfare organisations on a rand for rand basis for expenditure incurred as a result of feeding schemes for needy African families.

Personal Social Services
Unemployment Insurance is linked to the registration of the contributor as unemployed, after which the Department of Manpower attempts to place unemployed persons in suitable employment. This function was further extended by the Manpower Training Act (1981) to the provision of training of work-seekers. This development is in accord with the report of the Wiehahn Commission, which found that South Africa, in common with many developing countries, faced not one but two major problems in manpower, namely, a shortage of skilled and a surplus of unskilled manpower (Department of Foreign Affairs 1985).

Manpower training is also provided by sectors of private industry.

In the 1985-6 budget the state allocated R100 million for the creation of new job opportunities. In October 1985 a further R500 million was allocated for this purpose. An inter-departmental committee was appointed to oversee this project and to decide about the allocation of the available funds. The intention is to cover the entire spectrum of the economy and thereby to create new job opportunities, for example in small business corporations, agriculture, mining and construction.

South Africa

Evaluation
The existing social security system is inadequate and unable to cope with the rising unemployment, and state and employer contributions, especially to the UIF, are not sufficient. All economically active persons should be included in the existing schemes, both as contributors and beneficiaries. Moreover, human dignity should not be threatened by the need to rely on charity in the form of social relief and minimal social pensions or grants.

The recent schemes launched by the state to create new employment opportunities and to improve training facilities are, however, a positive attempt to respond to both the present economic depression and the country's long-term need for skilled manpower.

THE SICK AND INJURED

Philosophy. The basic concept of 'health for all' is accepted in South Africa. The ultimate objective, therefore, is a balanced, comprehensive approach, whereby preventive, curative, health promotive and rehabilitative services are each allocated their rightful role, and will put an optimal service, in terms of total available resources, within the reach of the entire population whether in the cities or in the most remote rural areas.

Need. All persons in urbanised areas have health services of a similar nature available to them. In rural areas however, there is a lack of basic health services. Professor Ralph Kirsch has noted that rising costs and the trend towards medical specialisation have been particularly harmful to South Africa's vast rural population, which still lives in unhygienic conditions where infectious diseases are common (The Argus, 2 August 1984).

In the rural areas the doctor-to-population ratio is 1:25,000, whereas in urban areas it is 1:750. 'It is not the lack of facilities or money but the lack of manpower that is responsible for the inadequacy of rural health services,' Professor J Gear, an expert on community health, has noted (Rand Daily Mail, 21 September 1984).

Health Administration. Central government state departments are primarily responsible for community health, the provincial administration of

South Africa

the four provinces for institutional curative treatment, and the approximately 430 local authorities for providing community and environmental health services.

Numerous voluntary agencies, many of which are registered welfare organisations, provide free health services. The South African National Tuberculosis Association is an example of such a voluntary organisation.

Social Security

Sickness Benefits. The Unemployment Insurance Fund, a contributor scheme, also makes provision for sickness benefits, payable at the rate of 45 per cent of weekly earnings, after a three week waiting period, reimbursed at the rate of one day of each day's unemployment beyond two weeks.

Temporary Disability Benefits. Under the workmen's compensation scheme temporary work injuries attract a wage-related benefit, up to R600 a month. A total disability gains 75 per cent of previous wage. A partial disability gains a pro rata benefit, as determined by the Workmen's Compensation Commissioner, payable for up to 12 months.

There is no national medical insurance programme in operation. Any patient, except the genuinely indigent, has to pay for medical services. There are, however, more than 200 private medical insurance schemes which make provision for the necessary benefits.

Evaluation

Highly specialised health services of a preventive and curative nature are available in the Republic's urban areas. In rural areas, however, there is a shortage of all forms of health care, and in particular primary health care services. The state has begun to address this situation by means of extending health care services in rural areas, introducing the Population Development Programme, which is designed to increase the quality of life of all people in South Africa, and increasing training facilities for health care personnel.

South Africa

ASSESSMENT OF THE SOUTH AFRICAN WELFARE SYSTEM

Few countries reflect the universal link between prevailing political philosophy and the welfare system in as direct a way as South Africa. The predominant characteristic of South African society is differentiation on the basis of race, which is also the most notable trait in the welfare system. The persons who are best protected by social security and most adequately aided by personal social services are the white group. Whites, because of historical factors and socio-political forces that have promoted their interests, are also the most skilled, and, therefore, are perceived by the state as the key group to be protected if the economy is to grow and more jobs are to be created.

The existence of a welfare elite is not unexpected in a developing African country, since Mouton (1975) has shown that most nations in sub-Saharan Africa tend to have welfare provisions that advantage a select group, be it members of a particular tribe, civil servants, or those considered most important to the country's development thrust.

In the South African situation, however, where impermeable, caste-like, legal barriers exist to block inter-group mobility, the favouring of white people by the welfare and other systems of society is dysfunctional, since for enhanced economic development progressively more people must be drawn into the skilled work sector, and the white community does not itself have the numbers to provide the required manpower. This means that some profound changes in the ordering of society must take place before widespread economic growth can occur. Because the nature and structure of the welfare system in a developing country can be a fundamental ingredient in promoting the attainment of national development goals, the question can be posed of whether or not the South African welfare system seems to be changing to facilitate the achievement of national economic growth.

Undoubtedly the country's social welfare system is presently undergoing change. Preventive action is being emphasised, community care is taking precedence over residential facilities. Tangible evidence exists of efforts to remove racial discrimination by progressively reducing inequalities in social security payments to members of different race groups. However, the racial fragmentation of the welfare system itself is being consolidated, rather than dismantled. The 1985 Report on an Investigation into the Present Welfare Policy in the Republic of South Africa, which was commissioned by the Cabinet Committee for Social Affairs, advocates the complete splitting into uniracial units of all welfare services, including those sponsored by the community (Department of Constitutional Development and Planning 1985b). Those who favour this proposal believe that 'separate' does not mean 'unequal', and that uniracial welfare facilities will permit services for each group to be tailored to specific group wants and needs. Those against argue that increased racialisation will further entrench white advantage, that human beings have common needs whatever their cultural identifications, that separate services by definition cannot be equal, and that efficiency, effectiveness, economy and humanity would be promoted by organising services on a common, multiracial basis.

A second feature of the welfare system earmarked for significant change is the present division of responsibility between state and community sectors. The 1985 Report also advocates an accelerated 'privatisation' of welfare, which in practice will mean reduced state involvement and correspondingly increased activity and self-funding by the private sector. While the motivation for this can be understood in terms of the state's desire to steer clear of socialism and to channel a growing proportion of tax monies into activities that will directly promote national economic growth, privatisation is not a viable option at a time of economic recession. Moreover, in an increasingly racialised welfare structure, disadvantaged uniracial groups will be made especially vulnerable by privatisation, as community-sponsored services for people of colour will be totally divorced from those for whites, and it is whites who currently control the wealth of the private sector.

Thus, the remedies proposed by the 1985 Report are unlikely to correct fundamental deficiencies in the Republic's welfare system, and indeed may even worsen them. In particular, the recommendations in the Report do not represent a realistic attempt to remould the welfare system in a form that will make welfare a front-line

South Africa

Department of Social Welfare and Pensions (1976), Report on an Investigation into the Possible Establishment of a Contributory Pension Scheme in South Africa, Pretoria.

Eales, J. (1980), Urban Black Aged: A Study by the Transvaal Region of the Urban Foundation, Johannesburg: The Urban Foundation.

Estimates of Expenditure to be Defrayed from the State Revenue Account During the Financial Year Ending 31 March 1985 (1984), Pretoria: The Government Printer.

FAMSA (1985), Annual Report, April 1984 - March 1985, Kempton Park.

Foster Care Action Group (1985), 'Memorandum', Johannesburg.

Hare, I. and McKendrick, B.W. (1976), 'South Africa: Racial Division in Social Services', in Thurz, D. and Vigilante, J.L. (eds), Meeting Human Needs, (Vol. 2) London; Sage.

Joseph, T.W. (1977), 'Planning for the Elderly: A Policy Framework for the Urban White Population of South Africa', unpublished B.Sc. (Town Planning) Dissertation, University of the Witwatersrand, Johannesburg.

McKendrick, B.W. (1985), 'Charting a National Course for Rehabilitating Newly-Blind Adults', Rehabilitation in South Africa, 29(1), 2-6.

Mouton, P. (1975), Social Security in Africa - Trends, Problems, Prospects, Geneva: International Labour Office.

Orange Free State Province (1984), Estimates of Revenue and Expenditure for the Year Ending 31 March 1985, Bloemfontein, PR-PC-2/1984.

Province of the Cape of Good Hope (1984), Estimates for Provincial Revenue to be Collected and Expenditure to be Defrayed from the Provincial Revenue Fund During the Year Ending 31 March 1985, Cape Town, CP1/1984.

South Africa

constituent of national growth strategy.
What of the future? The country's constitutional development is the subject of active concern and vigorous, on-going debate within South Africa, but whatever new philosophies and structures evolve, they will be certain to also affect the nature and purpose of the country's social welfare system. It is to be hoped that South Africans will be able to devise a political model that will permit all people to participate actively and constructively in building a new society, and that their plans for the new society will embrace a reshaped social welfare system that will support and protect people as they strive to realise their latent potential, thereby enabling them to contribute optimally to the nation's development.

REFERENCES

Department of Constitutional Development and Planning (1985a), <u>Proposed National Family Programme</u>, Pretoria.

Department of Constitutional Development and Planning (1985b), <u>Report on an Investigation into the Present Welfare Policy in the Republic of South Africa</u>, Pretoria.

Department of Co-operation and Development (1984a), <u>Annual Report April 1982 - March 1983</u>, Pretoria: The Government Printer, RP12/84.

Department of Co-operation and Development (1984b), <u>Annual Report April 1983 - March 1984</u>, Pretoria: The Government Printer, RP90/84.

Department of Foreign Affairs (1985), <u>South Africa 1985 - Official Yearbook of the Republic of South Africa</u>, Pretoria.

Department of Health and Welfare (1984), <u>Annual Report</u>, Pretoria.

Department of Internal Affairs (1984), <u>Annual Report</u>, Pretoria: The Government Printer, RP47/84.

South Africa

Province of Natal (1984), <u>Estimates of Expenditure to be Defrayed from the Provincial Revenue Fund and Revenue to be Collected During the Year Ending 31 March 1985</u>, Pietermaritzburg, NP2/1984.

Province of Transvaal (1984), <u>Estimates of the Revenue to be Collected and Expenditure to be Defrayed During the Year Ending 31 March 1985</u>, Pretoria.

<u>Report of the Commission of Inquiry into the Collection of Voluntary Financial Contributions from the Public</u> (1976), Pretoria: The Government Printer.

South African National Council for the Blind (1985), <u>27th Biennial Report, 1983 - 1985</u>, Pretoria.

<u>Survey of Race Relations</u> (1983) (Vol. 37), Johannesburg: South African Institute of Race Relations.

<u>Survey of Race Relations</u> (1984) (Vol. 38), Johannesburg: South African Institute of Race Relations.

Unemployment Insurance Fund (1985), <u>Report for the Year Ending 31 December 1984</u>, Pretoria: Pretoria Printers.

TANZANIA
William J. Mallya and Haynes A. Mwankanye

THE WELFARE SYSTEM ENVIRONMENT

Ideological Environment
Tanzania, a republic in East Africa, aspires to become a socialist, self-reliant society in which co-existence between a millionaire and a poor man is unaccommodatable, a society in which there is exploitation by none and work by all. Observation of a just return of one's labour, coupled with an administration of social equity, is the basic pillar of the ideology of socialism embodied in Arusha Declaration of 1967.

In the context of the national policy, social welfare is seen as a vehicle for the development of the people. The chapter on 'Objectives and Strategy' in the Second Five Year Development Plan points out that development includes the provision for all people of a healthy diet, adequate clothing, acceptable housing and access to basic education as well as health facilities.

By and large, the socialist philosophy dictates that existing welfare arrangements should be evenly distributed, so as to respond to the needs of the majority, who in many cases are marginally poor.

Incidentally, welfare support expands correspondingly with government or private initiative directed at financing the expansion of basic services, based upon a maximum rate of consumption of goods and services at the disposal of the society. Tanzania's welfare values are inseparable. Health and housing services, proper nutrition and clean water are the elements of social welfare that cannot be obtained except on the basis of a sound economy. Helping the people to move towards increased self-actualisation is one of the basic themes of Tanzanian social welfare administration, while some calculated dependence is, to a certain extent, permissible with certain disadvantaged groups specified in the Arusha Declaration, including small children, people who are too old to support themselves, the disabled, and those whom the state at any one time cannot provide with an opportunity to work for their living.

The underlying twin purposes are thus to create conditions that promote and sustain social welfare arrangements for the people's development and the deployment of such arrangements in the furtherance of socialist goals.

The prevailing welfare system is seemingly a function of a number of factors.

Traditional Moral Values. Various sub-social systems that constitute present day Tanzania have had, for many decades, in-built values of mutual aid and protection with characteristic emphasis on interdependence between the family, clan and village members. Since these values are still strong, it is no surprise that the political machinery encourages its promotion in the spirit of nation building.

Collective Working. A strong sense of survival is an inherent value in all Tanzanian sub-cultures, and its significance rests on the understanding that it imbues people with the spirit of hard work, which the ruling party, the Chama Cha Mapinduzi (CCM), uses as a rallying point for people to improve their welfare. The ethic of hard work is, itself, enmeshed in the Tanzanian welfare system, to ensure that the welfare of both workers and peasants remains a major preoccupation of welfare administrators.

Social Equity. Socialist reconstruction in Tanzania demands that the proceeds of labour be proportionately distributed according to an individual's labour contribution. Indeed, income differentials should reflect labour contribution differentials. These enhance the functioning of the Tanzanian welfare system.

Self-reliance. The concept of self-reliance permeates the entire Tanzanian culture. It provides the socio-economic framework within which individuals, communities and the nation as a whole strive to attain higher standards of living, using, primarily, locally-available resources.

Tanzania

Human Equality. According to the philosophy of the ruling party (CCM) all human beings are equal and must be treated as such. Everyone should have equal access to the benefits of development in terms of social service, freedom of worship, freedom of expression and so forth. The dehumanising concept of racial segregation is considered both contemptible and detrimental to the promotion of human welfare.

Grassroots Development. Communal spirit is reputed for enhancing the ideals of shared leadership and collective responsibility at the village level. Decisions affecting the development and welfare of the community are arrived at only after formal and informal discussions between community members and responsible government and party functionaries.

Historical Origins
By the time the country gained its independence from Britain in December, 1961, the groundwork for social welfare administration had already been laid down. The tradition in most British colonies had been that of leaving social welfare provision to private charity and voluntary enterprise. This applied to the then Tanganyika too.

Since independence, and the subsequent Arusha Declaration, both the ruling party and the government have made concerted efforts to restructure the entire social welfare system under the auspices of relevant government Ministries, and to expand social welfare services so as to meet a wider range of community needs.

Social Security. The first programme was introduced by the defunct colonial administration in 1949 by means of the Worker's Compensation Act, which required employers to compensate manual workers and labourers sustaining injury while on duty. In 1983, however, Tanzania made substantial amendments to some of the basic provisions in this Act. Employers are now required to compensate every worker injured in the course of duty and to extend compensation to legally recognised relatives of a worker who loses his life while on duty. The Labour Department collaborates with the Ministry of Health, as well as the National Insurance Corporation, in dispensing this compensation, under the watchful eye of the National Union of Tanzanian Workers.

Tanzania

The Tanzanian National Provident Fund was established in 1964 to provide long-term social security protection.

Rural Social Support. Rural Tanzania is characterised by strong extended family ties, evoking mutual understanding and co-operation between members, and upon which a sense of communal obligation and mutual support prevails. Present government effort of encouraging peasants to live and work collectively in villages has ushered in the setting up of cooperative enterprises. Furthermore, the National Insurance Corporation provides group insurance to Ujamaa Villages, co-operative societies and Marketing Boards.

Urban Community and the Personal Social Services. In the late 1960s the government adopted a programme which encouraged institutions and work units to provide essential personal services (including canteens, day-care centres and so forth) and some workshops have been set up to cater for the training needs of the handicapped and the blind. In addition, displaced persons in general, and the elderly in particular, have their security assured in homes set up by the state as well as religious organisations.

Rural Local Community and the Personal Social Services. Since the late 1960s the government has embarked on an elaborate policy of providing health care, a clean water supply and day-care centres in villages so as to promote the welfare of the peasants. These services are administered through rural extension workers.

Municipal Authorities and Personal Social Services. For many years municipal authorities had played a major role in providing homes for the destitute, dispensaries and schools. From the late 1960s however, the central government gradually took over such responsibilities, especially following the abolition of local governments in the 1970s. With the restoration of local governments in 1985 it is quite feasible that municipal authorities will once again provide those services.

Tanzania

Political Environment

Any serious discussion on Tanzania's post-independence development policies in general, and socio-economic transformation in particular, has to centre around the Arusha Declaration of 1967 and the subsequent acceptance of socialism and self-reliance (Ujamaa) principles. These constitute both the framework and the basis upon which development efforts have progressed, notably in the rural areas. In fact, the Arusha Declaration provided a new blueprint for Tanzania's socio-economic and political development along socialist lines, pledging, among other things, to ensure that the major means of production were brought under the control of peasants and workers, with less reliance on grants and loans from outside, less emphasis on heavy industry, and a decided emphasis on agriculture. The policy of villagisation was adopted as a rational panacea for implementing the broad objectives of the Arusha Declaration. This involved the bringing of the peasant producers together in villages for co-operative production. This means that most of the farming could be done by groups of people who live as a community and work as a community. Indeed local services are locally provided to meet community requirements.

Tanzania is a one party state, and <u>Chama Cha Mapinduzi</u> (CCM) commands supremacy over the political machinery. It is the ruling party which shapes the broad economic and development policies, which are then translated into relevant programmes for implementation by the government.

Party organisation springs from the cell (comprising ten households) into the Branches, District, Regional and National organs. These organs function, at various levels, to guide and supervise development activities, and, in doing this, the party links the people with the government. At the same time, the ruling party works closely with the government in promoting the policy of socialism and self-reliance through the mobilisation of peasants and workers to strive for increased productivity.

It has, in fact, been the policy of the ruling party right from the time of independence in 1961 that, while other nations go to the moon, Tanzania should focus on developing the village. Villagisation has since then been considered as an innovative and potentially effective means of realising a broadly participatory economic growth

(Mallya 1980) which should accommodate distributive justice. In keeping with this policy there has been an extensive investment directed at the village in terms of improved water supply, construction of health centres, schools, roads, the establishment of cooperative shops and so forth.

Furthermore, the traditional forms of leadership which evolved through inheritance rights have been supplanted by the democratic process, which is scrupulously safeguarded by the ruling party. Such a form of political organisation and decision-making machinery reinforces the socialist virtue of achieving meaningful political participation by peasants and workers (Pratt 1976). At the same time, political participation is seen as a form of mobilisation and persuasion for the peasant to give up his old habits of raising production as well as adherence to tribal organisation which has meant security to him in the past.

Nonetheless Tanzania has an economic base with a strong state command, and with co-operative economic activities widespread both in urban and rural areas.

Economic Environment

The Tanzanian economy is mainly agricultural and much of the farming is at subsistence level. The main cash crops and export earners are coffee, cotton, sisal, tea and cashew nuts, although farmers have been encouraged in recent years to concentrate on essential food crops. The industrial sector is small and dominated by para-statal enterprises. The most important industries are food processing, textiles, brewing and cigarette manufacture. The service industry has experienced a rapid growth in recent years.

In 1983 Tanzania's Gross National Product (GNP) per capita was $US240 and over the period 1965-83 this indicator had grown by a modest 0.9 per cent a year (see World Bank 1985). In absolute terms, Tanzania's growth performance has been more impressive (averaging 3.6 per cent per year for 1973-1983) but only marginally higher than the prevailing population growth rate (averaging 3.3 per cent per year over the same period) (World Bank 1985). The growth in agricultural output (averaging 2.6 per cent per year between 1973 and 1983) has in recent years failed to keep pace with population growth.

Tanzania

Inflation has remained quite modest by Third World standards, averaging 11.5 per cent for the decade 1973-83 (World Bank 1985).
Tanzania's evident withdrawal from the international economy and its policy of economic self-sufficiency has insulated it from international economic cycles in recent years. Its international debt is modest by Third World standards (debt services constituted only 1.5 per cent of GNP in 1983).

Social Environment
Tanzania's population in mid 1983 was 20.8 million (World Bank 1985). It comprises some 120 ethnic groups, nearly all of which speak the Bantu language. The Sukuma, who live just south of Lake Victoria, are the largest group, other large groups include the Chagga, Ha, Haya, Makonde and Nyamwezi. The Masai are a large non-Bantu-speaking tribe. Small Arab and Indian communities live along the coast and in Zanzibar.

A combination of a high and growing crude birth rate (50 per thousand in 1983) and a modest and falling death rate (16 per thousand in 1983) has resulted in Tanzania's population expanding rapidly in the decade from 1973 (at an average annual rate of 3.3 per cent (see World Bank 1985)). Thus by 1990 its population is likely to be 27 million (World Bank 1983).

Urbanisation in Tanzania is quite modest, with only 14 per cent of the population living in urban areas. But this population is expanding rapidly (8.6 per cent average annual growth for the decade prior to 1983) (World Bank 1985). Indeed half the urban population lives in the capital, Dar es Salaam.

Life expectancy at birth has increased markedly from the mid 1960s to 1983, when it reached 49 years for males and 52 years for females (World Bank 1985). Similarly, there has been a marked drop in the infant mortality rate to 97 per thousand in 1983 (World Bank 1985). The child death rate (aged 1-4) has also fallen noticeably to 18 per thousand (World Bank 1985). This can be attributed to improved health care in Tanzania.

In comparison with most low-income Third World countries, Tanzania is able to provide sufficient food to maintain an adequate calorie supply (World Bank 1985).

Tanzania

THE WELFARE SYSTEM: AN OVERVIEW

The Tanzanian welfare system is maintained by and heavily dependent on the government in terms of funding as well as personnel. The personal social services are partly financed through government resources, in the form of subsidies to privately or voluntarily run welfare institutions.

It has been argued of late that social insurance protection as such is not as yet established in Tanzania, ostensibly because of economic constraints and lack of highly trained and experienced manpower (Idd 1985). The prevailing pension, provident fund and compensation schemes do, however, point to the fact that some aspects of social security protection are already laid down. Furthermore, existing strong traditional value systems obtaining in rural areas ensure the provision of simple forms of social security protection, particularly for disadvantaged persons (Mwankanye 1985).

Social Security Administration and Finance
Tanzania has a three-pronged social security system: a national provident fund, a pension system for public employees and an employer liability system.

The Tanzanian National Provident Fund (TNPF).
This is an independent public agency operated by a tripartite board under the general supervision of the Labour Department. Contributions are paid by employers (5.0 per cent of payroll) and covered employees (5.0 per cent of wages). The TNPF covers employees of firms with four or more workers.

State Pension Schemes. Government employees covered by the Pensions Ordinance, the Political Leaders Pension Act and the Parastatal Pension Fund Act contribute, along with their employers to the National Insurance Corporation, which is administered by the state. The Corporation processes applications for injury, death and survivors' benefits. The Labour Department scrutinises these applications before they are forwarded to the Ministry of Health for confirmation.

Tanzania

War Service Pension Scheme. Under the Defence Forces (Service Pension and Gratuities) Regulation a range of non-contributory war-service pensions and benefits are provided for in the state budget.

Employer Liability Schemes. Manual workers, non-manual employees earning 24,000 shillings a year or less, and apprentices are covered by a workmen's compensation scheme. This involves participating employers providing a range of work injury benefits by means of compulsory insurance with private carriers, where the insurance premiums vary according to risk. Law enforcement responsibilities rest with the Ministry of Labour and Social Welfare, which must also approve settlements and pay benefits.

The labour laws also require employers to pay severance indemnity, which is also enforced by the Ministry of Labour and Social Welfare.

Personal Social Services Administration and Finance

The administration of personal social services is mostly undertaken by the central government through the Social Welfare Department except for the Dar es Salaam City Council which has some extensive autonomy in running such services in the city. Services include primary education, health services, special education, and maternal and child health services.

Welfare Facilities. Welfare facilities are provided by municipal and town councils in urban areas, and by village governments in the rural areas. Sanatoriums are run by the central government, while old people's homes are maintained by the central government, religious organisations, and in some few cases, by Ujamaa Villages. Homes administered by religious organisations receive subsidies from the state. Access to these welfare facilities is free except for old people's homes, which usually demand that admission be extended only to individuals with no one to care for them.

Furthermore, some canteens, nurseries and day-care centres are run by industries, parastatal organisations, as well as UWT (the national women's organisation, affiliated to CCM). Such services are financed by the respective institutions operating them, while the Social Welfare Department provides technical advice on the running of day-care centres.

Tanzania

<u>Sheltered Employment Facilities</u>. The state operates welfare workshops for various vocational skills, aimed at providing the handicapped with paid employment. After training, the handicapped persons are encouraged to organise themselves into work units. Government support includes the provision of skilled staff in such workshops, who provide the needed guidance in their management.

<u>Counselling and Interpersonal Helping</u>. Professional social workers, welfare workers and local community leaders involve themselves in counselling and helping. Whereas professional social workers and welfare workers operate in institutional settings, local community leaders operate voluntarily (Mwankanye 1985). The forms of counselling provided range from resolving matrimonial conflicts and matters relating to family maintenance, to education and vocational guidance, to reconciliation, to referral services and so forth.

<u>Rural Support Services</u>. Displaced rural persons do receive government assistance and through the Social Welfare Department may be placed in government-supported centres. In some isolated cases Ujamaa Villages such as Isansa Ujamaa Village, Mbozi District and Mbeya Region have taken the initiative to set up homes for the disabled, aged and orphaned, supported by the village fund. In such cases it is the village which assesses the degree of individual need and makes a decision.

THE AGED

It is inferred in the Arusha Declaration that the ruling party (CCM) sees the care for the aged as being the shared responsibility of the family, the village community and the state. It is generally accepted as a cultural norm that aged parents enjoy the support of their grown-up children in terms of meeting their material as well as psychological needs (Castle 1966). The exemption from work of the aged, however, can not be made merely out of reverence for old age, but rather has to do with the fact that, for most people, old age marks a stage in the life cycle when working power has very much been drained out of the body. One then needs support in old age, just as one needed support in the early years of life.

Tanzania

The support to the aged is not given merely because they, or the majority of them, are weak and cannot work. It is given essentially in recognition of their past contribution to society during their active years.

Understandably, in the majority of cases there is a strong bond between the parents, their children and their grandchildren. This is true even where the children are grown up and have established their own families. Indeed urbanisation has not snapped the bond that joins these generations. Old people in a family are therefore not regarded as a burden, for there is mutual satisfaction in living together. Cultural factors are still strong enough to ensure that it is anathema not to provide care for elderly relatives. Be that as it may, care that is combined with social contacts provides greater satisfaction and a sense of security for the aged. It helps meet the emotional needs of the elderly. Within the family unit help rendered by, or offered to, a member is not obligatory. It is bound by a moral rather than a legal force. This means that family members may provide reciprocal help to one another, although they are not legally bound to do so. Yet when considering the security of the aged in Tanzania it must be recognised that there are two social groups: peasants and workers. The word retirement is of no substance to peasants; for peasants do not retire from work. They are tied to the land, as well as to their families, throughout their life span. As for the workers, it is not a common practice for all those who retire to go back to the land. Many aged workers do not see the horizon of life becoming brighter in terms of meeting their daily basic needs after their retirement. In fact, they view life as becoming more difficult after retirement. This attitude is probably formed by the prevailing economic difficulties and the way of life generally experienced in the urban world. Under these circumstances, those without family care receive guaranteed care by the state, if not by the community in which they reside, while retired pensionable persons have an additional degree of security.

Social Security

Retirement and related social security benefits are provided to retirees formerly in covered employment.

Tanzania

State Retirement Benefits. Those in parastatal work units qualify for retirement pension if they meet the following eligibility conditions: firstly, that they have attained the minimum pension age, 50-54 years, with the mandatory retirement age being 55 years, for both sexes; secondly, that they have been employed for not less than 10 years; and, thirdly, that they suffer from invalidity sustained during the working period.
Pension laws covering civil servants allow for commutation of 25 per cent (Vaides 1985). A worker qualified for retirement in parastatal service is granted a lump sum equivalent to 12.5 times one-quarter of the specified amount, plus an annual pension for the rest of their lives equal to three-fourths of the specified amount (Rugaika 1980). Appropriate retirement travel allowances are provided to retirees and their dependants.

National Provident Fund Benefit. Covered workers upon obtaining the age of 55 who retire from regular employment can withdraw the balance standing in their provident fund account. It is payable to employees under the age of 55 if they are unemployed or in uncovered employment for at least six months: one-third payable after six months, the balance after 18 months; or if they retire from employment to return to live in a co-operative village.

Personal Social Services
Aged persons with families receive partial supportive services from their children. Those without families who are displaced receive supportive services in homes administered by either the central or city governments in urban areas, villages or religious organisations in rural areas. Those admitted in homes are encouraged to be engaged in some active work such as gardening, poultry keeping, and helping in the distribution of rations.

Evaluation
The elderly (those aged 60 and above) constitute between 16 and 20 per cent of the total Tanzanian population. On the whole the elderly in Tanzanian society are poor and frugal. During their active years they are unable to save systematically and so find themselves experiencing falling standards of living. They are thus ill-prepared for

retirement. It is common, for example, for a civil servant to be ignorant of his pension entitlements at any particular time during his employment. In any event accrued pension entitlements could be lost if dismissal occurs. Needless to say the present state pension schemes and provident fund benefits are not subject to inflationary adjustments.

Nevertheless, with the introduction of Ujamaa Villages there has been a systematic development of a broad range of personal social services to which the elderly have access. This is in addition to any support services that the village community might render to them.

The policy of deploying all human resources in productive activities has, likewise, come a long way toward encouraging the elderly to reactivate their commitment to their social and economic roles. All these arrangements minimise the costs that the state would have incurred in the protection of the elderly.

At the moment, however, the elderly are not organised in a formal association to look after their interests, problems and future prospects. The youth and women, for example, are organised under <u>Chama Cah Mapinduzi</u>. <u>Jopo la Wazee</u> or Elders Councils initiated by the Ministry of Labour and Social Welfare may probably be the embryo of such associations, for the experiences of the elderly need to be tapped in an orderly manner.

THE DISABLED AND THE HANDICAPPED

Provision for the welfare of the handicapped and disabled in Tanzania is guided by the ruling party (CCM) ethic as enunciated in the Arusha Declaration. The socialist philosophy piloting development in the country demands that society should bear the obligation to promote the welfare of the disabled and handicapped. For the disabled and handicapped who are potentially productive the state offers vocational training in skills they can sell in the employment market. On the other hand, those with severe handicaps and disabilities are cared for in 19 homes run by the government and 24 homes run by voluntary organisations, where they are assured of social and economic protection. Family care, however, is highly appreciated where it is provided.

Tanzania

Social Security
Social security policy relating to the handicapped and disabled puts emphasis on compensating workers who, in the course of duty, sustain injury. Income support is however not provided to handicapped and disabled persons who sustain injury outside the work context.

Workmen's Compensation Benefits. Most workers in both state and privately owned enterprises and institutions qualify for disability pension if they are totally and permanently incapacited as a result of their work (Workmen's Compensation Ordinance Cap.263) (excluded are casual workers, family labour and non-manual employees earning over Tshs 24,000 a year). A lump sum of 54 months' earnings are paid in the event of a total disability, up to a maximum of Tshs 38,000. A constant attendance supplement equal to 50 per cent of the benefit payable is also available.

The partially but permanently disabled are paid a disability benefit proportionate to the degree of disability sustained.

Temporary disability benefits are payable after a three-day waiting period, for up to 76 months, at the rate of half-pay.

Medical benefits are also provided, covering medical and hospital care, subsidised medicines, appliances and transportation.

National Provident Fund Benefit. Covered workers who become permanently incapacitated for work can withdraw the balance standing in their provident fund account.

Personal Social Services
The handicapped and disabled are provided supportive services by their families, including, among other things, home help and day-care, the result of which is full integration of the handicapped and disabled in the family unit. In the event of a family being unable to cope, institutional care is available from state or privately-run organisations. Rehabilitation of the handicapped and disabled is one among the many main foci of government activity.

Institutional Care. The Disabled Persons Act of 1982 puts responsibility of caring for the disabled on parents and relatives, so as to minimise problems of dehumanisation and patronisation. Only in the absence of such support does the government accept the responsibility for their welfare by placing them in homes. These homes are available free of charge, including any medical and para-medical services provided. There are 19 homes run by the government and 24 run by voluntary organisations. General hospitals admit handicapped and disabled patients needing treatment into specialised units, while mental patients are cared for in the few available 'half way' homes after receiving treatment in psychiatric units (Ndaka 1985).

Rehabilitation. Vocational rehabilitation has occupied a central place in the government's strategy to promote the welfare of the handicapped and disabled in Tanzania. Yombo Rehabilitation Centre and Tanga Production Workshop have been established for this purpose and are financed by the government. After training, the handicapped and disabled are encouraged to work in special integrated factories, while those unable to work in such factories are encouraged to form co-operative enterprises.

For Tanzania, however, institution-based rehabilitation seems to be very expensive. Hence the government is now attempting to set up a community-based rehabilitation programme which is expected to be cheaper and which can operate nationwide (Ndaka 1985).

Rehabilitation Aids. The handicapped and disabled persons have easy access to a limited range of rehabilitation aids. Walking callipers, artificial legs and tricycles are available but not to the satisfaction of everyone. Audio-visual aids are also available to a limited extent.

Evaluation

Although the 1973-4 census indicates that there are 40,000 disabled persons in Tanzania, it is likely that this is an under-enumeration of the total disabled population (Ndaka 1985). (It may even be valid to suggest that the actual number is unknown but not less than 500,000 people.) The state encourages the exploitation of volunteerism, which has its underlying basis in the mutual concern of human beings for one another in recognition of their oneness. This value is strong in the community support system. Hence the introduction of community-based rehabilitation

Tanzania

programmes. The state's role is defined as the provision of institutional care, when community or family support is no longer functional, and includes provision of vocational rehabilitation, supportive appliances and learning aids. Personal social services, including sheltered employment in integrated factories and co-operative undertakings, all serve the purpose of relieving most families of the burden of attending to all the needs of handicapped and disabled persons.

NEEDY FAMILIES

The family unit in Tanzania is primarily responsible for its own welfare. The state's role is quite limited, focusing on providing social security protection in the event of the contingencies of child bearing and death.

Pregnant Women
There is no clearly established programme for welfare support in Tanzania during pregnancy. Usually, expectant mothers are encouraged to use maternal and child-health clinics which provide advice on the need to use cheap and locally available nutritious food items and monitor conditions essential for the good health of both the mother and the baby.

Social Security. Working expectant mothers receive paid maternity leave covering a maximum period of three months, including full fare for mothers and their offspring. In the past married expectant mothers were denied this right and had no entitlement to have access to free medical services as is currently the case.

Low-Income Families
Only low-income workers are allowed to gain additional income through working overtime. Low-income families can, however, gain assistance from voluntary organisations if they need material or financial resources and technical know how to run small scale economic projects.

Personal Social Services. Some supportive services are generally available to families in need. In urban areas they include the provision of pre-natal and ante-natal care and services to malnourished children. Moreover, recreation facilities have been established to cater for a

Tanzania

wide range of human needs including the need for association, improved physique and accomplishment. Some of these services may be available in rural areas, but on a much smaller scale. Moreover it seems that such services are not fully appreciated by rural residents, who prefer to use traditional ways of helping. Also the limited services available in the rural areas are quite isolated because of poor communications. As for the recreation facilities, these are basically developed around schools, thus they mainly benefit school-going children. Notwithstanding this some well advanced Ujamaa Villages (such as Butiama) have already established such facilities with their running costs being met by the village government.

Families Without a Breadwinner
Survivors of deceased workers receive welfare support.

Social Security. If a state or parastatal worker's death is the result of work activities after having served at least 10 years, those who wholly or substantially depend on him will be granted survivors benefit. The amount payable is a lump-sum death benefit four times the worker's annual salary at death. If death follows a non-occupational illness then a lump-sum equivalent of an annual salary is paid to the widow and orphans. For both occupational and non-occupational reasons the employer feels the obligation of meeting burial expenses such as the contribution of a coffin and some small amount of money is given to the bereaved family.

Survivors of deceased workers who participated in the Tanzania provident fund scheme qualify for a lump sum benefit equal to the balance remaining in the deceased member's account at the time of death.

Survivors of deceased workers covered by the Workmen's Compensation Ordinance receive a lump sum benefit of 41 months of the deceased's earnings, less any disability benefits paid prior to death, up to a maximum of Tshs 29,000. A reduced benefit is paid to partial dependants. A funeral grant of up to Tshs 500 is paid in the event that there are no eligible survivors.

Evaluation
Traditionally, the family has primarily shouldered

Tanzania

the obligation of promoting the welfare of its members and the state still considers the family useful in that regard. Additional social security protection, in certain respects, is assured by members in an Ujamaa Village in which collective productive ventures enable members to enjoy some support when the family is unable to provide for them. Collective working and sharing is viewed by the ruling party (CCM) as a healthy way of improving family welfare. It is also a way of ensuring that distributive justice is achieved amongst Ujamaa Village community members. It also fosters a positive community spirit and so enhances economic development.

CHILDREN AND YOUTH

Children and youths form a large section of the Tanzanian community, which is faced with many and complex problems and needs. These range from malnutrition to health problems, school dropouts to unemployment, loitering to drug-abuse and pick-pocketing to robbing and so forth. There is a trend towards a breakdown in the traditional family structures, which seems to deprive children and youth of the customary social values and norms without any new ideals being established to replace them.

General government concern has been directed at the mobilisation of young people for participation in development and their preparation for taking up citizen responsibilities. At the same time, the government is ensuring that the social welfare system is restructured and expanded to cater for the emergent needs of the children and youths with a view to preparing them for useful roles in national development.

Social Security
Family allowances are not provided in Tanzania although income tax relief is extended to families with up to four children. This benefit is, however, limited to salaried workers only.

Maternity Benefits. Maternity benefits are available to families with triplet births, who receive a subsidy from the Presidential Fund.

Personal Social Services
These are services meant to augment or substitute for parental guidance and support. A wide range

Tanzania

of family support is provided, mainly by the government, the ruling party and associations (such as the Girl Guides and Boy Scouts), which is generally available to children and youths. They are mostly intended for character training in preparing them for undertaking responsible future citizenship.

Institutional Child Care for Pre-School Children. Customarily, the care of children rests with grandparents and relatives while mothers are engaged in productive work. Significant changes have taken place since the late 1960s, however, when child welfare policies were developed by the government, the most important of which was the setting up of day-care centres. These provide a network of child-care facilities, in addition to those provided in nursery schools.

Out-of-School Care. School age children as well as adolescents, before and after school, receive substitute care through cultural, recreational, sporting and educational facilities provided by a wide range of institutions.

In rural Tanzania grandparents have continued and are still continuing to provide substitute care to children and youth.

Support for Children Affected by Marriage Breakdown. The state is always pre-occupied with the intent of helping married couples keep their marriage intact, although this is not legally binding. Nevertheless, upon the occurrence of a marriage breakdown, state attention is drawn to the maintenance and welfare of children who are finally covered by the Maintenance Ordinance. The monitoring of the welfare of such children is the responsibility of the Social Welfare Department. When child maintenance payments are not forthcoming social welfare workers report the matter to the appropriate legal organs for further action.

Support for Illegitimate Children. Legally, the state requires the putative father to pay child maintenance to the mother of the child born out of wedlock, according to a scale specified in the Affiliation Ordinance of 1964.

Institutional Care for Orphans. For more than two decades the trend in Tanzania has been to place

Tanzania

orphans without relatives to look after them into children's homes and orphanages. These are generally operated by religious institutions, while the government provides subsidies and advises on the operational standards to be followed.

Foster Care. Children after three years in a children's home, who are unlikely to be looked after by their natural parents or relatives, may be provided with foster parents. Procedural requirements are for prospective foster parents to submit an application to the Social Welfare Department, which is then reviewed to determine the extent to which they can afford to provide adequate care for the child. In Tanzania foster care is of a temporary nature but may be substituted by adoption, essentially if no natural parent or relative comes forth to claim the child.

Adoption. The Social Welfare Department arranges adoptions for children whose parents and relatives are deemed to be dead or untraceable. Applicants showing interest in becoming adoptive parents are assessed to ascertain their suitability.

Evaluation
Approximately 45 per cent of the Tanzanian population consists of children and the youth. The state's attitude towards providing them with welfare support is based on the principle that the family, including the village community, should still be responsible for them. Children of working mothers and those deprived of parental care and support receive welfare protection from the local community or voluntary organisations, at little or no cost to the state.

THE SICK AND INJURED

Government assumes full responsibility in guiding formulation of health policies in the country and it runs the majority of its services free of charge. Since the ruling party (CCM) and government uphold the view that social welfare cannot be fully enjoyed without good health there have been a number of occasions when campaigns such as 'Mtu ni Afya' ('Man is Health') have been organised and, mostly, aimed at promoting rural health, through the use of rural health centres, dispensaries and maternal and child health clinics.

Tanzania

Free access to government health institutions makes it possible for sick and injured workers to receive the required medical treatment. As for the sick and injured peasants free medical treatment is provided by rural government health centres and dispensaries.

Since the government is well aware that, by its own efforts alone, it cannot answer all the needs of sick and injured citizens, it values the role played by voluntary agencies which, at the present moment, run a large number of hospitals and dispensaries all over the country, in both urban and rural areas.

Parastatal organisations and private companies run hospitals and dispensaries to cater for the health needs of their workers and their dependants. To further augment government effort the workers organisation, JUWATA, also runs some dispensaries.

In addition, the state permits a small number of private practitioners to operate private hospitals with fees and scales of emoluments for medical workers regulated by the state through the Private Hospitals (Regulations) Act, 1977.

Since some of the workers and peasants still believe that sustaining injury and falling sick may be a result of witchcraft, traditional practitioners continue to play an important role in attending to the health needs of this particular group of people. Although traditional practitioners are not registered the Faculty of Medicine at the University of Dar es Salaam follows their activities closely by doing research on the traditional health care system.

The 'Mtu ni Afya' campaign is designed not only to spread awareness of the need to be healthy but also to acquire some knowledge on health and several preventive measures. They include the spread of clean water for drinking, washing and cleaning for the mass of the people and CCM has so far ensured that over ten million people have access to clean water. It has been made possible by drilling wells, supplying tap water and using bamboos. Likewise, community health is yet another major pre-occupation of CCM and the government. The objective is to stimulate people to improve sanitation by keeping residential areas clean and preventing water contamination; to immunise and inoculate children as a preventive measure against diseases such as small pox, meningitis and so forth; and to combat

Tanzania

malnutrition by introducing body-building, nutritious items into diets. In doing this the intention of CCM and government is to build a nation of healthy workers whose contribution to economic development leads, as a by-product, to the improvement in the welfare of Tanzanian society.

Social Security
Tanzania considers work by everyone as conducive to the promotion of economic development, which has a direct link with improved human welfare. The trend in Tanzania is for the injured and sick workers to have social security support from their employers, and for injured and sick peasants to have social support from their local community. In addition, a clear distinction is made between occupational and non-occupational sickness and injuries.

Occupational Injury and Sickness Benefits for State Workers. Workers in state work covered by the state insurance programme receive compensation with, sometimes, subsidised costs covering medication.
 A worker on sick leave after an occupational injury receives full pay up to six months and half pay for a further six months.

Non-Occupational Injury and Sickness Benefits for Workers and Peasants. This scheme covers two categories of workers: those in paid employment and those participating in collective work in Ujamaa Villages. Tanzania has no clearly designed sickness allowance and the discretion of providing security protection for peasants rests upon individual village governments (Village Government Act 1975). State workers suffering a work injury while not on duty are entitled to receive full pay for the first six months and half pay for a further six months.

Medical Care. Health care is freely provided to injured and sick workers and peasants in government hospitals, including diagnosis and treatment check ups, operations and registration. Workers in state and parastatal organisations and in privately-owned industries obtaining health care in private hospitals approved by the state receive subsidised medical costs.

Tanzania

Personal Social Services

Usually people in the neighbourhood, both in rural and urban areas, provide a varied range of support services for sick and injured workers and peasants, and their dependants. These include helping with domestic work, voluntary counselling and guidance and sometimes they receive visits and care from health workers.

Evaluation

Social support is available to the sick and injured, from the state, from the community and from their families. Emphasis is placed on the provision of health services.

It is not uncommon in some plants for some workers to deliberately sustain less serious injuries in order to be provided with injury benefits. Employment agencies repeatedly complain of workers' negligence which reduces production. Efforts to provide workers with protective clothing, likewise, are diminished by the workers' reluctance to wear them.

THE UNEMPLOYED

It is not easy to precisely assess the rate of unemployment in Tanzania for there is no law requiring them to register. Generally speaking, the unemployed fall into two categories: urban residents who do not have access to land and paid employment; and primary and secondary school leavers and graduates of institutions awaiting job placement.

It is estimated that the net increase of the young people into the labour market is 9.2 per cent a year and that the government has to create 24,000 jobs annually for the growing urban labour force. According to an ILO report (1982) Tanzania has undertaken major efforts to provide its youth with education and skills relevant to their surroundings and to engage them in gainful employment, but the youth unemployment problem has recently escalated due to the prevailing economic crisis and to the increasing number of primary school leavers resulting from the implementation of universal primary education.

Youth unemployment is a major problem in Tanzania. There are no jobs for most of the youth in the urban areas to which they are attracted because rural living is, to them, comparatively lacking in excitement, social amenities and the real satisfactions.

For many years the government has been trying to pursue policies aimed at solving the youth unemployment problem, starting first, in the early 1960s, with the 'go back to the land' policy and the policy of education for self-reliance, the implementation of which encountered difficulties because many youth still shun manual work. Furthermore, economic growth has been slower in relation to population growth and there has been a general scarcity of capital.

Government measures to reduce the work force in 1974 and 1985 should be seen as a silent admission that disguised unemployment exists in Tanzania. It is more pronounced in rural areas than in urban areas, because of prevailing social attitudes that sanction women to do more work than men. The traditional occupation of women in rural Tanzania is mainly agriculture, that is subsistence farming. Thus nearly all tasks connected with food production continue to be left to women. Implicitly, the male population in rural areas is under-employed.

Structural unemployment in industry occurs periodically, particularly where productivity is dependent upon water supply and electricity. Likewise, the decline in prices of raw materials sometimes occasions structural unemployment in the plantations, which, in turn, might spill over into plants that make use of such raw materials (Livingstone & Ord 1980).

Since the mainstay of the economy is agriculture, it is not surprising for Tanzania to experience seasonal unemployment, triggered by annual seasonal variations affecting agriculture and fisheries.

The serious intent of government to generate employment opportunities for the unemployed through the introduction of labour-intensive public-works programmes has not even been able to arrest unemployment in the country. Lack of significant economic development for the last 10 years has partly contributed to this. Chronic unemployment has led, in part, to an increase in urban crime and, at the same time, to insignificant petty trading greatly mushrooming in the streets, which is creating insanitary living conditions.

Although the CCM and government have, on many occasions, organised campaigns to motivate the

Tanzania

unemployed to migrate to agricultural areas there has been little response. Even worse, the unemployed continue to flow from rural areas into urban centres. At present, the government pins its hope on the success of the implementation of the Human Resources Deployment Act, which was occasioned by the CCM's and the government's realisation that it could no longer be assumed that Tanzania had no unemployment. Interestingly, the exercise undertaken to implement the spirit of this act is showing signs of succeeding, particularly in Morogoro Region.

Social Security. Workers laid off in Tanzania receive 15 days' wages for each year's employment from their employers. Moreover, those covered by the National Provident Fund may withdraw one-third of the balance in their account if they remain unemployed for six months, the balance after 18 months.

Personal Social Services
Opportunities exist for the unemployed and their families to receive personal social services.

Job Creation Programmes. In some cases unemployed people set up co-operative farms and small scale industries. In addition, the state encourages the unemployed to go back to the village and work on the land, and for those who are landless to move to other regions of the country where land is plentiful.

Training Centres. Seeing the need to help primary school leavers the state promotes post-primary technical education in three hundred and sixteen training centres.

Recreation Facilities and Programmes. The tendency for the unemployed youth in Tanzania to deviate from socially acceptable behaviour has attracted concern from the government. In an effort to curb this tendency the state encourages the setting up of various recreation facilities, such as community centres that will get the youth out of the streets and instill them with a sense of self-discipline.

Evaluation
Unemployment in Tanzania has become a major government concern and its efforts have been

directed at deploying human resources in different sectors of the economy. By way of the Human Resources Deployment Act 1983, the state is all set to engage all able bodied persons in gainful employment. The exercise is, thus, aimed at promoting individual welfare in terms of improved standards of living, together with general economic growth emanating from increased productivity.

ASSESSMENT OF THE TANZANIAN WELFARE SYSTEM

The spirit underpinning the welfare system in Tanzania is a function of the traditional sense of communal obligation and mutual support, combined with current ethics embodied in the ideology of socialism. The state continues to appreciate and support the use of the existing community support system since it is, primarily, the one which provides a built-in means by which the welfare of Tanzanian community can be ensured. The philosophy of socialism has fundamentally re-cast the traditional value of mutual aid from a community basis into a state basis, whereby concern is focused on those unable to enjoy welfare support from within the family structure.

Tanzanian welfare philosophy is built upon the principles of family support, which is inherent in traditional society, and the CCM creed that all human beings are brothers. In order for human welfare to be improved it is believed that the scourge of poverty, ignorance and disease must be combated at all costs. A substantial part of state efforts is thus directed at ameliorating the impact of these conditions upon human functioning. Since living conditions in the rural sector of the economy are worse than those in the urban sector, the CCM directs the government to design policies aimed at improving conditions in the rural areas. Moreover, since one of the pillars of socialism is the execution of distributive justice, income tax is severe for high income earners and constitutes one of the main sources of government revenue.

Although income redistribution is intended to arrest income inequalities the problem of poverty still lingers on, putting a strain on economic development. This factor alone is a sufficient for the state not to institute a social welfare scheme with cash benefits. Hence Tanzania's social welfare system emphasises use of collective self-reliance and mutual aid, particularly in village settings, whereas in urban areas the state might step in to aid those who are disadvantaged as well as deprived, including the old, children and the disabled, all of whom may receive institutional care. However, the able-bodied unemployed do not receive any welfare support because land abounds on which they could work for a living.

Community-based welfare support has the great advantage of reinforcing a sense of belonging and, therefore, security between the members. It is long-rooted in the past, serving to provide security, food and shelter. Government intent, at present, is to maintain this traditional approach, where it is still intact and capable of meeting social welfare needs, and to intervene only where complex modern welfare problems have emerged. Taking into account the existing character of the economic, political and cultural variables in Tanzania it must be appreciated that Tanzanian workers and peasants are assured of at least a minimum welfare support.

FURTHER READING

Bakengesa, S.K.S. and Mallya, W.J. (1983), Old Age in Tanzania: Problems and Prospects, an unpublished manuscript, National Social Welfare Training Institute, Dar es Salaam.

Castle, E.B. (1966), Growing up in East Africa, London: Oxford University Press.

Farrant, M.R. (1971), Destitution. An Investigation into Patterns of Destitution in Rural-Urban Tanzania and Examination of the Welfare Policy, 1974 Social Welfare Option, Dar es Salaam: Department of Sociology, University of Dar es Salaam.

Government of Tanzania and the United Nations International Children's Emergency Fund (UNICEF) (1985), Analysis of the Situation of Children and Women and Priorities for Children Survival and Development Vol.I, Dar es Salaam: Government Printer.

Idd, M.R. (1985), Pension Schemes: Product Development, Dar es Salaam: Insurance Institute of Tanzania.

Tanzania

International Labour Office (ILO) (1982), <u>Basic Needs in Danger: A Basic Need-oriented Development</u>, Addis Ababa, Ethiopia: African Regional Office, ILO.

Keneth, C. (1968), <u>Social Theory and African Tribal Organisation,</u> Chicago: University of Illinois Press.

Livingstone, L. and Ord, H.W. (1980), <u>Economics for Eastern Africa</u>, London: Heinemann.

Magangika, J.P. (1985), <u>Provident Funds: Their Development and Future Prospects,</u> Dar es Salaam: Insurance Institute of Tanzania.

Mallya, W.J. (1980), <u>A Review of Prospects and Constraints in Tanzanian Agriculture</u>, unpublished M.Sc Dissertation, University of Swansea, Wales.

Ministry of Health (1979), <u>Main Report: Inventory of Health Facilities 1978,</u> Dar es Salaam: Government Printer.

Ministry of Planning and Economic Affairs (1980), <u>National Social Economic Profile</u>, Dar es Salaam: Government Printer.

_____ (1982), <u>Population Census Vol. VII,</u> Dar es Salaam.

Mwankanye, H.A. (1985), '25 years of Social Welfare Administration', <u>Tanzanian Social Workers Association Papers</u>, Dar es Salaam.

National Social Welfare Training Institute (1979-80), <u>Preliminary Study/Survey of the Disabled in Tanzania,</u> an unpublished manuscript, Dar es Salaam.

Ndaka, M.A. (1985), 'Development in the Field of Social Services for the Disabled', <u>Tanzanian Social Workers Association Papers,</u> Dar es Salaam.

Oget, B.A. (1968), <u>Zamani: A Survey of East African History,</u> Nairobi: East African Publishing House.

Tanzania

Pratt, C. (1976), The Critical Phase in Tanzania, Cambridge: Cambridge University Press.

Report of the Welfare Organisation: Tanganyika for Year 1949 and 1950, Dar es Salaam: Government Printer.

Rugaika, W.K (1980), 'Parastatal Pension Scheme: Benefits and Unresolved Issues at Stake', Institute of Finance Management Papers, Vol.2, Dar es Salaam.

Tuinginie, S.A., A Short History of Tanganyika: The Mainland of Tanzania, Dar es Salaam: Longman Tanzania.

United Nations International Children's Emergency Fund (UNICEF) (1985), Hali ya Watoto Tanzania, 1985, Dar es Salaam: Tanzania Publishing House.

Vaides, W. (1985), Critical Evaluation of Pension Scheme for Workers in Tanzania, Dar es Salaam: Insurance Institute of Tanzania.

World Bank (1985), World Development Report 1985, New York: Oxford University Press.

Yimam, A., (1982), The Organisation and Delivery of Social Services to Rural Areas, Addis Ababa: African Social Work Education Association, Document 19.

ZAMBIA
Elizabeth E. Brooks and Vukani G. Nyirenda

THE WELFARE SYSTEM ENVIRONMENT

Ideological Environment
Zambia is a large country comprising 752,620 square kilometres in area. In this respect, Zambia is greater than the combined area of France, Belgium, the Netherlands and Switzerland. Located in the south-central part of Africa, Zambia is completely land-locked and is bordered by Zaire, Angola, South-West Africa, Botswana, Zimbabwe, Mozambique, Malawi and Tanzania.

Formerly known as Northern Rhodesia, Zambia became an independent Republic within the Commonwealth on 24 October 1964. Its population of nearly six million consists of 72 tribes unevenly distributed over the nine provinces. The large number of tribes means that there are an equally large number of languages. For this reason, it has not been possible to develop a lingua franca for Zambia. The nearest the government has come to finding a linguistic common denominator is the recognition of about seven languages used in mass media and on radio.

The vast extent of land, the uneven dispersal of the population and the large linguistic diversity have an important bearing on the country's level of, and approaches to, social development. Long distances have to be covered in order to reach people in need. In addition, for social development workers to be effective they must be able to speak, or at least understand, the language of the community, which creates another problem, that of having to learn a new language.

Perhaps, the most important element of the Zambian context is its political philosophy: the philosophy of humanism. At the core of this philosophy is the belief that Man is the centre of all human endeavours. Thus, all political, economic and social activities must be centred on Man. This philosophy, as conceived in Zambia, is an embodiment of the Zambian, indeed, traditional African, way of life which has always characterised a mutual-aid and Man-centred society. It is perhaps for this reason that Zambia has chosen socialism as a vehicle for achieving the principle of the philosophy of humanism. Accordingly, Zambia can be characterised as a Welfare State in so far as it has chosen to provide all the basic social services (such as health and education) free of cost to its citizens.

It was particularly after Independence that this guiding philosophy began to play a major role in shaping the structure and content of services. Emphasis was placed on services of a developmental nature - moving away from the typical remedial type of services. Communities were encouraged to, once again, begin playing a major role in the improvement of their lot through self-help activities.

This change in policy has led to the merging of the departments that were involved in the provision of social welfare and community development services into the Department of Social Development.

The focus of people as the centre point for planning has also led to the development of a social security system which is all-embracing: the National Provident Fund, which is a contributory social security system covering all workers in all walks of life.

At the level of implementation of programmes, the philosophy of humanism has also encouraged the active participation of voluntary, non-governmental organisations in social development. The basic tenet here is the use of people in creating conditions for self-improvement on a communal basis - approximating what was normally done in the traditional Zambian communities which were basically self-reliant.

Historical Origins

The historical evolution of the welfare system in Zambia must take into account the political and socio-economic environments. The move from the traditional rural system of indigenous Africans through a colonial period, with European domination and industrial expansion, to an independent nation, where the indigenous population is again in control, has moulded the shape of the welfare system. It should be noted that the subsequent description of the historical development of social welfare takes a narrow definition of social welfare that omits housing, health and education services, although the level of these services does affect what will be required of the social services and, in fact, these will be referred to in the description of actual services.

Traditional Society Pre-1896. The typical Zambian village was a group of people related by blood and marriage ties living and working together. It was essentially a mutual aid society where the rights and obligations of each person were clearly defined. In this way the 'extended family' met the needs for social services of its own members. The only exception was a misfit who was deemed to be a threat (witchcraft, theft, continuous adultery) to the group and was therefore ostracised by the village.

Colonial Rule: British South African Company 1896-1924. During this period, there was very little concern about the welfare of people. The Company's chief concern was to exploit the natural resources of the country. The Hut Tax was a major impetus to force men to work on the mines, but they came alone. There were a few regulations to control sanitation and health. Missions did carry out social services but this was secondary to their spiritual work.

British Rule: 1925-1963. The British assumption of administration in the mid 1920s marked the beginning of mining on a big scale. It was to the social problems created by the growing industrial urbanised centres that any welfare measures were directed. For example, a Workmen's Compensation Ordinance was established for whites in 1930 and extended to Africans in 1944. A Minimum Wage Ordinance was passed in 1932. The mining companies provided welfare halls which specialised in recreational activities. Welfare associations which grew up at this time provided a forum for Africans to discuss some of their social problems, but they had no power. Provincial Commissioners provided some welfare relief for whites but only repatriation for Africans. Some specialised individual and family services were available to the European population (for example, the Adoption Ordinance 1941), but African families were not supposed to move to the urban areas.

The appointment of the first welfare officer in 1945 was followed by the establishment of the Department of Social and Probation Service which had been proposed in Bain's report (1950). The early officers in this Service were from the British Probation Service and not surprisingly there followed the passing of the Juvenile Ordinance in 1953. In 1954, the Department started case work and handed group work over to the urban local authorities. The eventual recognition of the urban African family brought in its wake a new emphasis in welfare services, that of 'mitigating the violence of change'. Voluntary agencies increased (including the YWCA in 1956) but their services were particularly directed towards expatriate needs. 1960 saw the establishment of community development services aimed at creating basic facilities in the rural areas, where the majority of Africans still lived. 1961 brought the opening of the Oppenheimer College of Social Service which took over the training of welfare officers from Mindolo, a mission school that provided a minimal level training.

Independent Zambia: Since 1964. Independence found Zambia with a Department of Social Welfare providing probation, public assistance and child care, but enforcing a policy of promoting extended family responsibility. Urban local authorities and mining companies provided group activities, mostly of a recreational nature. The Community Development Department provided women's clubs, literacy clubs and basic facilities (such as housing and roads). Voluntary organisations provided recreational training, health and child welfare. The services of these organisations were eventually coordinated with the establishment in 1974 of the Zambia Council for Social Development. A major step forward for social security was achieved in 1965 when the Zambia National Provident Fund was established. The 1984 merger of the Social Welfare Department with the Community Development Department, to become the Social Development Department, provided an opportunity for uniformity in welfare services across Zambia and for community involvement in the

Zambia

meeting of human need, as envisioned in the 1980 Local Administration Act.

The Political and Socio-Economic Environments

Zambia adopted a Westminster-type republican constitution shaped by its British colonial experience. The basic tenets of this constitution include the protection of human rights for individuals and the assumption of the responsibility by the state for the welfare of its citizens. This responsibility has its origin and base in the philosophy of humanism. Legislative power rests with a unicameral National Assembly. Executive power is held by the President, who is elected by popular vote.

At the operational level, Zambia has adopted a decentralisation system of administration. The main objective of this approach is to ensure that there is sufficient power sharing within the Zambian society. Ultimately, such power sharing should result in transfer of political power from the state to the people. Even more important, the system ensures active participation of people in all walks of life in their own development.

The same philosophy is followed even in the area of political party organisation. The machinery for the organisation of the United National Independence Party (UNIP) is basically located in the Section at the grass-roots level. The UNIP structure builds on from here to the Ward, District, Province and, finally, National level. Additionally, the UNIP organisation is intertwined with other aspects of the socio-economic infrastructure to ensure that all organs of society work for the benefit of Man as required by the philosophy of humanism.

As shown above, there is sufficient political will to discharge the moral responsibility of the state to provide for the welfare of its citizens. However, when it comes to implementation of the intention - the policy - other factors come into play and must be taken into full account. Firstly, there is the question of population dynamics. At the time of Independence, the total Zambian population consisted of 3.49 million people of whom 80 per cent lived in the rural areas and 20 per cent in the urban centres (CSO 1985). In less than 22 years this population has grown to 6.8 million people of whom 43 per cent live in the urban areas (UNDIESA 1982).

Zambia

HISTORY OF FORMAL WELFARE SERVICES IN ZAMBIA

DATE	AGENT	SERVICE
1917	Government	Mines Health and Sanitation Regulations
1930	Government	Workmen's Compensation Ordinance (covered Whites only)
1932	Government	Minimum Wage Ordinance
1933	Voluntary	United Welfare Association
1924-38	Mines	Recreational Services
1933	Government	Juvenile Ordinance
1941	Government	Adoption Ordinance
1944	Government	Workmen's Compensation Ordinance (extended to Africans)
1945	Government	First Welfare Officer appointed - mostly for whites
1946	Voluntary	United Federation of Welfare Societies
1947	Gray	Report advocating social security for whites
1950	Bain	Report recommending creation of a social welfare department
1952	Government	Department of Social and Probation Services
1953	Government	Juvenile Ordinance (urban areas only) and probation of offenders
1954	Government/ Voluntary	Split between group work (responsibility of the local authority) and case work (responsibility of the Government)
1960	Government	Community Development Commissioner appointed
1961	Government/ Voluntary	Oppenheimer College started
1965	Government	Zambia National Provident Fund created
1968	Government	Handicapped Act
1974	Government	Zambia Council for Social Development created
1984	Government	Merger of the Community Development Department and the Social Welfare Department to become Social Development Department

Zambia

The sheer size of the population has serious implications for social service provision. In 22 years, the demand for goods and services has increased at a rate unparalleled. In the growth and expansion of the capacity to meet such demands: more school places are required, more hospital beds, more houses and more services to cater for persons outside the normal operations of the money economy.

Secondly, the rapid growth of the population has occurred unevenly. In the majority of cases the urban population has grown at a much faster rate. Furthermore, Zambia has witnessed one of the most serious examples of the rural-urban drift, leaving the previously densely populated rural areas with virtually no people while urban centres are bursting at the seams with the unplanned-for growth in population.

A further complication with respect to Zambian population is the issue of dependence ratio. More than 58 per cent of the total population is under the age of 21 (UN DIESA 1982). A sizeable portion of the population consists of persons over the age of 60. This leaves a very small work force of a little more than 400,000. It is this small group that must raise the revenue to support the rest of the population.

The basis of the Zambian economy is the mining of copper and cobalt, although over 70 per cent of the population is engaged in agriculture. Over the decade prior to 1983 economic growth was negligible; instead, as a result of rapid population growth and modest inflation, living standards fell (World Bank 1985).

THE WELFARE SYSTEM: AN OVERVIEW

Structure and Administration
The attainment of independence on 24 October 1964 found Zambia with two separate social service departments: the Social Welfare Department and the Community Development Department, located in different Ministries and focusing on different problems (that is, public assistance versus clubs and literacy) in different areas (that is, urban versus rural). Of course the urban areas also had the community development services provided by the local authorities (government and mines).

By and large, these services were centralised both in terms of policy and service delivery. There was very little input from the social workers, let alone the communities served. The 1971 Registration and Development of Village Act made provision for the establishment of Village Productivity Committees (VPC) and Ward Development Committees (WDS) which were designed to facilitate the participation of people in development. A similar system of Section Development Committees (SDC) and Ward Development Committees (WDC) was envisaged for the urban areas. However, the intention of these VPCs, SDCs and WDCs was never fully realised. Their requests tended to get lost in the hierarchy of government bureaucracy (see Brooks 1974). As long as services were controlled and directed from Lusaka there was very little communication, let alone impact, from outlying areas.

In 1974, the Community Development Department was transferred to the Ministry of Labour and Social Services where the Social Welfare Department already resided. However, this made virtually no difference to their service nor to their service delivery. It was not until 1984 that the two services joined hands to become the Social Development Department. Thus began the transformation of services towards the ideals of being uniform in scope, developmental in focus and professional in character. This process is still going on. There is extensive need for re-orientation and re-training of staff as well as re-drafting policies, programmes and practices.

As far as service delivery is concerned the most significant step towards real community participation was taken in 1980 with the passing of the Local Government Act. It provided for the decentralisation of government administration.

Under this system the 57 districts became the major administrative units. The District Council oversees the affairs of each District. It is chaired by the District Governor and has representatives from each Ward within the District. The District Secretariat is the administrative arm of the Council. The Secretariat is made up of various departments each headed by a Secretary: Political, Security, Administration, Legal, Developmental, Social, Commerce, Trade and Finance.

The Social Secretary has the following responsibilities:

Zambia

- Community development service
- Social welfare
- Public health
- Public education
- Training
- Housing & estates
- Public amenities
- Sports and youth
- Tourism & parks
- Clubs & societies
- Regional affairs
- Social security
- Cultural affairs

The implication of this structure is that, with decision-making occurring at the local level (the District), there can be genuine community involvement in that decision-making. With one Secretary responsible for so many welfare services, true integrated planning and development is possible. But if this is to succeed professional social development workers and politicians will need to accept their new roles as partners rather than the antagonists of the past (see Brooks and Nyirenda forthcoming).

Implementation of this Act has been understandably slow. Now, four years later we can see that urban districts are well launched into the system. Much of the responsibility proposed was already theirs. In contrast, the rural District Councils are much further behind having less access to professional staff and revenue and the Mine Township Councils have maintained their somewhat independent position. A notable gap for all of these local authorities is the activities of the Social Development Department and those of the Zambia National Provident Fund which have remained outside their control.

The Act itself is not clear in regard to the division of responsibility between the central government ministries and the district councils. Even where tasks are transferred, as long as finance is still the prerogative of the central ministry then real power has not been transferred. There seems to be no plan for the transfer of revenue sources or financial control of the district councils.

The Zambia National Provident Fund (ZNPF) was established in 1965 and covers over one million employed persons, including agricultural workers. It is administered by a tripartite Board and a Director, under the general supervision of the Ministry of Labour and Social Services. It has six regional offices and 32 district offices.

The workmen's compensation scheme, comprising an employer-financed compulsory work injury insurance programme, is administered by the

Zambia

Workmen's Compensation Control Board, which is managed by a Board and a Commissioner, under the general supervision of the Ministry of Labour and Social Services.

Private voluntary agencies in Zambia are for the most part governed by a board which sets policy while the day-to-day tasks are carried out by a small body of professional/sub-professional staff. Government involvement in voluntary agencies is minimal other than the Social Development Department's general watchdog function and the 'grants in aid' given to a few agencies. The Zambia Council for Social Development provides consultative and information services but has no controlling function. Voluntarism is not a popular ideal and this is a constraining factor for membership drives. More popular politically and generally is the 'self-help' concept. Such efforts tend to make use of informal committee structures that exist only for the duration of the project. More voluntary agencies are tapping into this resource for the promotion of social development.

Financing Social Welfare
Zambia's political and sociological philosophy, as well as its ideological position, can only be seen as good intentions. For them to be transacted into programmes and activities, they need to be supported by resources, both human and material. Futhermore, the resources must be paid for in one form or another. They need to be backed by financial arrangements.

In Zambia the state has chosen to provide the basic social services, including personal social services, free of cost to its citizens. Consequently, the state, through its departments and other organs, provides the funds for the provision of basic social services. Thus, in 1980, out of a total Government budget of approximately K838,000,000 over K185,000,000 went to the provision of social services in the basic needs areas of education, health and social welfare. In 1986, this figure rose to more than K377,000,000 (Estimates, 1980, 1986).

Within the Ministry responsible for social welfare, funds allocated to the department responsible for social welfare programmes represent a sizeable proportion of the Ministry's budget, 29 per cent in 1980 and 37 per cent in 1986 (Estimates 1980, 1986). In general, this is

Zambia

to be seen as a demonstration of the country's commitment to welfare.

In addition to these arrangments, the ZNPF collects contributions from both covered employees and employers. Employees contribute five per cent of their earnings, which is matched by their employers. A contribution earnings ceiling of K200 per month applies. Also employers pay risk related premiums to the Workmen's Compensation Fund. This again, is a demonstration of the commitment of employers to the welfare of their employees.

When taken in general terms, the financial commitments for the provision of social services look impressive. However, when examined closely, a different picture emerges: a greater part of the financial resources are consumed by personal emoluments and collateral expenses for the staff employed in the social service sectors. For example, in 1980, programmes-related expenditure represented 2.3 per cent.

The conclusion to be drawn from this apparent disparity between the policy and operational practices can only be attributed to faulty planning. Deliberate efforts have to be made to ensure that the value premises and policy objectives are adequately translated into programmes and activities and are actually supported by adequate funding and other resources.

THE AGED

> We live in a world that discards the old like broken bottles. By denying old people a place in society we make rubbish of a valuable resource. And we don't realise what we are throwing away (Debbie Taylor, <u>Zambia Daily Mail</u>, 26 April 1982).

This attitude derives from the myths that have been developed regarding the aged. In most societies, the aged are seen as inevitable victims of the ravages of time. In their old age, they are not expected to be happy, creative, active and productive members of society; they are miserable, ugly, senile or simply dead. Indeed this is an attitude alien to the traditional Zambian society.

In Zambia, the elderly have always been seen as a family and community resource because of their wisdom derived from long-life experience. As a result, the care of the aged has always been seen as a family and community responsibility. Even in the urban areas where the traditional family ties are fast diminishing, official Government policy on the care of the aged would tend to lean towards family care within communities. This is a drastic departure from the welfare policies inherited at independence, which had led to the development of institutional care in the form of homes for the aged. Some of these still remain.

Personal Social Services

In 1980, there were three such homes and a geriatric centre serving 96 persons (MOLSS 1981) and there are many informal set ups such as the granny villages that have sprung up around mission stations in the rural areas. It has been argued that aging in itself is not a disease (Debbie Taylor, Zambia Daily Mail, 26 April 1982). However, in a developing country like Zambia, a host of factors contribute to the poor condition of the aged. These include poverty, disease and malnutrition. Given the changed circumstances that the aged are experiencing in today's Zambia, organised services outside the family have become a necessity.

Social Security

Under ZNPF covered employees upon retirement at age 50 (or at age 55 without retirement) receive a lump sum benefit equal to the combined contributions of the employee and his or her employer, plus accrued interest (about five per cent a year). This may be paid in installments or as an annuity. Unfortunately, Zambia is still very far from developing a comprehensive social security scheme that can embrace all categories of the aged. The only general financial aid is public assistance and its administration is very limited. Only 55 persons received it in 1980 (MOLSS 1981).

Evaluation

What makes the aged a significant group among the needy section of the Zambian society is the fact that, with improvement in health care and general conditions of living, there is a steady increase in both the numbers of the aged and the life expectancy. Whereas in 1974, those aged 60 and above constituted only 4.6 per cent of the population, in 1980, the aged constituted more than seven per cent of the population (CSO 1980). Consequently, a future problem is developing for which there are no adequate services in the current arrangements. Zambian society would therefore be better advised to look back into the past and learn from the way the traditional communities looked after the needy, including the aged.

THE DISABLED AND HANDICAPPED

Current estimates have put the number of handicapped persons in Zambia at about 88,000. In the absence of an accurate census, this is a very crude estimate. Indications are that the number of disabled and handicapped persons in Zambia could be much larger. The blind form the largest single sub-group of those identified as handicapped. With their obvious and conspicuous handicaps and disabilities, this sub-group has tended to be the most vocal and for a long time monopolised not only sympathy, but also the services that were provided for all the handicapped.

The physically handicapped are the next largest sub-group whose needs have been recognised by the Zambian society. Together with the blind, they dominate the Government-sponsored Zambia Council for the Handicapped. A much more neglected group comprises the intellectually handicapped, especially children.

Personal Social Services

Long ignored and in some cases written off as 'irreparable', the physically handicapped are slowly beginning to attract the attention of both government and the non-governmental organisations. The latter include Cheshire Homes, Da Gamma Home, and various other mission operated facilities. The result is that their needs are beginning to be taken into account in planning such services as education and health. A teacher training college to train teachers specialised in dealing with physically handicapped children has been established.

Until recently the intellectually handicapped were not recognised. A few severe cases of physically and mentally handicapped were housed at Chainama Hills Hospital and there was a class for those from the community who demonstrated some potential. But it would not be surprising if these were not included in the current estimates of the handicapped. However, with the development of psychiatric services, more recognition is being given to the existence of this group. Most of the work has been spearheaded by voluntary organisations. A Mental Health Association has been in operation for some years. More recently (1981) the Zambia Association for Children with Learning Disabilities was formed. It works hand in hand with the Ministry of Education. As a result, there are now 21 classes for children with mental disabilities in the regular school system, nine of which are supported by a parent interest group. Teachers specialised in dealing with children that have learning disabilities are also being trained.

It has taken time to recognise the presence of the handicapped in Zambian communities mainly because of traditional attitudes regarding the source of handicaps and disabilities, especially if not brought about by physical accidents. Any form of congenital disability is regarded as a bad omen to the family or a form of punishment for the misdeeds of that family. In the mid-1970s, a team of mental health workers discovered a 12-year old mentally retarded child in hiding in a dingy lean-to for almost ten years who had never been seen by neighbours.

Social Security
There is no general social security protection from any source for those who are disabled. but ZNPF does provide an invalidity benefit for permanent incapacity for work in the form of a lump sum equal to 40 per cent of the total employee and employer contributions paid plus accrued interest (about five per cent per year). It also pays a survivor's benefit in the case of death equal to the unclaimed benefit and a funeral grant of K80, if 24 contributions have been paid by the deceased.

Evaluation
The negative attitudes combined with the lack of proper information about real needs and possible services mean that the handicapped and disabled in Zambia remain largely an ill-serviced group. It is the non-governmental organisations and the service clubs that have been in the forefront providing services for and to this group. However, these have usually been on an *ad hoc*

basis. Apart from remedial services, little is done in the area of rehabilitation and creative use of some of the talents possessed by handicapped persons. Even where such persons have been trained and have acquired skills, they do not find jobs easily because of the negative attitudes inherent in Zambian society.

CHILDREN AND YOUTHS

Nearly half (47.6 per cent) of Zambia's population of 6.8 million (1985) is under 15 years of age. Another 10.3 per cent is between the ages of 15 and 19 years. Thus 3.8 million of Zambians are either children (0-12 years) or youth (13-18 years) (UNDIESA 1982). This number will continue to sky-rocket as long as Zambia keeps up its growth rate of 3.1 per cent per year (NCDP 1984, p.5). The problem of effectively serving such vast numbers is mind-boggling. Even minimal service is bound to be expensive.

However, Zambia has risen to the challenge. Early in post-independence days, Zambia identified the basic needs of children and youths to lie in the areas of education and health facilities. Changes were made to provide free medical care for all and steps were taken to provide primary education (Grades 1 to 7) for all children of the relevant age group. By 1971, most seven year olds managed to find a place in Grade 1. By 1978, it was estimated that about 84 per cent of the relevant age group was in primary school (ILO 1981, p.110). Unfortunately, economic problems coupled with population increases made it very difficult to maintain these gains. Similarly, despite a colossal increase during the post-independence years in secondary school facilities that resulted in a progression rate from primary to secondary school of 23.16 per cent in 1975 (NCDP 1979, p.338), the rate is now reducing and is less than 16.6 per cent.

The same kinds of problems have been experienced in the health field. Medical facilities have been increased in absolute numbers and expanded in scope, but they are hard pressed to cope with pressures of an expanding population. In addition there has been inequity in allocation of such facilities so that urban areas are favoured over rural areas and maintenance of present services is virtually nil.

This is the problematic context in which

Zambia

social welfare services operate. It is a situation so overwhelming that solutions seem impossible. Very few children and youths are not in need in one way or another, but some specific groups do stand out as particularly needy.

Grade 7 School Leavers. In the period from 1969 to 1977, there was a total of 100,000 grade seven school leavers unable to proceed to secondary school. In 1978, another 100,000 were added and this number (or even greater) has been added each subsequent year (ILO 1981, p.67). These youths do not have any saleable skill. Their hopes have been raised by an education system that prepares for higher education rather than for life or specific employment. They rapidly become a problem to themselves, their families and the nation. Frustration and despair are common among such youths. Their families castigate them for failing grade seven and as a frustrated semi-educated group of considerable size, they represent a security threat to the nation. At the same time they are a large untapped resource of the country.

It should be noted that this analysis has ignored the 20,000 grade four students (in rural areas) unable to proceed to grade five in 1978.

Delinquents. In 1979, the Ministry of Labour and Social Services, through its then Social Service Department handled 873 cases of delinquency. Of these, 636 (72.8 per cent) were offences relating to property and theft (MOLSS 1979). Considering the amount of petty theft rampant in the country, it seems likely that those dealt with by the Department represent but a small sample of delinquent youth in Zambia.

There is certainly a lot of public outcry against Mishanga boys. These are youths who buy goods that are in short supply and then sell them at inflated prices. Just where their behaviour should be regarded as delinquent or applaudable self-reliance is hard to say.

The Malnourished. Malnutrition is the number one killer of children in Zambia. It is estimated that between 20 and 40 per cent of child deaths after the first week of life are at least partially caused by malnutrition. The seriousness of the situation is mirrored in the rate of infant mortality - 23 per thousand (ILO 1981, p.117). In

Zambia

1979, out of 4,795 deaths, 1,240 or 27 per cent were children under one year and another 17 per cent were one year olds (CSO 1975).

The 1970-1 National Nutrition Survey established that 20 per cent of the children under the age of five had second or third degree malnutrition (NCDP 1984, p.31). This situation has persisted or perhaps worsened according to smaller more recent studies. UNICEF estimates that 34 per cent of Zambia's population is malnourished (UNICEF 1983) and, of course, the children would be the hardest hit.

Malnutrition is related to poverty as shown by its high incidence in remote rural areas and the squatter sections of the urban centres. The present economic crisis has worsened the problem.

The Neglected. No one has done a survey of the incidence of neglect of children in Zambia. The extended family traditionally protected children from neglect in any instance where parents were unable to provide adequate care. However, the urban way of life has, to some extent, eroded the role of the extended family. From time to time, reports are made of newborns being abandoned and it is not uncommon to be accosted in a town centre by young boys begging for money. There seem to be hordes of 'street boys' engaged in various economic ventures - Mishanga, car washing, tyre mending, car protecting and, one suspects, theft. There is a Child Labour Law, but it only prohibits work in mines, industry, construction and transport. Agriculture and commerce are free to hire children (Laws of Zambia, Vol. VI, Cap.191). It has long been recognised that rural children participate in agriculture production. Weeding, grass cutting, maize shelling and cattle herding are all identified as activities for children and youth (see Brooks 1985; Chilivumbo 1984). Such activities must, of necessity, clash with the time requirements of formal education. But education is not compulsory.

Personal Social Services
The Ministry of Labour and Social Services provides most of the services for children and youths. But these benefit only a very small number as will be seen from the bracketed numbers indicated with each service given in 1979 (MOLSS 1979).

Under Corrections, the Ministry prepares

Zambia

social histories for the courts (873), offers a probation service (271) and supervises an approved school at Nakambala (64) and a reformatory at Katombora (120).

Under Family and Child Welfare, it supervises orphanages (102 children), vets the work of the Child Care and Adoption Society who provide fostering (41) and adoption (11) services, and very occasionally provides counselling in cases of marital conflicts or motherless children. The small numbers involved here probably reflect the responsibility taken by the extended family in these matters, but it may also reflect the inappropriateness of the service.

The General Welfare Section takes the form of rations, clothing, accommodation, rent payments and travel assistance. Such service would usually only be given to a mother with dependent children and even that only temporarily. Extended family members are expected to step in and take over the responsibility. An able-bodied youth would not receive any service.

It will be noted that these services are curative rather than preventative in nature and are primarily provided in the urban areas. Preventative services in the urban area are the responsibility of the local authorities - District Councils or Mine Townships. They include recreational clubs, homecraft training, pre-school and an increasing number of training programmes for grade seven school leavers. The latter are supported jointly by Ward Councils, the Ministry of Youth, and the Ministry of Higher Education. Voluntary organisations (such as churches, YWCS, YMCS, Boy Scouts, Girl Guides) provide limited recreational and educational programmes for youth. The Zambia Pre-School Association provides guidance to an increasing number of community pre-schools.

The rural areas are largely left without service. There are a few Rural Reconstruction Camps and a few training centres, but most rural children and youths receive neither curative nor preventive service.

On the macro level attempting to serve the majority of Zambian children and youth, the following programmes are in embryo. The Ministry of Health has committed itself to primary health care which puts an emphasis on maternal and child health and involves co-operative effort with the National Food and Nutrition Commission (MOH

Zambia

1981). The Ministry of General Education and Culture is seeking ways to implement the educational reforms which will provide a more vocationally oriented curriculum lasting for nine years. The Ministry of Youth, in conjunction with the Ministry of Higher Education, is seeking ways to expand the grade seven leaver training programmes (NCDP 1979).

Social Security

The only social security benefits paid with respect to children are those provided for orphans by the ZNPF and the Workmen's Compensation Fund. The former involves a refund on past contributions, with accrued interest. The latter is an earnings-related pension.

Evaluation

Thus, it can be seen that health and education are the major areas of service to children and youth. There is no family allowance for the rearing of children and, in the main, parents are expected to care for their own offspring. Some minor attempts are being made to service those whose needs are not being met by their own family. Any service that is provided tends to be in the urban area.

NEEDY FAMILIES

In traditional Zambian society of the pre-colonial times, there was no room for a needy person, let alone a needy family. Dr K. D. Kaunda has described the traditional Zambian community as a mutual aid society which:

> ... was organised to satisfy the basic human needs of all its members ... Most resources such as land might be communally owned and administered by Chiefs and Village Headmen for the benefit of everyone. If, for example, a villager required a new hut, all the men would turn to the forests and fetch poles to erect the frame and bring grass for thatching. The women were responsible for making the mud-plaster for the walls and two or three of them would, undoubtedly, brew some beer so that all the workers would be refreshed after a hot, but satisfactory day's work. In the same spirit, the able-bodied would accept the responsibility of tending and harvesting the garden of the sick and infirm ... Human need

Zambia

was the supreme criterion of behaviour. The hungry stranger could, without penalty, enter the garden of a village and take, say, some peanuts, a bunch of bananas, a mealie cob, or a cassava plant root to satisfy his hunger. His action only became theft if he took more than was necessary to satisfy his need. For then, he was depriving others.

The Zambian society of today has gone through drastic social change, thanks to the introduction of the modern state and the money economy. In traditional society, the family played a key role in providing for the needs of its members and ultimately of society. One African Minister once asserted that '... no nation is stronger than its families'. However, the agents of modernisation have more or less destroyed the main fabric of the traditional Zambian family. The result is the absence of a natural institution to turn to in times of need.

In Zambia the incidence of destitution among the masses is on the increase. Part of the reason for the increase in urban destitution is the drift of large numbers of people from rural areas to urban areas in search of paid employment. However, since the majority of the migrants have few or no skills and since jobs in the towns are few anyway, many of the migrants simply end up joining the swelling numbers of the urban unemployed. As such they have no means of maintaining themselves and thus join the groups of the needy.

In the rural areas, the problem arises from the fact that most of the able-bodied leave the rural areas for the towns, leaving behind mostly the aged, women and children who cannot adequately look after themselves. It has been estimated that the rural female-headed households constitute about 25 per cent of all rural households. These are the most vulnerable of the rural poor. The ILO basic needs mission to Zambia (1981) summarised the situation of the rural female-headed household thus:

> They suffer the full range of rural disadvantages, including adverse terms of trade, difficulties in obtaining basic goods, lack of markets for subsistence staple crops, and poor access to services. But on top of these, they are faced with acute labour

Zambia

scarcity. Where a woman lives alone with her children, she has to struggle to fit into one life the activities of mother, housewife, farmer, food-processor, water-carrier, wood-gatherer and even a marketeer. If she is sick, there is no-one else in the household to take over.

Personal Social Services
There are limited personal social services provided for destitutes in the form of food rations, some clothing and repatriation to rural areas. In 1980, such services were given in response to 886 applications for long term help and 1,903 applications for short term help (MOLSS 1981). Other than this, there are no services or facilities specifically designed to cater for the needy families in Zambia.

Social Security
Zambia does not have a comprehensive social security system that protects needy families.

Evaluation
There are few services and facilities specifically designed to cater for Zambia's needy families. The majority of the needy families are not protected by the welfare system.

THE UNEMPLOYED

Zambia is now approximately 43 per cent urban. Urban centres are under severe financial pressure partly because of the world wide economic recession in which Zambia suffers acutely because of its over-dependence on copper, but also because of the increase in the number of people in town as against the decrease in the number of jobs:

> Between 1974 and 1979, the urban population is estimated to have increased by about 615,000, just over half from natural increase and just under half from net migration from the rural areas (MOLSS 1983, p.62).

But between 1975 and 1979, wage earning employment in the formal sector dropped by 21,000 jobs. In 1979, 21 per cent of the labour force were in wage employment and it is predicted that if present conditions persist only 13 per cent will be able to find wage employment in 2000 (ILO 1981, p.4).

Zambia

In 1983, the estimated number of wage employees was 363,800 (CSO 1984). Those registered as unemployed were 41,067, but it is obvious that the majority of the unemployed do not register. With an urban labour force of something in excess of 689,000 (the 1979 figure), there must have been at least 325,200 unemployed persons.

Unemployed youths are mostly unskilled with limited education. Their numbers are being constantly increased by the grade seven school leavers. Even if we ignore those aged 14 to 18 years as being too young for employment, there are several thousands who have already reached adulthood (19 years): 100,000 from 1978, another 100,000 from 1979 and another 100,000 from 1980. For them, there are few prospects of either further education or employment. Some of them have remained in the rural area and, more by default than by choice, have taken up subsistence farming. But the majority no doubt have remained in, or migrated to, the urban areas in search of work. Thus, the rural areas have been denuded of their most promising labour resource and the urban areas have grown to proportions beyond the coping capacity of their services. Furthermore, individual families have been burdened with dependants whose chances of wage employment in the formal sector are nil. Even the informal sector offers little hope. Establishing oneself there requires capital and that is a very scarce commodity for such people. In addition, most are ill-equipped to deal with the vagaries of the informal sector whether in retailing, manufacturing or producing and many lack the necessary skills.

Particularly vulnerable in the ranks of the unemployed are the women. They tend to be less well educated and therefore less skilled. The majority do not register as seeking employment. For example, in 1969, out of 1,139,786 women (15 years and over) only 179,445 were listed as seeking employment while 776,154 were listed as student, housewife, aged, sick (CSO 1984). But, particularly with the pressures of the failing economy, housewives do try to contribute to the household income.

This must, of necessity, be in the informal sector. There, gender seems to be a critical variable so that women are precluded from the petty manufacturing found in the informal sector and relegated to petty retailing where the profit is much lower and there is a greater chance of failure (Bardouille 1982).

Of course, there is also the dilemma of the rural woman who is unable to progress beyond subsistence level farming. Where she is also the head of the household her problems are complicated by lack of labour and immobility (ILO 1981, p.118).

The Government Response. Wage employment is dependent on the economic expansion of the mines, industry and manufacturing. However, in recent years, Zambia has seen the opposite. The Third National Development Plan admitted that the actual level of employment in 1977 was lower than that in 1976 (NCDP 1979). Unfortunately, there has been no reversal in this trend. 1984-5 has witnessed a series of redundancy announcements. October 1985 found the Government announcing its intention of streamlining its own work force as a means of economic expedience. Tracts of land for agricultural development are offered to all those who are laid off.

This particular compensation reflects the government view that only in agriculture can a solution be found to Zambia's economic woes. In 1983, a 10-year plan was drawn up to promote agricultural development and aid agencies were asked to direct their funds to these projects. Some response has been forthcoming, but examination of government expenditure does not reveal any major shift from its earlier urban emphasis, as might have been expected if rural agriculture is to become a major focus of the development thrust in this country. In any case, even success in this area will still not provide wage employment.

Another area deemed to have some potential for relieving the unemployment problem is the informal sector or that of the self-employed. With this in mind the government launched the Small Industries Development Organisation (SIDO) in December 1982. Included in its mandate were technical and practical aid to small industries and the promotion of investment in small industries. The Village Industry Service (VIS), started even earlier and on a voluntary basis, carried out similar work, but with smaller units emphasising village craft. While both these efforts are commendable, they could not as yet be seen to be making a major impact on the problem of unemployment.

Zambia

Social Security

For those who are unemployed, there is virtually no relief. There is no social security protection given to the able-bodied unemployed. For example, in 1980, short-term public assistance was given to only 69 job seekers (MOLSS 1981).

Personal Social Services

The unemployed may register at the Ministry of Labour and Social Services, but the possibility of gaining a job is something less than 50 per cent. For example, in 1983, there were 41,067 new registrations and only 18,268 jobs were filled out of the 22,162 vacancies reported (CSO 1984, p.5). Considering that only about 10 per cent of the unemployed register for the service, it cannot be said to be anwering the problem of unemployment. No doubt it is a valuable service for matching employees with prospective employers. But it is really designed for an economy with something approximating full employment to deal with the temporary unemployment characteristic of the administration of free enterprise.

Evaluation

Thus, it is evident that the state has no machinery to deal with the hardships caused by unemployment. Here again, the extended family is expected to exercise its traditional role and take responsibility for its unemployed and therefore dependent members. Women are particularly disadvantaged in relation to finding employment as are young people. The various attempts of government to meet this problem have not met with a great deal of success in terms of the reduction in the total size of the problem.

THE SICK AND INJURED

Zambia, with the low standard of living so typical of Third World countries, finds it difficult to maintain a high standard of health for its populace. In 1983, life expectancy was 48.3 years (MOH et al. 1984, p.8). While government medical services are free, access is in favour of the urban Zambian. There are approximately 3.5 beds or cots per 1,000 people available, but 25 per cent of the rural population are considered to be unserved because of remoteness from the service (MOH et al. 1984, p.8). In addition to using government medical services people in both urban and rural Zambia make use of home remedies and traditional healers in their search for health (see Frankenberg and Lesson 1976; Nanchengwa 1984; Spring 1978).

There is a generally low level of nutrition. For example, one researcher estimated that the average rural worker's calorie intake will sustain only five hours of light work three-to-four days a week (Gertzel 1973). Only 48 per cent of the population have access to safe water and only 47 per cent have access to adequate sanitation (MHO et al. 1984).

Zambia has a creditable record for expanding its road system. It is estimated that by 1978, there were 5,000 kilometres of tarred roads (Kaplan 1979). However, the slumping economy since 1978 has made it very difficult to maintain these roads. The same slumping economy has resulted in a scarcity of vehicles. As is true for almost all services, the rural population struggles most with poor road maintenance. Poorly maintained vehicles and roads are major contributors to increasing road accidents.

Approximately 60 per cent of the population live in the rural areas, and most of these exist on the proceeds of subsistence farming (MAWD 1983). The urban areas which have burgeoned particularly since Independence are dominated by the capital intensive copper mining and all the related industry.

Only 43 per cent of births take place in health institutions (MOH et al. 1984, p.8). The rest are either unsupervised or supervised by traditional birth attendants most of whom have not received any formal training. Even among those who were admitted to hospitals in 1981, there was a maternal mortality rate of ten per thousand (MOH et al. 1984, p.8). In 1983, the total expected confinements was 312,290 (MOH et al. 1984, p.32). Presuming the 1981 mortality rate 3,123 women would have died in the process of giving birth in 1983.

In 1982, Zambian outpatient facilities reported treating 6,879,718 children and 6,457,817 adults. These were supposedly new cases, but presumably refer to new diseases rather than new patients. Nevertheless, with the population standing at something just under seven million, this report does suggest a very high use of medical facilities.

Zambia

Diseases most commonly reported for the children were respiratory (19.93 per cent), digestive (19.08 per cent) and malaria (9.40 per cent). For adults they were digestive (17.55 per cent), respiratory (16.97 per cent) and injury (8.48 per cent) (CSO 1985, p.55). The ultimate of illness is death. In 1982 there were 17,887 hospital deaths. Among the children, the greatest killer was malnutrition (22 per cent), followed by perinatal death (18 per cent), respiratory (13.5 per cent) and measles (8.8 per cent). For adults, the big killers were heart (13.4 per cent), respiratory (10.3 per cent), tuberculosis (9.8 per cent) and malignancy (9.1 per cent) (CSO 1985).

What is most distressing is the finding of the Ministry of Health that 77.9 per cent of the deaths and 62.5 per cent of the admissions to hospital are preventable with means presently available in Zambia (MOH 1981).

In 1983, 2,818 persons were seriously injured and another 1,519 slightly injured as a result of road accidents. Another 747 were fatalities. Between 1966 and 1980, 'car crashes have gone up by 77 per cent, indicating a 50 per cent rise in deaths, 60 per cent in the number of motor vehicles and 55 per cent increase in population' (*Times of Zambia*, 19 February 1985). The 1983 road accident figure stood at 7,697.

In 1982-3, the Workmen's Compensation Fund processed 3,937 claims which included 166 fatalities, 526 permanent disabilities and 3,245 temporary disabilities while the government processed claims for 20 fatalities, 65 permanent disabilities and 95 temporary disabilities (Workmen's Compensation Fund Control Board 1984). The mining and quarrying industry is by far the greatest contributor of both fatalities and disabilities. The Mines Safety Department estimated the percentage of these fatalities and disabilities against working men to be 0.37 and 32.68 respectively (MOM 1984). It is perhaps noteworthy that the claims accepted by Workmen's Compensation have dropped from 5,143 (1981-2) to 3,937 (1982-3) and this downward trend has been continuing over several years.

However, the seriousness of road and work related accidents cannot be downplayed. A major cause for adult hospital death is accidents and injuries (CSO 1985, p.56). In addition:

Zambia

80 per cent of orthopaedic beds are occupied by accident victims, 60 per cent of whom spend more than 90 days in hospital, plus a further period of rehabilitation (<u>Times of Zambia</u>, 19 February 1985).

Personal Social Services
Prevention is the first level of defence against sickness and injury and this is the intention of the newly introduced Primary Health Care Programme (in 1981) with its slogan 'Health for all by the year 2000'. It includes health education, nutrition, sanitation, maternal and child health, immunisation, control of endemic disease, mental health and treatment of common diseases (MOH 1981).

The same principle is the operative guideline for the Inspectors of Factories (Ministry of Labour and Social Services), the Mines Safety Department (Ministry of Mines), the Workmen's Compensation Fund Control Board, and the Roads and Road Traffic Board. Their safety programmes include education, publication and inspection.

Social Security
The ZNPF provides a gratis maternity benefit of K65.00 for its members (wage employees only), if they have contributed for 24 months (US, SSA HS 1984). Such women would also qualify under the labour law for 90 days maternity leave in addition to their regular 30 days sick leave per year.

In addition, the Workmen's Compensation Fund provides a compulsory insurance against work injury for employed persons, but not casual workers or teachers (US, SSA 1984). There is also a special system for public employees. The benefits provided are as follows:

- <u>Temporary disability</u>: pro-rata according to the salary level from 100 to 30 per cent of the salary, payable up to 18 months.
- <u>Permanent disability</u>: pro-rata according to the salary level from 100 to 10 per cent of the salary. Child supplement of 15 per cent of pension for first child and five per cent for each other child under 18 years through to the eighth child.
- <u>Partial disability</u>: per cent of full pension proportionate to the degree of the disability. Periodic adjustment for cost-of-living changes.

Zambia

- **Medical benefits:** (work injury) medical, dental nursing and hospital care up to K1,500, artificial limb up to K500; and transportation.
- **Survivors benefit:** 80 per cent of disability pension of insured payable to widow or invalid widower; orphans: 15 per cent of insured's pension for first; five per cent for each other orphan under the age of 18 (older, if full time student). Full orphans 30 per cent for first; ten per cent for each other (maximum eight children). Payable to other survivors, if no widow or orphans (according to amount of dependence). Periodic adjustment for cost of living. Funeral grants cover the cost of burials up to K50 each.

Evaluation

It should be noted that employed persons are relatively well covered for work injury, probably reflecting the long history of copper mining in Zambia. But there is virtually no financial help for the sick or for an injury of a non-wage earner. It is assumed that the extended family will provide for such people, even when that provision includes extended nursing care of the chronically ill. There are no nursing homes or home care services.

AN ASSESSMENT OF THE ZAMBIAN WELFARE SYSTEM

It is very clearly Zambia's intention to provide its people with opportunities for earning income sufficient to meet their needs and access to community services that will support both families and communities. However, the foregoing description of unsolved problems and groups of people in situations of particular risk makes it obvious that this intention has not been realised.

There have been a number of contributing factors. As a Third World country, Zambia has suffered greatly from the global economic recession. This situation matched with a phenomenal population growth means that the few Kwacha have to be spread to more people. The result is less service and even this limited service is not distributed evenly so that the rural areas receive much less than their share.

There has been growth, not only in the population, but also in the 'social bureaucracy' - growing number of employees receiving a salary but 'contributing little if anything, to the effectiveness of essential government services' (ILO 1981, p.8). What is required is basic structural change. Without it this burgeoning bureaucracy will be a positive hindrance to the social welfare of Zambia.

The social situation in Zambia is very complex. Services must be planned for people as diverse as the non-educated peasant farmer living in a traditional village environment to the university graduate living in the capital city and working as a managing director of a large international organisation. Definitions of need vary greatly and even the solutions for one group can be a problem for the other. For example, the education system that opened doors of opportunity for the successful graduate can be a cause of frustration and unfulfilled expectations for the school leaver.

With the mounting pressure of problems in the society, it is very tempting to see those persons most affected as being problems themselves. This negative attitude militates against a creative use of these people in finding solutions to their problem situations.

What is the way forward? Planning is certainly required if the best use of scarce resources is to be achieved. But it must be planning at a very practical level - including who, what and how. It must also be at a very basic level. Zambia cannot afford the frills. Basic needs must be met and anything else reserved for a future, hopefully more prosperous, time.

Additionally, it must be coupled with a recognition that structural changes, although painful to execute, are necessary. Resources cannot be wasted on the salaries of unproductive people.

The execution of the plans must be continually monitored and special consideration must be given to the maintenance of a positive attitude towards people that will foster their participation in the building of themselves and of the nation.

REFERENCES

Bardouille, Raj (1982), <u>Manpower Research Report No. 10, Men and Women's Work Opportunities in the Urban Informal Sector: The Case of Some Urban Areas in Lusaka</u>, Lusaka: Institute of African Studies.

Zambia

Brooks, Elizabeth E. (1974), 'Village Productivity Committee and Social Development in Zambia', <u>International Social Welfare</u>, XVII(1), 35-42.

_____ (1985), 'Field Testing of Appropriate Technology', TDAU, University of Zambia.

_____ and Nyirenda, V. G. (forthcoming), 'Decentralisation: New Partnerships for Social Service Delivery in Zambia', <u>Journal of International and Comparative Social Welfare</u>, 2.

Central Statistical Office (CSO) (1975), <u>Registered Births, Marriages and Deaths</u>, Lusaka, Zambia.

_____ (1980), <u>Monthly Digest of Statistics</u>, Lusaka, Zambia.

_____ (1984), <u>Monthly Digest of Statistics</u>, Lusaka, Zambia.

_____ (1985), 'Paper on Population Trends and National Development', prepared for the National Seminar for Policy Makers, Lusaka, Zambia.

Chilivumbo, A. (1984), 'Population Consequences of Agricultural Development: The Case of Zambia', Inaugural Professional Address, University of Zambia.

<u>Estimates of Revenue and Expenditure (1980, 1985, 1986)</u>, Lusaka, Zambia: Government of Zambia.

Gertzel, Cherry (ed.) (1973), <u>The Political Process in Zambia, Documents and Readings</u>, Lusaka, Zambia: The University of Zambia.

Frankenberg, K. & Lesson, J. (1976), 'Disease, Illness and Sickness: Social Aspects of the Choice of Health in a Lusaka Suburb', in Lauden, J. (ed.), <u>Social Anthropology and Medicine</u>, London: Academic Press.

International Labour Office (ILO) (1981), <u>Zambia Basic Needs in an Economy Under Pressure</u>, Addis Ababa: Jobs and Skills Programme for Africa.

Zambia

Kaplan, Irving (1979), Zambia: A Country Study, Washington DC: The American University.

Ministry of Agriculture and Water Development (MAWD), Planning Unit (1983), Food Strategy Study, Lusaka, Zambia.

Ministry of Health (MOH), Planning Unit (1981), Health by the People: Implementing Primary Health Care in Zambia, Lusaka, Zambia.

_____ World Health Organisation and United Nations International Children's Emergency Fund (1984), Report of a Joint Evaluation of Primary Health Care in the Republic of Zambia, Lusaka, Zambia.

Ministry of Labour and Social Services (MOLSS) (1979), Annual Report, Lusaka, Zambia.

_____ (1981), Department of Social Service, Annual Report, 1900, Lusaka, Zambia.

_____ (1983), Report on the National Seminar on 'Basic Needs in an Economy under Pressure' 28-30 March 1983, Zambia, Lusaka, Zambia.

Ministry of Mines (MOM) (1984), Annual Report of Mines Safety Department for the Year 1983, Lusaka, Zambia.

Nanchengwa, Violet M. (1984), 'People's Beliefs about Causation of Disease and Implications for Choice of Health Care in Lusaka', unpublished MA Dissertation, University of Zambia, Lusaka, Zambia.

National Commission for Development Planning (NCDP) (1979), Third National Development Plan, 1979-83, Lusaka, Zambia.

_____ (1984), 'Deliberation of the Committee Selected to Study the World Bank Recommendations in Draft Report No. 4715 - ZA on Population, Health and Nutrition', Lusaka, Zambia.

Spring, Anita (1978), 'Faith and Participation in Traditional Versus Cosmopolitan Medical Systems in North-West Zambia', unpublished paper presented at the African Studies Association Annual Meeting, Baltimore, 1-4 November 1978. Wotham, Mass: USA (Mimeo).

Zambia

United Nations: Department of International Economic and Social Affairs (UNDIESA) (1982), 'Demographic Indicators of Countries and Estimates and Projections as Assessed in 1980', New York.

United Nations International Children's Emergency Fund (UNICEF) (1983), <u>1982 World's Children Data Sheet of the Population Reference Bureau Inc</u>, New York.

United States of America, Department of Health and Human Services, Social Security Administration, US, SSA (1984), <u>Social Security Programs Throughout the World, 1983</u>, Washington, DC.

Workmen's Compensation Fund Control Board (1984), <u>Annual Report 1982/83</u>, Lusaka, Zambia.

World Bank (1984), <u>Draft Report on Health Care Population and Nutrition No. 4715 - ZA</u>, Washington DC.

_____ (1985), <u>World Development Report 1985</u>, New York, Oxford University Press.

ZIMBABWE
Joe Hampson and Edwell Kaseke

THE WELFARE SYSTEM ENVIRONMENT

Historical Origins and Ideological Environment
Zimbabwe is the latest African country to join the world stage of independent sovereign states, but its birth-pangs started over a century before. The first Chimurenga or revolt in 1896 against white settlers is often used as a convenient way of dating the modern nationalist movement and sense of statehood, although there were great nation states in the region as early as the thirteenth century. The greatest was Great Zimbabwe, which reached the height of its influence before the end of the fifteenth century. Its surviving buildings are the largest ancient stone buildings in black Africa. The pre-capitalist Shona civilisation was violently disturbed in the nineteenth century by the advent of white settlers from South Africa, who were initially lured to the area by the dream of large gold deposits. This failed to materialise in any sizeable way, but the settler communities had, by the beginning of the twentieth century, already discovered the region's considerable agricultural potential. In the 1930s iron and steel works were started, rapid expansion in the commercial, agricultural and industrial sectors took place after 1945, but it was the manufacturing sector that was to prove the most successful developer.
   All this growth in prosperity, of course, took place against a backdrop of increasingly severe racial repression, black disenfranchisement, and an ultimately successful attempt by white farmers to force Africans into proletarianism. Social welfare programmes were designed with the intent of providing a labour pool. Indigenous

agriculture was seen as the only welfare system possible for the local population. The country's land was divided, chessboard-like, into areas of white commercial land and poorer quality 'Reserve' or 'Tribal Trust Lands' (TTL).

Various efforts were made by a few individuals and groups to promote liberal reformism in issues connected with welfare services, social security and unemployment, but the settler economy was geared more to the dictates of capitalism. For example a Government Report of 1944, written by Frank Russel, a Social Security Officer, criticised the prevailing attitude that 'the home of the native and his economic and social security is to be found in his Reserve ... [and] the years he spends in towns are merely an interlude' (Rhodesia 1944, p.230). He proposed a pension scheme for blacks and whites, and also, summing up provisions at the time, he said that:

> Social assistance is afforded on the basis of need to all European, Asiatic and Coloured Persons in age, by old age pensions; in destitution, by the payment of rations or by the payments of maintenance grants at home or in institutions; and in sickness, by the provision of health services free or at reduced rates. Natives receive no Old Age Pensions and very little in the way of relief, the general assumption being that the reserves will support their old, sick and destitute. Social insurance exists in the sphere of occupational disability where all races are covered, and all employees earning less than 270 pounds per annum, with the exception of casual workers and domestic workers in private households. Voluntary insurance against the cost of medical service and loss of earnings through sickness and old age covers in each case roughly 1/4 of the gainfully employed European persons, together with their dependants ... Few Coloured and Native employees, apart from those engaged on the railways, are provided for by sick pay schemes. (Rhodesia 1944, p.203).

The first official welfare provision in Rhodesia was the introduction in 1936 of the probation and school attendance officer programme, which solely dealt with non-Africans. It was not until 1948 that a duly constituted Department of

Social Welfare was established. Amongst its functions was the investigation of juvenile delinquency among all races. The first African probation officer started work in 1952. It was not until 1964 that the Department of Social Welfare provided a public assistance programme, but after four years less than 400 African families were eligible for any help. The assistance provided was in the form of rations, or a cash equivalent, with a rent allowance.

Municipal authorities very largely reinforced the public welfare system but, after the appointment of a Senior Welfare Officer in Bulawayo in 1955, that city's welfare provisions were acknowledged to be wider in scope than any other municipality. It had built up a net of services embracing: public recreation, social group work, case work and community development, all financed through the municipal monopoly on production and sale of opaque beer (Gargett 1977).

There was, of course, no social security provision for unemployment. Consequently, large numbers of the unemployed joined the informal sector in order to survive. In many cases they were subsidised, both in cash and in kind, by their families in the rural areas. Kinship ties became powerful instruments for securing employment and for gaining financial assistance. The influx of able-bodied males into the urban areas meant that only women, young children and old people remained in the rural areas and thus the rural areas were denied effective manpower. Consequently, the productivity of the subsistence agricultural sector suffered. The situation was worsened by the introduction of the 'white agricultural policy', which relegated black farmers into the periphery by making them sources of cheap labour for the white farmers (Stoneman 1978). This undoubtedly contributed to rural impoverishment thus increasing the propensity among rural Africans to migrate to the urban areas; hence creating a vicious circle of poverty and underdevelopment. The results were manifold: great rural poverty within a subsistence economy, and a cheap pool of labour to service the industrial, commercial and agricultural sectors for the benefit of whites. The Rhodesian Front election victory of 1962 marked the growing consolidation of white settler power, and a refusal to acknowledge the increasingly severe pauperisation of both rural and urban blacks. The official ideology saw blacks as living in a self-sufficient 'tribal' and peasant society. Any sector employment or commercial involvement in the formal sector was considered only an interlude; the Reserves constituted both the home and the all-encompassing social security system. The contradiction between that view and the enforced pauperisation of the Reserves, so as to create a motive for joining the labour force in an effort to alleviate their poverty, was never acknowledged but always obvious.

After the prolonged and severe armed struggle in 1979 Mugabe's party and Nkomo's party negotiated a cease fire that was to lead to settlement and talks and the election of Mugabe's party to government of Zimbabwe in April 1980. The nationalists have inherited a country not only severely affected by the civil war (most rural infrastructure had been damaged or destroyed) but also with an inherently dualist economy where the industrial and agricultural sectors were geared to catering for the needs of 250,000 whites, largely ignoring the country's five million or more black population. Upon attaining independence Zimbabwe adopted as its ideology scientific socialism, based upon Marxist-Leninist philosophy. By adopting this socialist ideology, Zimbabwe has thus commited itself to the creation of a new social order, through an economic policy of growth with equity and geared towards an equitable distribution of resources. There is thus an aim of redistribution of the national wealth.

Rhodesia has always been reckoned to be a country with one of the greatest inequalities in income distribution in the world. Chenery et al. (1974) found the income share of Rhodesia's lowest 40 per cent of the economically active population to be 8.2 per cent of the total income in the country. Although in terms of Gross Domestic Product (GDP) per capita Zimbabwe is in the World Bank's middle-income lower group of countries, and although the glaring racial disparities in wealth in Zimbabwe are no longer so stark, the gap between rich and poor is still very wide.

Minimum wage levels have been legislated for, but the income gap has not been narrowed much, because of the differential effects of inflation (12.1 per cent for high-income urban dwellers in 1984, compared with 20.1 per cent for low-income earners); the wide gap in income levels (for example, in 1981 in the civil service pay scale

Zimbabwe

the highest level was 34 times the lowest); and a regressive tax system. In the rural area it would seem the commercial farmer's better infrastructure and credit arrangements have allowed that group to capitalise on the prevailing producer prices to a greater extent than those in the peasant sector can.

Socio-Economic Environment

Zimbabwe, land-locked in south-central Africa between the Zambezi and Limpopo Rivers, and covering an area of some 391,000 square kilometres, has a population of 7.9 million of which 24 per cent is urban based (World Bank 1985). Some 656,000 people live in the capital Harare. There are approximately 125,000 Europeans in Zimbabwe. The crude birthrate is high (53 per thousand in 1983) while the crude death rate is quite low (13 per thousand in 1983).

Agriculture accounts for 60 per cent of the labour force, 11 per cent of GDP and 45 per cent of exports (Zimbabwe is almost alone in black Africa in being a net exporter of maize). The mining sector is the most important source of foreign exchange earnings (about 30 per cent).

Since independence in 1980, Zimbabwe has suffered from a three-year drought, which produced a negative GDP growth rate of 3.5 per cent in 1983, but 1984 showed an upturn to 1.0 per cent, and 1985 evidenced a 6.0 per cent growth rate.

Zimbabwe's unemployment rate is, like many other Third World countries, notoriously difficult to estimate. Part of the difficulty lies in defining the actual labour force, and in computing the number of people employed in peasant farming and in the informal sector. The Riddell Commission (1981) estimated that about 40 per cent (1.0 million) of the labour force is in formal employment with the remaining 60 per cent (1.5 million) either engaged in peasant or informal sector activities, or unemployed. Another government report (Zimbabwe 1983) estimated unemployment or informal sector employment at 24 per cent of the labour force, by assuming peasant agriculture employed 43 per cent and the formal sector 32 per cent. Out of the approximately 1.0 million people formally employed the domestic service sector employs 10 per cent, manufacturing 17 per cent, public administration eight per cent, education eight per cent, construction five per cent and agriculture 26 per cent. Moreover, the

Zimbabwe

future rise in youth unemployment rates will be considerable as the gap between the demand and supply of labour widens.

From 1982 to 1985 the economy has only managed to create about 7,000 new jobs a year, yet some 80,000 school leavers enter the labour force seeking employment and nearly 200,000 young people come of working age. Secondary school enrolment in 1983 stood at 313,297, up from the previous year's 224,109, and primary school enrolment in 1983 reached 2,042,543, up from the previous year's 1,935,962.

Political Environment
Under the 1980 Constitution, legislative power is vested in the bicameral Parliament, comprising a House of Assembly (with 100 members elected by universal adult suffrage from 80 'common roll' constituencies and 20 separate 'white roll' constituencies) and a Senate (with 40 members: 14 elected by the 'common role' members, 10 by the 'white roll' members, 10 by the traditional House of Chiefs, and six presidential nominees). Executive authority is vested in the President, who is elected by Parliament for six years and who acts on almost all matters on the advice of the Cabinet, and the Prime Minister, who is appointed by the President. The Cabinet must have the confidence of Parliament, to which it is responsible.

The major political party (Zanu), led by Mr Robert Mugabe, has been in power since independence in April 1980. Zanu was partner to Mr Joshua Nkomo's Zapu in the Patriotic Front during the liberation war. Both parties infiltrated armed cadres into the then Rhodesia to fight the war of liberation, but Zanu had control over a much greater area of the country and operated a much larger guerilla force. Zanu enjoys majority support in Mashonaland, Manicaland, Masvingo and Midlands provinces. Zapu, on the other hand, enjoys greater support in Matebeleland, its traditional stronghold. The Zimbabwe government is, however, committed to the creation of a one-party state, and the abolition of the separate 'white' voters' roll, and it hopes to implement this by 1990.

Zimbabwe

THE WELFARE SYSTEM: AN OVERVIEW

The Zimbabwean social welfare system is, like all other institutions in the country, a product of a dual economy, where welfare was conceived in a residual model; and a racial history, where whites controlled and benefited disproportionately. Thus government welfare provisions are still basically residual and urban-biased. Social security programmes are primarily targeted at producing an efficient pool of labour, although recent health and educational provisions by the government tend to redress this imbalance by a considerable spread of services in rural areas.

The Administration of the Personal Social Services

Department of Social Welfare. The administration of the personal social services in Zimbabwe is the responsibility of the Department of Social Welfare (henceforth the Department) within the Ministry of Labour, Manpower Planning and Social Welfare (henceforth the Ministry). The Department is headed by a Director, assisted by two Deputies. At the Provincial level the Department is headed by a Provincial Social Welfare Officer, below whom are District Social Welfare Officers, who are in charge of Districts within the Provinces. Field Officers, that is Social Welfare Officers, operate at the District level.

The functions of the Department include the promotion of child welfare, usually through foster care, adoption and supervision, registration and periodic inspection of creches; registration of voluntary welfare organisations; handicapped; family casework; working with the aged and working with courts in the disposal of juvenile delinquency cases; rehabilitation of physically handicapped.

Voluntary Organisations. There are a number of voluntary organisations that provide personal social services. These are of significance in Zimbabwe in that they fill in the gaps left by the state in the provision of welfare services. Some of the voluntary organisations are church-related, and their activities include the provision of old people's homes (for example, Bumhudzo Old People's Home run by the Salvation Army Church), children's homes for orphans and children in need of care (for example, Matthew Rusike Chilren's Home run by

Zimbabwe

the Methodist Church, and <u>Makumbi</u> orphanage run by the Catholic Church). Other notable voluntary organisations include <u>Jairos Jiri</u> Association and St Gils, both of whom provide rehabilitation services for the physically handicapped; Island Hospice, which provides counselling services for work with dying, and CADEC and Christian Care, two church-related development organisations which have relief of distress as part of their function.

Any voluntary organisation involved in social welfare is required to be registered as a welfare organisation in terms of the Welfare Organisation Amendment Act (1976). Registration is a responsibility of the Department, but the Registrar is assisted by a Welfare Advisory Board appointed by the Minister of Labour, Manpower Planning and Social Welfare.

<u>Local Government</u>. Some local authorities provide welfare services for their residents, although they are very limited in scope. The most comprehensive welfare programmes are those run by the Bulawayo City Council. The City Council provides family casework for families experiencing marital or adjustment problems. Youth programmes are also run, which are geared toward instilling discipline and a sense of direction among youth and providing them with income generating skills.

<u>The Administration of Social Security</u>
The Department also operates three social security programmes. Firstly, there is an old age pension for non-Africans, which was introduced in 1936, but it was discontinued at the time of independence in 1980. Only those who were in receipt of assistance before independence continue to receive such pensions. This pension is non-contributory, but means-tested. Secondly, there is a public assistance programme which provides financial assistance to destitute members of society on a non-contributory but means-tested basis. Thirdly, there is the War Victims Compensation Act (1980) which provides disability pensions for those injured as a result of the independence war, or for the families of those who died in that war.

The Workmen's Compensation Insurance Fund is administered by the Department of Occupational Health, Safety and Compensation within the Ministry.

Zimbabwe

Financing the Welfare System

Social Security. The single broadest social security programme is the Workmen's Compensation Insurance Fund, financed by contributions from employers. (Additional penalty assessments are made on employers with unfavourable accident claim rates.) Out of this Fund come pensions, lump sum awards, and allowances during temporary disablement, and medical and rehabilitation expenses are paid to workmen or their dependants after a work-related injury or death. The scheme has a wage ceiling of Z$16,000 per annum for members, thus making some 900,000 in the private sector eligible for compensation benefit. Table 1 presents income and expenditure for 1983 and 1984.

TABLE 1 : WORKMEN'S COMPENSATION INSURANCE FUND INCOME AND EXPENDITURE

Income	1983 Z$	Percentage	1984 Z$	Percentage
Contributions	12,604,376	(76.2)	5,550,123	(54.2)
Additional Penalty Payments	141,138	(0.8)	1,646	( )
Investment	3,743,732	(22.7)	4,644,007	(45.4)
Miscellaneous	50,724	(0.3)	40,870	(0.4)
Total	16,539,970	(100.0)	10,236,646	(100.0)
Expenditure				
Pensions and Allowances	5,707,883	(70.8)	6,621,956	(75.4)
Medical Aid Expenses	744,339	(9.2)	312,043	(3.6)
Lump Sum Benefit	1,357,567	(16.8)	1,514,042	(17.3)
Rehabilitation Expenses	256,161	(3.2)	330,570	(3.7)
Total	8,065,950	(100.0)	8,778,611	(100.0)
Surplus:	8,474,020		1,458,035	

Zimbabwe

Unfortunately little data is available on numbers of workers aided but for 1984 there were 13,700 injuries and 213 fatalities reported to the Workmen's Compensation Insurance Fund.

The costs of public assistance and drought relief came to Z$42 million for the 1983-4 period. During that year it was claimed that 2.1 million people were receiving drought relief in the form of a monthly per capita average of 1kg beans, 15kg mealie meal and 0.51 oil. Some Z$66 million was spent on lump sum gratuities for ex-combatants. In respect of the different pension funds for that period, old age pensions involved Z$2.6 million, disability benefits involved Z$1.8 million, war pensions Z$0.5 million and war victims compensation pension Z$11.8 million.

Personal Social Services. All public welfare services are financed from general revenue by means of a government-determined annual vote to the Ministry, provided on the basis of expenditure estimates submitted by the Department.

Registered welfare organisations are eligible for per capita grants from the Department to meet some of their running costs.

The financing of health services is almost exclusively from general taxation.

The financing of local government welfare and community services throughout Zimbabwe is achieved through the monopoly sales of traditional beer. Beer halls are operated by the municipality and profits, in turn, finance community and welfare activities.

THE AGED

Serious welfare problems confronting the aged relate to the different economic sectors of commercial farming, peasant subsistence farming and urban wage employment. Within the commercial farming sector, the elderly have no tenure, and few if any social security benefits. Within the urban wage employment sector few workers participate in the pension programmes that will even take them beyond a Poverty Datum Line (PDL) existence. Indeed, the urban elderly are over represented among the recipients of public assistance. Within the peasant subsistence farming sector, the elderly are losing the protection afforded by extended family networks,

Zimbabwe

and, in spite of cultural sanctions, are often poorly treated by family members, lacking both health and educational facilities relevant to their needs.

Demography. In 1969 the European aged formed 9.5 per cent of the white population, whereas the African aged comprised 2.69 per cent of the African population. In 1982, however, the elderly African population of Zimbabwe was estimated at 213,000, some 2.8 per cent of the total African population, whereas the European elderly numbered 24,500 or 13.3 per cent of the total white population. The small percentage change in the proportion of African aged tends to hide the fact that, absolutely, the elderly African population increased by 72 per cent in 13 years.

The life expectancy for males and females in 1983 was 52 years and 60 years respectively (World Bank 1985).

Rural Elderly. For those elderly who were never in formal employment, or who never received a pension, their usual source of subsistence is peasant farming – 75 per cent of elderly men and 83 per cent of elderly women live in rural areas. Although evidence is scanty, it seems that rural households containing elderly are particularly poor, in comparison with elderly-headed urban households. Households with elderly members are under capitalised, with few or no cattle. (Over half the rural household have no cattle, a serious deficiency when considering the economic, cultural, and productive significance of livestock.) Previous reliance on household members remitting cash to their rural homes seems to be becoming less common. In one study of rural elderly fewer than 14 per cent were in receipt of monthly remittances, and one-third of the elderly whose children were in paid employment reported as never receiving remittances (Hampson 1985). During the three years of drought (1982-1984) both government and voluntary agencies were deeply involved in the provision of drought relief throughout drought hit areas.

Personal Social Services
For the elderly these tend to be located almost exclusively in urban areas. There are some 52 or so old folks homes provided by the voluntary sector, housing over 2,000 residents. There are

Zimbabwe

three types of homes: the sheltered or cottage type (Model A); hostel accommodation with meals (Model B); and a nursing home for the very disabled or frail (Model C). Government provides 25 per cent of the building costs, state lotteries match another 25 per cent, and the balance is contributed over 20 years. The Department of Social Welfare provides Z$30 per resident for homes with destitute elderly, and the Ministry of Health provide bed grants for model C homes. Most of the African residents of old folks homes tend to be alien ex-farm workers, mine workers, or domestic workers. The form of institutional structures adopted makes for a 'warehouse' model of care. The large number of elderly destitute who are alien is a feature of previous Rhodesian policy of relying on importing workers for commercial agriculture and domestic services from Malawi, Zambia and Mozambique. In theory repatriation is always possible, but absences for decades mean that the returning worker has lost all meaningful contact with any family, and the cost of post-retirement care is transferred from the country of employment to the country of origin.

Social Security

For both urban and rural elderly participation in non-formal activities is an essential requirement for obtaining a livelihood. One study by Tarira found a wide variety of rural income-generating activities: breeding poultry and rabbits, mat making, brewing spirits or beer, making clay pots, yokes for ploughs, hoe handles. Urban activities include petty trading activities (especially vegetable and fruit selling by elderly women) selling tobacco, snuff, beer, clothes, service activities like washing and ironing clothes, herbal healing and n'anga (traditional healer) activities. In a survey of one Harare market, elderly formed 19 per cent of all sellers, but 40 per cent of the alien sellers. Most of the sellers seemed to have settled in the city for a considerable period and have been employed, demonstrating Brand's (1982) thesis that the urban informal sector in Zimbabwe is, in large measure, a safety net for those who were once in the formal sector, rather than a stepping stone for rural migrants seeking urban employment. One of the principal forms of mutual aid societies for the urban poor in Zimbabwe is the burial society, usually an ethnically-based grouping where

Zimbabwe

insurance is purchased by monthly payments against the very high costs of funerals (Hall 1985).

Old age pensions are still provided subject to a means-test under the 1936 programme, but only to non-Africans who qualified prior to independence in 1980.

The elderly are entitled to public assistance, but few satisfy the qualifying conditions, especially in the rural areas. The Department has been active in opening up a considerable number of rural offices, but public assistance continues to be an urban phenomenon, and the largest single category of public assistance applicants are elderly destitute.

Evaluation
As in many Third World countries, the personal social services targeted at the aged tend to be located predominantly in urban centres. Access by the rural elderly is severely limited.

The main problem for the vast majority of the elderly is income security.

By the mid 1970s it has been estimated that about 70 per cent of all whites in employment were covered by private pension plans. For Africans, only some 17 per cent of the agricultural labour force, and 44 per cent of all formal sector employees, are covered by such plans, contributions to which are tax-free, which tend to pay very small benefits. The Whitsun Foundation (1980) noted that only 1.3 per cent of urban Africans in wage employment will receive pensions above the urban PDL.

CHILDREN AND YOUTH

Zimbabwe has a relatively young population age structure, which makes children and youth a major welfare target group.

Personal Social Services
The legal instrument that promotes and safeguards the welfare of children is the Children's Protection and Adoption Amendment Act (1979) (Chapter 33). The Act 'provides for the establishment of juvenile courts and for the protection, welfare and supervision of children and juveniles'. The Act also provides for the setting up, registration and supervision of institutions as places of safety for children and for the rehabilitation of problem-children.

Zimbabwe

In terms of the Children's Protection and Adoption Amendment Act, the Minister of Justice appoints a magistrate to preside over a juvenile court. The presiding officer may require the assistance of one or two assessors depending on the nature of inquiry. If the inquiry is in respect of a female child the presiding officer is required to seek the services of a female assessor. In order to ensure adequate care and supervision for children and young persons, the Act makes it an offence for a parent to fail to meet the basic needs of his child. However, if a parent's failure to provide adequate care for his child is due to destitution then the parent may not be prosecuted. The Act further states that it is an offence for a person to allow a child or young person to patronise a brothel or to beg or to cause the abduction, seduction or prostitution of a child.

A child alleged to be a child in need of care is brought before the juvenile court for an inquiry in terms of Section 20 of the Act. A child can be alleged to be a child in need of care if the child is destitute in that his parents are deceased or can not be traced, or if his parents or guardian are unable to exercise proper care and control over him or if a child cannot be controlled by his parents or guardian. On the basis of the inquiry, the juvenile court can commit a child to a certified institution or order the child to be placed in the custody of a person capable of exercising good care and supervision of the child. The court can also order the child to be returned to the custody of his parents or guardian with or without a probation officer's supervision.

Adoption and Fostering. The Department of Social Welfare is responsible for the adoption and fostering of minor children: Section 58(2) of the Children's Protection and Adoption Amendment Act provides for the appointment of a probation officer 'to act as guardian ad litem' of the child in the case of an application for adoption. The probation officer's appointment serves to safeguard the interests and needs of the child. In safeguarding such interests the probation officer assesses the circumstances of the applicant, particularly the motive for adoption; the applicant's socio-economic background; and the ability of the applicant to provide emotional

Zimbabwe

security for the child. In general, adoption cannot be effected if the applicant is less than 25 years old or if the applicant is less than 21 years older than the minor, without the special consent from the Minister of Labour, Manpower Planning and Social Welfare. The Minister's consent is usually given in cases where the minor is the child of one of the spouses or in cases where applicant and minor are within the 'prohibited degrees of consanguinity'.

Foster care is another option for dealing with children in need of care. The probation officer and the courts have to be satisfied that the prospective foster parents will be able to provide adequate care and supervision for the child. The court order placing the child in foster care is rescinded when the child attains the age of 18 years. Foster fees (Z$45 per child per month) are paid to the foster parents. There is periodic supervision from a probation officer in order to safeguard the interests of the child.

In 1980 there were 285 cases of fostering and adoption.

Juvenile Delinquency. The Criminal Procedure and Evidence Act (1976) (Chapter 59) calls for a social inquiry report to be completed by a probation officer in respect of juveniles under the age of 18 who have committed offences. This report provides the magistrate with relevant information upon which a decision on sentencing can be made. The options open to a probation officer in the disposal of juvenile delinquency cases include whipping (boys), suspended sentence, postponed sentence, committal to a training institute, or, in some cases, a discharge but with a strong reprimand. First offenders, or those who have committed minor offences, are often given suspended or postponed sentences or are simply reprimanded. Those juveniles with a criminal history, or those who have committed serious offences, are committed to training institutions for rehabilitation. Juveniles below the age of criminal responsibility (14 years) cannot be prosecuted without the special consent of the Attorney-General.

In 1980 some 530 juveniles were put on probation, of whom 465 were committed to institutional care.

Zimbabwe

Children's Homes. Although the personal social services for children and youth are provided in the main by the Department of Social Welfare, voluntary organisations often try to fill the gaps left by the state. Their main contribution is in the provision of children's homes, which get per capita grants from the Department (currently Z$45 per child).

Child care. Urban local authorities provide day-care and pre-school centres for use by residents. These centres have to be registered and supervised by the Department.

Youth Services. Municipal authorities are also responsible for a large range of youth programmes, the most comprehensive of which is found in Bulawayo. Recreational, vocational and occupational activities and training are provided, funded from traditional beer sales. The churches and the ruling party also provide programmes of activities. The Ministry of Youth, Sport and Recreation is in the process of building and administering a training centre in each of the seven Provinces to provide skills and training for youth, but in the four year period to 1985 lack of funds meant that only some 1,900 youths have gone through these training centres.

Social Security

The state provides a fiscal welfare benefit in respect of children of better-off families. For those paying income tax, there is a Z$500 abatement for each child in the family to a maximum of six children (Z$3,000). For non-tax-paying families there is no comparable support.

Evaluation

The welfare of children is protected by law in Zimbabwe. The state's role is to protect children at risk. To this end a legal and administrative infrastructure has been created, which works reasonably well.

The voluntary sector's major contribution is in the provision of children's homes for orphans and homeless youths. These attract a government subsidy.

Municipal authorities provide child-care and arrange youth programmes, but only in urban centres. In rural areas youth programmes tend to be church-sponsored or arranged by Zanu's youth wing.

Zimbabwe

As in most Third World countries only limited access to the personal social services is available to children and youths living in rural areas.

Fiscal welfare benefits are only available for the better-off families with up to six children.

NEEDY FAMILIES AND THE UNEMPLOYED

Many types of needy families exist in Zimbabwe, including families of the unemployed, which are disadvantaged, especially those containing agricultural workers and refugees.

Agricultural Workers. Families of agricultural workers can be classified as 'needy families' because of poor nutritional status, poor health and hygiene facilities, poor education facilities, poverty wages, lack of tenure, and lack of extended family contacts. Some 20 per cent of the country's population live on commercial farms, yet in many ways are 'a forgotten group' (Riddell Commission 1981, p.156). (One provincial hospital in the middle of such an area set up a farm health worker project, whereby health workers are trained on different farms to animate the farm-worker communities, monitor children's health, advise on setting up clean water supplies, VIP (Ventilated Improved Pit) latrines, irrigated vegetable garden plants, and pre-schools.) Yet the Riddell Commission argued for a more radical approach to providing social services for such groups. Land, it was argued, should be set aside within close proximity to a grouping of commercial farms for the establishment of worker villages. These villages should contain acceptable-standard housing, water, sewage, schools, health facilities and stores. Not only would such a scheme reduce the almost total dependence such workers presently have upon their employers, but it would allow for a nucleus that later could improve its infrastructure in terms of transport, electricity, post, banking and so on.

Refugees. In 1986 Zimbabwe is host to some 100,000 plus Mozambican refugees (technically referred to as displaced people) who have come to Zimbabwe partly as a result of the drought, partly fleeing from the South African-sponsored MNR operations in the Tete province. About 25,000 of these refugees are being assisted by the United

Zimbabwe

Nations High Commission for Refugees (UNHCR), government and voluntary agencies (such as Save the Children Fund, Oxfam (USA), Oxfam (UK), Christian Care, CADEC) in the provision of health facilities, educational and skills training, and income generating activities, but are housed and fed in camps organised by the Zimbabwe government. Most of the rest live in Zimbabwean villages and are cared for by the villagers themselves. Because of language difficulties, security problems and the absolute poverty from which they fled, these refugees are particularly disadvantaged, and are often willing to work on nearby commercial farms for below minimum wages. A very small group of political refugees, mainly South Africans, are within Zimbabwe, and receive financial assistance from UNHCR, channelled through the Department of Social Welfare, in the form of a monthly payment, currently Z$56 per adult and Z$28 per child, plus a housing allowance.

Social Security
There is no comprehensive social security scheme in Zimbabwe.

Public Assistance. The Department of Social Welfare runs a non-contributory public assistance scheme geared towards providing financial assistance to the destitute whose circumstances have been caused by, among other things, unemployment, or a breadwinner's death or desertion. Assistance is only granted when it can be proved, beyond doubt, that an applicant holds Zimbabwean citizenship or resident status for at least one year, and who is unable to get assistance from his or her family. (Non-citizens are usually granted public assistance pending repatriation to their countries of origin.) The basis for assistance is the payment of cash allowances of 50 per cent of the established level of past earnings, up to a maximum of Z$200 per month. Thus those who were higher paid are given a higher level of public assistance (Riddell Commission 1981, Kaseke 1982).

Investigation of degree of destitution of an applicant is a responsibility of the District Social Welfare Office. A home visit forms the basis for determining the degree of destitution. On the basis of the findings from the home visit an investigating officer can recommend the granting of assistance. If unemployment is the

Zimbabwe

reason for destitution, applicants must prove that they are actively looking for employment, so as to discourage the development of a dependency syndrome. Those who have little chance of securing employment because of lack of skills are encouraged to settle in the rural areas, where they are expected to be productive. The level of assistance is dependent upon degree of individual and family need. However, on average the level of assistance is calculated at Z$10 per month for the husband, Z$10 for his wife and Z$5 per child per month. In addition, a rent and fuel allowance is paid. However, investigating officers are granted discretionary powers which allow them to adjust the level of assistance in order to meet the individual family need. Recipients of public assistance also receive free medical treatment and are assisted with the payment of tuition fees for their children attending secondary schools. Tuition for primary school is free.

Pauper Burials. The Department can assist destitute families in the event of death within the family by meeting the costs of burying the deceased. In 1980 some 28,000 pauper's funerals were financed

Personal Social Services
Various personal social services are provided for needy families and the unemployed. There is a partnership between government and voluntary organisations in the provision of such services. The Department of Social Welfare also provides counselling services for needy families and the unemployed. Other voluntary organisations such as the Citizens Advice Bureau offer advice and referral services. Many Municipal authorities provide welfare services for their residents, including counselling services, promotion of interest groups, and self-help projects. In cases of divorce social workers in the Department are usually asked by the courts to assist in determining which parent receives custody of the children. The husband is usually asked to pay a maintenance allowance to his ex-wife and children. The payment of a maintenance allowance will be discontinued once the woman remarries.

Evaluation
The needy family is not well protected in Zimbabwe. Most neglected are the families of

Zimbabwe

agricultural workers and refugees, but even those who might qualify for public assistance may not be able to gain access to such assistance.

Although the Department has made great strides in decentralising its services, the offices are still not within easy reach of the majority of the poor people. The real poor in most cases fail even to raise a bus fare in order to travel to their nearest District Office.

Indeed, because the public assistance programme provides earnings-related benefits (up to a maximum monthly level) it favours those who were in higher paid employment.

THE SICK

Before Independence the gap between urban and rural health service (very closely paralleling the gap between white and black service) was extreme: the capital's main hospital (white) absorbed over 25 per cent of the health budget, yet the capital's black hospital found 31 per cent of infant and child deaths were primarily caused by malnutrition. Infant mortality in rural areas was estimated at 300 per thousand. The national ratio of one hospital bed for every 452 people hid a rural provision that was three times as scarce. Urban workplace clinics and hospitals were well-provided, but rural health care was mainly of an inferior standard and often voluntary agency or mission sponsored.

State health services are free for those earning less than $150 per month, yet the spread of availability is still rather uneven, with the cities well served at the expense of rural populations. State pharmacies are often short of many drugs which can be purchased at considerable expense on the open market. Zimbabwe's access to health care professionals is highly skewed (Faruqee 1981): with an average population per physician of 8,056, the urban population's average is 2,000 while the rural population is 33,000 per physician. The national average population per nurse and midwife is 1,190, but in the towns it is 320 while in rural areas it is 2,020.

Municipal clinics charge small fees for services, as do mission health services, because they often find government financial assistance unable to cover their costs. The government spends around 1.4 per cent of GNP on health services. Life expectancy in Zimbabwe is 56 years.

Zimbabwe

Private medical aid is available through a number of private insurance schemes, providing cover for the sophisticated and expensive facilities in private ownership. Such schemes typically have tax-free matching contributions from both employer and employee. At government request one of the leading medical insurance companies launched in 1986 a cut-rate insurance scheme costing $15.20 per month (or half to employees) to cover cost of government doctors and dentists, ambulance fare and artificial limbs. Until that time some 273,000 workers and their families were covered by medical aid societies. One survey, however, showed that some 150,000 to 200,000 urban workers (excluding their families) were not covered by medical aid. It is expected that the cut-rate scheme may give coverage to a significant proportion of those 200,000 workers.

The Ministry of Health targets a number of programmes aimed at preventing the onset of malnutrition and disease, and consequent disability, in the childhood population. During the drought a supplementary feeding programme was set up, which at its peak was feeding 1 million children. Yet malnutrition remains a problem, with 25 to 30 per cent of urban children in one 1985 survey diagnosed as having mild to severe malnutrition, and 39 to 42 per cent of rural children were so diagnosed. Although Zimbabwe is a food exporter, the daily calorie supply per capita is estimated at 2,025, some 90 per cent of requirements. The Extended Programme of Immunisation (EPI), which started in 1982, has resulted in 42 per cent of the Zimbabwean children under six being inoculated against the six major childhood diseases (measles, TB, polio, whooping cough, diptheria and tetanus).

Non-government health care for children is founded on well-baby clinics and collective monitoring of weight for age. Supplementary feeding schemes are now being used by some voluntary agencies to initiate vegetable and ground-nut plots where creches can be set up (Johnson 1986).

Social Security

<u>Non-Occupational Sickness</u>. Workers are usually granted sick leave on full pay for six months, thereafter on half pay. Peasants and workers earning less than Z$150.00 per month are entitled

Zimbabwe

to free medical services. Those who lose their earning capacity as a result of non-occupational sickness can be considered for means-tested public assistance.

Evaluation
Emphasis has been placed on the provision of health services in both urban and rural areas, although disparities still exist. Welfare services are minimal, but sick leave is provided, along with free medical care for low-income peasants and workers.

THE DISABLED AND THE HANDICAPPED

A disability survey undertaken in Zimbabwe in 1982 revealed that there are over 300,000 disabled people in Zimbabwe and of these only two per cent have access to rehabilitation services (Nyathi 1986). Some 25,000 were considered to be critically disabled, and some 10,000 were disabled through war injuries before independence. Services tend to be urban based and curative, although a number of programmes are now initiated that will bring welfare services to rural disabled and handicapped.

Personal Social Services

Institutional Care. Institutionalisation of the disabled and handicapped is only provided for those who lack family support or those whose disability warrants institutional care for effective rehabilitation. The Ministry of Health has established a few psychiatric units in major hospitals in order to cater for the mentally handicapped. In Harare a Half-way House for mental patients (Tariro) was established to prepare for the eventual release of these mental patients back into their communities.
    Jairos Jiri, the largest voluntary agency for disabled, which offers the widest range of services, has a training centre in Bulawayo for 350 disabled clients, a sheltered workshop for 25 employees, and a small hostel for disabled. A workshop is located at Mutare (18 employees), and a training centre at Masvingo (16 trainees). Jairos Jiri also runs three farms, where they employ disabled. It also has a range of services for disabled children.

Zimbabwe

Rehabilitation. Rehabilitation for the disabled and handicapped is carried out in special schools such as the Emerald Hill School for the Deaf in Harare, Capota School for the Blind in Masvingo, Zimcare Trust for the Mentally Handicapped in Harare and Bulawayo. In addition, there are also sheltered workshops, which provide not only employment but also opportunities for self-reliance and re-integration into society. Students in the special schools are expected to pay for their board and lodging, but destitute parents can get assistance from the Department of Social Welfare.

The Ministry of Health now trains and employs around 90 rehabilitation assistants whose role is to assist in the rehabilitation of the disabled and handicapped in rural communities. These rehabilitation assistants enable the disabled to have access to rehabilitation services and rehabilitation aids.

The Cheshire Foundation launched a pilot programme of disability detection and prevention in rural areas by employing two teams of nurses, physiotherapists and social workers, travelling in rural areas, and employed to help educate and rehabilitate disabled, and make appropriate referrals where treatment was necessary. It is anticipated that the Ministry of Health will take over this programme.

Children. There are believed to be some 14,000 disabled children in Zimbabwe, with varying degrees of handicap. In one survey of mental handicap among children by NASCOH (1985) it was found that Down's Syndrome accounted for three-quarters of the congenital disorders; half of the acquired disorders relate to conditions occurring in the pre-natal period.

In respect of physical disability a nationwide survey of the disabled showed that out of the 29,500 total of children disabled, lower limb disability was the commonest form of disability, for children under 15 years of age. The second largest grouping for the under 15s is visual disability, over one-third of whom are totally blind.

The biggest provider of welfare services for physically disabled children is Jairos Jiri. In Harare there are two centres, one for 35 pre-school children (mostly with cerebral palsy) and another a residential rehabilitation centre

Zimbabwe

for 200 resident children. Another residential centre for disabled is located in Rusape (for 60 disabled children, mostly polio victims), and Jairos Jiri also runs a school for the blind for 111 partially and totally blind children in Kadoma, a small hostel for blind children in Bulawayo, and a school for deaf children (185 enrollment).

Social Security

Workmen's Compensation. The Workmen's Compensation Insurance Fund is the main source of social security for those in formal employment with a wage up to a maximum of Z$1,333 per month, but excluding the large number of domestic workers. The fund will pay a maximum of Z$2,000 towards hospital and medical expenses, including artificial appliances. The disability benefit payments, payable for up to 18 months, are determined by the degree of disability and previous earnings:

- 80% of first $300 of monthly earnings: Z$240
- 60% of next $300 of monthly earnings: Z$180
- 50% of next $400 of monthly earnings: Z$200

A ceiling of Z$620 per month applies. Permanent disability pension benefits are also determined by degree of disability and previous earnings. A children's allowance is payable for up to five children to a maximum of 32.5 per cent of the pension (a discretionary rate applies for more than five children.) A widow's allowance is two-thirds of the worker's pension (a lump sum equivalent to 24 months pension is payable upon re-marriage.) The Workmen's Compensation Insurance Fund contributes up to Z$800 for funeral expenses. The rehabilitation services provided include a large complex in Bulawayo, with facilities for 60 residents, as well as outpatients care, offering retraining in a wide variety of trades (such as carpentry, leatherwork, welding and tailoring) as well as literacy classes and bookkeeping.

War Victims Compensation. The War Victims Compensation Act of 1980 was enacted 'to provide for the payment of compensation in respect of injuries to or the death caused by the war'. The Act is administered by the Department of Social

Zimbabwe

Welfare and covers war-related injuries and deaths which occurred before 1 March 1980. The claimants are those who sustained an injury or those who were dependent upon a person who died as a result of the war. A medical board assesses the degree of disablement for the purpose of determining the level of compensation to be awarded. A disablement pension is calculated as follows: 45 per cent of the claimant's earnings immediately prior to the date of his or her injury, up to Z$7,041 per annum, plus 30 per cent of his or her earnings (if any) between Z$7,041 and Z$14,076 per annum. These rates are awarded to those whose occupations have not been affected by the injuries. For those who have been forced to change occupations because of injuries higher rates are awarded.

<u>Public Assistance</u>. The disabled and the handicapped can be awarded public assistance if they are considered to be destitute. This target group tends to be given priority in public assistance over the able-bodied. The handicapped also get free medical services and get assistance with payment of tuition fees for their children attending secondary school.

AN ASSESSMENT OF THE ZIMBABWEAN WELFARE SYSTEM

Whilst Zimbabwe is wealthy, relative to its neighbours and even within the African context (GNP per capita was US$850 in 1983), the country's great inequalities in the distribution of wealth and income mean that many of her rural population receive hardly the basic necessities of life, in terms of adequate nutrition, shelter and access to safe water. Social security operates within a framework of social welfare that favours the better off and employed.
Zimbabwe's socialism and desire for redistribution of wealth is tempered by her desire to increase production and generate wealth. This latter goal is of necessity being implemented at present through an inherited capitalist mode of production in industry, in services and in agriculture. Social policy and social welfare issues have not been debated within a meaningful socialist framework, and hence there seems little prospect yet of altering social welfare programmes from a residual to an institutional mode.

Zimbabwe

Important external influences also mean that Zimbabwe is not entirely the master of her own fate, for situations like drought, military strife in Mozambique, the contradictory relationship with South Africa, and others, all determine the economic base on which social welfare decisions are being made.

Issues on social welfare are little known and even less discussed. The statistical bases upon which policy decisions are made are often very thin, and a system of centralised bureaucratic control allows little opportunity for exploratory research and for data to be used to monitor and evaluate programmes. Hence it is imperative that Zimbabwe begin to debate the issues of formal, structural, institutional care and welfare, and how such systems can best complement the informal support systems still available through extended family and kin networks. Where informal care has collapsed completely (often among aliens, elderly destitute, physically handicapped) planning for the best mix of formal and newly-created informal support networks must be initiated, so that social security and personal social services can be capable of meeting the needs of Zimbabwe's total population, and not just a tiny fraction of the marginalised.

Almost all African countries have failed to extend social security coverage to their rural population, largely because of the difficulty of administering a social security scheme for people with often unreliable and inadequate incomes. Many of Zimbabwe's rural farmers are relatively fortunate in that they currently grow enough food for their consumption as well as surplus for sale, thus contributing significantly to the nation's wealth. However, there exists a paradox: while government uses the foreign exchange earned from rural exports to boost the urban economy very little is ploughed back for the development of the rural areas. Social justice and the philosophy of egalitarianism demands that social security for the peasants be given priority, as a clear recognition of that sector's original contribution to national income; and that government and the urban sector should contribute towards the funding of social security programmes for peasants. Very often, government finds itself subsidising the richer (by, for example, child abatements on income tax) and thus perpetuating inequality.

Zimbabwe

The provision of social security and personal social services should not be divorced from an overall developmental strategy designed to improve the quality of life in the rural areas. This implies an increase in the productivity of the poor through improvement of infrastructure and greater access to extension services, credit and marketing facilities.

FURTHER READING

Brand, V. (1982), 'Social Security Provisions and the Informal Sector: Some Options for Zimbabwe', an unpublished paper, School of Social Work, Harare (mimeo).

Brand, V. (1984), 'Socio-Economic Factors Associated with Paraplegic', an unpublished paper, School of Social Work, Harare (mimeo).

Chenery, H. et al. (1974), Redistribution with Growth, London: Oxford University Press.

Clarke, D. (1976), Economics of African Old Age Subsistence in Rhosesia, Gweru, Rhodesia: Mambo Press.

Faruqee, R. (1981), Social Infrastructure and Services in Zimbabwe, Staff Working Paper, Washington: World Bank.

Gargett, E. (1977), The Administration of Transition: African Urban Settlement in Rhodesia, Gweru, Rhodesia: Mambo Press.

Hall, N. (1985), 'A Survey of Burial Societies in Harare', an unpublished paper, School of Social Work, Harare (mimeo).

Hampson, J. (1982), 'The Organisation and Delivery of Social Services to Rural Areas - A Zimbabwean Perspective', a paper presented at the ASWEA Seminar, Minia, Egypt.

Hampson, J. (1985), 'Elderly People and Social Welfare in Zimbabwe'. Aging and Society, V, 39-67.

Zimbabwe

Johnson, N. (1986), 'Rural Health Care Delivery Systems and the Social Development Task'. *Journal of Social Development in Africa*, 1(1) 49-60.

Kaseke, E. (1982), 'Social Assistance in Developing Countries: the Case of Zimbabwe', an unpublished paper, London School of Economics (mimeo).

Midgley, James (1984), *Social Security, Inequality and the Third World*, London: Wiley.

NASCOH (1985), *Seminar on the Disabled Child In Zimbabwe, April 1985*, Harare: NASCOH.

Nyathi, L. (1986), 'The Disabled and Social Development in Rural Zimbabwe'. *Journal of Social Development in Africa*, 1(1) 61-5.

Rhodesia (1944), Government of, *Report of the Social Security Officer*, Salisbury: Government Printer.

Riddell Commission (1981), *Report of the Commission of Inquiry into Homes, Prices and Conditions of Service*, Harare: Government Printer.

Stoneman, C. (1978), *Skilled Labour and Future Needs*, Gweru, Rhodesia: Mambo Press.

Whitsun Foundation (1980), *Social Security Study*, Harare.

World Bank (1985), *World Development Report 1985*, New York: Oxford University Press.

Zimbabwe (1983), Government of (1983), *Annual Review of Manpower 1983 Volume 1*, Harare: Government Printer.

APPENDICES

COUNTRY	SERVICE PROVIDERS	THE AGED	THE DISABLED AND HANDICAPPED	CHILDREN AND YOUTH
Ethiopia	Central government administrative agencies		Permanent disability (work injury) benefit (workman's compensation)	
			Medical care (workman's compensation)	
	Private enterprise	Occupational retirement benefits		

NEEDY FAMILIES	THE SICK AND INJURED	THE UNEMPLOYED	METHODS OF FINANCING	RESPONSIBLE GOVERNMENT ADMINISTRATIVE AGENCIES
Funeral grants (workmen's compensation)	Paid sick leave		Direct provision by employers (workman's compensation)	Ministry of National Community Development (Labour Department)
			Employer financed	

COUNTRY	SERVICE PROVIDERS	THE AGED	THE DISABLED AND HANDICAPPED	CHILDREN AND YOUTH
Ethiopia	Central government administrative agencies	Development centres		Reform schools
				Development centres
	Voluntary agencies		Training schools	Hostels
			Institutional care	Training centres
			Vocational rehabilitation	Orphanages
				Youth facilities

NEEDY FAMILIES	THE SICK AND INJURED	THE UNEMPLOYED	METHODS OF FINANCING	RESPONSIBLE GOVERNMENT ADMINISTRATIVE AGENCIES
Community centres		Job-search programme	Government allocation	Ministry of National Community Development
Development centres			International charity	
Food supplementaiton		Vocational training	International charity	Ministry of National Community Development
Emergency relief				

COUNTRY	SERVICE PROVIDERS	THE AGED	THE DISABLED AND HANDICAPPED	CHILDREN AND YOUTH
Ghana	Central government administrative agencies	Lump-sum provident fund retirement payment	Lump-sum provident fund invalidity payment	Lump-sum provident fund orphan's payment
		Subsidised health care	Lump-sum disability (work injury) grant (workmen's compensation)	Orphan's benefits (workmen's compensation)
		Subsidised food allocation	Pro-rata partial disability (work injury) benefit (workmen's compensation)	
			Medical care and hospitalisation (workmen's compensation)	

NEEDY FAMILIES	THE SICK AND INJURED	THE UNEMPLOYED	METHODS OF FINANCING	RESPONSIBLE GOVERNMENT ADMINISTRATIVE AGENCIES
Lump-sum provident fund survivors payment	Paid sick leave	Earnings-related benefits (provident fund members only)	Employer provident fund contributions	Social Security and National Insurance Trust
Paid maternity leave	Earnings-related temporary disability (work injury) benefit (workmen's compensation)		Employee provident fund contributions Direct provision by employer (workmen's compensation)	Labour Department
Subsidised health care	Medical care and hospitalisation			Ministry of Health
Tax exemptions				
Food supplementations				
Paid maternity leave				
Subsidised health care				

COUNTRY	SERVICE PROVIDERS	THE AGED	THE DISABLED AND HANDICAPPED	CHILDREN AND YOUTH
Ghana	Central government administrative agencies	Destitute homes Rural support services	Registration Vocational rehabilitation Preferential employment Sheltered workshops Institutional care Educational programmes Rehabilitation aids	Food supplement Foster care Children's homes Adoption Recreational activities Juvenile care
	Regional government administrative agencies			Day-care centres
	Voluntary agencies	Mutual aid associations Domiciliary support services General support services	Rehabilitation services Rehabilitation aids Training	Food supplements Day-care centres Out-of-school care Voluntary work camps
	Private enterprise			Day-care centres

NEEDY FAMILIES	THE SICK AND INJURED	THE UNEMPLOYED	METHODS OF FINANCING	RESPONSIBLE GOVERNMENT ADMINISTRATIVE AGENCIES
Emergency relief	Rehabilitation services	Public employment centres	Government allocation	Department of Social Welfare
		Youth employment centres	International aid	Department of Community Development
		Vocational guidance		Ministry of Education
		Employment information centres		Department of Labour
		National mobilisation programmes		
			Government allocation	Regional Secretaries
Emergency relief	Emergency relief	Vocational training centres	Government allocations	Department of Social Welfare
Counselling	Hospital visits		Donations	Department of Community Development
	Food supplementation		Fund-raising	
			Membership dues	
Housing subsidies	Sponsored hospital wards		Employer grants	
Food subsidies			Employer initiated fund raising	
Transport subsidies				
Recreational facilities				

COUNTRY	SERVICE PROVIDERS	THE AGED	THE DISABLED AND HANDICAPPED	CHILDREN AND YOUTH
Ivory Coast	Central government administrative agencies	Earnings-related retirement pension Retirement settlement Solidarity pension Retirement allowances to foreign workers Elderly dependants allowance	Earnings-related invalidity pension Earnings-related permanent (work injury) disability pension	Orphan's pension Children's allowances to pensioners Family allowances School allowance

NEEDY FAMILIES	THE SICK AND INJURED	THE UNEMPLOYED	METHODS OF FINANCING	RESPONSIBLE GOVERNMENT ADMINISTRATIVE AGENCIES
Survivor's pension	Earnings-related temporary (work injury) disability pension	Unemployment relief	Employer social insurance contributions	Ministry of Labour and Social Affairs
Funeral grant				National Fund for Social Contingencies
Maternity benefit			Employee social insurance contributions	
Birth grant			Government allocation	

COUNTRY	SERVICE PROVIDERS	THE AGED	THE DISABLED AND HANDICAPPED	CHILDREN AND YOUTH
Ivory Coast	Central government administrative agencies		Rehabilitation centres	Foster homes
				Kindergartens
				Vacation camps
	Voluntary agencies		Institutional care	Foster homes
			Rehabilitation centres	SOS villages
			Schools for the handicapped	

NEEDY FAMILIES	THE SICK AND INJURED	THE UNEMPLOYED	METHODS OF FINANCING	RESPONSIBLE GOVERNMENT ADMINISTRATIVE AGENCIES
Low-cost housing			Government allocation	Department of Labour and Social Affairs
				National Fund for Social Contingencies
	Rehabilitation centre		Donations	Ministry of Labour and Social Affairs
			Government subsidies	
			International relief	

COUNTRY	SERVICE PROVIDERS	THE AGED	THE DISABLED AND HANDICAPPED	CHILDREN AND YOUTH
Kenya	Central government administrative agencies	Lump-sum (or instalments) after 60 years of age equal to total employer & employee contributions plus accrued interest	Lump-sum disability grants for total disability after 50 years of age equal to total employer & employee contributions plus accrued interest	Survivors of provident funds receive balance in deceased's account National youth services Primary schools consultation and supervision of programmes
	Regional government administrative agencies	Health care clinics and dispensaries	Clinics and health care centres Hospitals	Clinics, health care, nursery-schools Teachers and supervisors
	Voluntary agencies	Housing Programme development	Clinics	Orphanages Foster care Child welfare Nurseries
	Private enterprise			

320

NEEDY FAMILIES	THE SICK AND INJURED	THE UNEMPLOYED	METHODS OF FINANCING	RESPONSIBLE GOVERNMENT ADMINISTRATIVE AGENCIES
Pension for widows and children	Health care clinics	Training programmes	Provident fund (contributions from employers and employees)	Kenyan Social Security Fund Ministry of Labour
Self-help programmes	Temporary disability allowances	Unemployment relief	Government allocation	Ministry of Housing and Social Service Ministry of Education
Health care clinics	Mobile clinics			Ministry of Agriculture Ministry of Health
Housing development	Out-patient services			
Mobile clinics	Clinics and dispensaries		Taxes	
Self-help programmes			Agricultural levies	
Self-help programmes	Medical care		Donations	Ministry of Housing and Social Services
	Health centres		Government grant	
Training programmes			Foreign aid	
		Day labour	Union fees	

COUNTRY	SERVICE PROVIDERS	THE AGED	THE DISABLED AND HANDICAPPED	CHILDREN AND YOUTH
Kenya	Central government administrative agencies	Housing age grants for retirees after 60 years of age	Vocational rehabilitation programmes	Foster care
				Child welfare services
				Institutional care
				National youth programmes
	Regional government administrative agencies	Social services		Development programmes
				Social Service in primary schools
	Voluntary agencies	Community kitchens	Dispensaries	School leavers programmes
		Housing		Institutional care
		Funeral grants		
		Programme development		Nursery schools

NEEDY FAMILIES	THE SICK AND INJURED	THE UNEMPLOYED	METHODS OF FINANCING	RESPONSIBLE GOVERNMENT ADMINISTRATIVE AGENCIES
Adult education	Health care centres		Government allocation	Ministry of Housing and Social Services
Training programmes	Health service programmes			National Council of Social Services
Family planning	Health care teams for rural areas			
Literacy classes		Self-help programmes	Grants-in-aid from Ministries and local government	Ministry of Education
Training for farmers				Ministry of Housing and Social Services
Formal education				
Care of widows and needy children	Communal services for the sick and diseased		Donations	
Community kitchens			Government subsidies	

COUNTRY	SERVICE PROVIDERS	THE AGED	THE DISABLED AND HANDICAPPED	CHILDREN AND YOUTH
Mauritius	Central government administrative agencies	Social assistance	Social assistance	Orphan's pension revision
		Retirement pension	Invalidity pension	
		Rent allowances	Total disability (work injury) benefit	Orphan's (work injury) benefit
		Medical and hospital care	Partial disability (work injury) benefit	Family allowances for families with three or more children
		Inmates allowances		
			Permanent incapacity (work injury) benefit (workmen's compensation)	Tax deductions for children
	Voluntary agencies		Allowances for blind persons	

NEEDY FAMILIES	THE SICK AND INJURED	THE UNEMPLOYED	METHODS OF FINANCING	RESPONSIBLE GOVERNMENT ADMINISTRATIVE AGENCIES
Social assistance	Social assistance	Social assistance	Government allocation	Ministry of Labour and Social Security, Women's Rights and Family Welfare
Funeral grant	Temporary total incapacity (work injury) benefit (workmen's compensation)		Employer national pension contributions	
Widow's pension			Employee national pension contributions	
Survivors benefit (workmen's compensation)	Paid sick leave		Direct provision by employers (workmen's compensation)	
Paid maternity leave				
Maternity allowance				
Fishermen's allowance				
Emergency relief			Donations	Ministry of Labour and Social Security, Women's Rights and Family Welfare
			Government subsidies	

COUNTRY	SERVICE PROVIDERS	THE AGED	THE DISABLED AND HANDICAPPED	CHILDREN AND YOUTH
Mauritius	Central government administrative agencies	Residential care in government sponsored institutions Community centres	Residential care and rehabilitative services	Residential care for neglected or abandoned children Day nurseries, foster homes Youth training centres Adoption
	Regional government administrative agencies	Senior citizens clubs catering for recreational needs		Support to youth clubs affiliated to the local authority
	Voluntary agencies	Recreational facilities for senior citizens	Recreational facilities Schools for the physically and mentally handicapped	Residential institutions for neglected and destitute children
	Private enterprise			Day nurseries

NEEDY FAMILIES	THE SICK AND INJURED	THE UNEMPLOYED	METHODS OF FINANCING	RESPONSIBLE GOVERNMENT ADMINISTRATIVE AGENCIES
Loans to small farmers and small entrepreneurs Community development projects in rural areas Maternity, child care and family planning services	Free medical care Rehabilitative services	Projects aimed at reducing unemployment and encouraging self-employment	Government subsidy Bank loans and external funding arrangements for development projects only Local authority's revenue	Department of Social Security Development Bank of Mauritius Mauritius Co-operative Bank Ministry of Health Ministry of Local Government (Supervision)
Residential care facilities Homes for unmarried mothers and deserted wives	Aids to children and adults inoperable in Mauritius		User charges and government subsidies	Mauritius Council of of Social Services Ministry of Education, Arts & Cultural Affairs
		Entrepreneurship initiation course for unemployed graduates	User charges Government subsidies Profit on sales	Department of Social Security Ministry of Economic Planning and Development University of Mauritius

COUNTRY	SERVICE PROVIDERS	THE AGED	THE DISABLED AND HANDICAPPED	CHILDREN AND YOUTH
Nigeria	Central government administrative agencies	Lump-sum provident fund retirement payment	Lump-sum provident fund invalidity payment	
			Permanent disability (work injury) benefit (workmen's compensation)	
			Pro-rata partial disability (work injury) benefit (workmen's compensation)	
			Medical and hospital care	
			Appliances	

NEEDY FAMILIES	THE SICK AND INJURED	THE UNEMPLOYED	METHODS OF FINANCING	RESPONSIBLE GOVERNMENT ADMINISTRATIVE AGENCIES
Lump-sum provident fund survivor's payment	Temporary disability (work injury) benefit (workmen's compensation)	Lump-sum provident fund unemployment payment	Employer provident fund contributions	Ministry of Employment, Labour and Productivity
Lump-sum survivor's payment (workmen's compensation)			Employee provident fund contributions	Nigerian National Provident Fund
			Direct provision by employers (workmen's compensation)	

COUNTRY	SERVICE PROVIDERS	THE AGED	THE DISABLED AND HANDICAPPED	CHILDREN AND YOUTH
Nigeria	Central government administrative agencies	Homes for the aged	Rehabilitation centres	National youth services scheme
	Regional government administrative agencies	Homes for the aged		Foster care
				Adoption
				Remand Homes
				Approved schools
				Rehabilitation centres
	Voluntary agencies	Homes for the aged		Services for abandoned and neglected children
				Youth services

NEEDY FAMILIES	THE SICK AND INJURED	THE UNEMPLOYED	METHODS OF FINANCING	RESPONSIBLE GOVERNMENT ADMINISTRATIVE AGENCIES
		Job-placement service	Government allocation	Ministry of Social Development
		Small industry assistance		Ministry of Youths, Sports, and Culture
				Ministry of Employment, Labour and Productivity
				Ministry of Health
			Central government allocation	State Ministries
			State government allocation	
			Donations	
			Government allocation	

COUNTRY	SERVICE PROVIDERS	THE AGED	THE DISABLED AND HANDICAPPED	CHILDREN AND YOUTH
South Africa	Central government administrative agencies	Social assistance	Social assistance	Social assistance
		Medical care		
			Constant attendance allowance	Family allowances (whites with three or more children only)
			Medical care	Maternity benefits
			Permanent disability (workmen's compensation)	Orphan's benefit (workmen's compensation)
			Pro-rata partial disability (work injury) benefit (workmen's compensation)	
	Regional government administrative agencies			

NEEDY FAMILIES	THE SICK AND INJURED	THE UNEMPLOYED	METHODS OF FINANCING	RESPONSIBLE GOVERNMENT ADMINISTRATIVE AGENCIES
Survivors benefit (workmen's compensation)	Earnings-related illness benefit	Earnings-related unemployment benefit	Government allocation	Department of Health Services and Welfare
Funeral grant (workmen's compensation)	Temporary disability (work injury) benefit (workmen's compensation)	Social relief	Employer social insurance contributions	Workmen's Compensation Board
Social relief			Compulsory insurance premiums paid by employer	Department of Labour Manpower
				Unemployment Insurance Fund
				Department of National Health and Population Development
		Social relief	Government allocation	Department of Health Services and Welfare
				Workmen's Compensation Board
				Department of Labour Manpower
				Unemployment Insurance Fund
				Department of National Health and Population Development

COUNTRY	SERVICE PROVIDERS	THE AGED	THE DISABLED AND HANDICAPPED	CHILDREN AND YOUTH
South Africa	Central government administrative agencies	Old age homes	Medical social work services	Services to children at risk
			Agricultural settlements	Adoption
				Foster care
				Residential care
	Voluntary agencies	Community services	Vocational rehabilitation	Foster care
		Housing units	Training colleges	Day-care services
		Domiciliary services	Rehabilitation aids	Services to neglected children
		Homes for the aged	Institutional care	Youth services
		Service centres	Income-generating projects	Creches
		Holiday schemes	Sheltered workshops	
		Group social work services		
	Private enterprise			

NEEDY FAMILIES	THE SICK AND INJURED	THE UNEMPLOYED	METHODS OF FINANCING	RESPONSIBLE GOVERNMENT ADMINISTRATIVE AGENCIES
Counselling		Job-creation programmes	Government allocation	Departments of Health Services
				Departments of Welfare
				Department of Constitutional Development and Planning
Marriage counselling	Free health services	Emergency relief	Government loans and susidies	Departments of Health Services
Emergency relief		Training facilities	Donations	Departments of Welfare
				Department of Constitutional Development and Planning
Day-care centres			User charges	Departments of Health Services
Youth services			Government subsidies	Departments of Welfare
				Department of Constitutional Development and Planning

COUNTRY	SERVICE PROVIDERS	THE AGED	THE DISABLED AND HANDICAPPED	CHILDREN AND YOUTH
Tanzania	Central government administrative agencies	Lump-sum provident fund retirement payment	Lump-sum provident fund invalidity payment	Maternity benefits (triplets only)
		Occupation retirement pensions	Permanent disability (work injury) benefit (workmen's compensation)	Income tax relief (salaried workers with up to four children)
			Pro-rata disability (work injury) benefit (workmen's compensation)	
			Medical and hospital care (workmen's compensation)	
			Occupational disability pension	

NEEDY FAMILIES	THE SICK AND INJURED	THE UNEMPLOYED	METHODS OF FINANCING	RESPONSIBLE GOVERNMENT ADMINISTRATIVE AGENCIES
Lump-sum provident fund survivor's payment	Paid sick leave		Employer provident fund contributions	Ministry of Labour and Social Welfare (Department of Labour)
Lump-sum death benefit (workmen's compensation)	Temporary disability (work injury) benefits (workmen's compensation)		Employee provident fund contributions	Tanzanian National Provident Fund
Funeral grant (workmen's compensation)	Medical and hospital care		Compulsory risk-related insurance premiums (private carrier) paid by employer	National Insurance Corporation
Maternity leave	Occupational injury and schemes benefit			Department of Labour
				Ministry of Health
Burial grant				
Occupational survivors pension				

COUNTRY	SERVICE PROVIDERS	THE AGED	THE DISABLED AND HANDICAPPED	CHILDREN AND YOUTH
Tanzania	Central government administrative agencies	Homes for the aged	Institutional care	Day-care centres
			Rehabilitation services	Nursery schools
			Medical and para-medical care	Protection of children at risk
			'Half-way' homes	Foster care
				Adoption
			Rehabilitation aids	Youth facilities
	Regional government administrative agencies	Homes for the aged	Homes for disabled	Orphanages
	Voluntary agencies	Homes for the aged	Institutional care	Out-of-school care
			Medical and para-medical care	Orphanages
				Youth services
			Sheltered workshops	
	Private enterprise		Vocational guidance	Day-care centres
				Nurseries

NEEDY FAMILIES	THE SICK AND INJURED	THE UNEMPLOYED	METHODS OF FINANCING	RESPONSIBLE GOVERNMENT ADMINISTRATIVE AGENCIES
Maternal and child health clinics		Job-creation programmes	Government allocation	Ministry of Labour and Social Welfare (Department of Social Welfare)
Food supplementaiton		Training centres		
Recreational facilities				
Counselling				
Community centres			Local resources	Municipal and Town Councils
Counselling			Government allocation	Ujamaa villages
Emergency relief	Domiciliary services		Government allocation	Social Welfare Department
Counselling	Counselling		Donations	
	Visits			
Canteens			Direct provision by employers	Social Welfare Department

COUNTRY	SERVICE PROVIDERS	THE AGED	THE DISABLED AND HANDICAPPED	CHILDREN AND YOUTH
Zambia	Central government administrative agencies	Lump-sum provident fund retirement payment	Lump-sum provident fund invalidity payment	Lump-sum provident fund orphan's payment
		Limited social assistance	Earnings-related permanent disability (work injury) pension (workmen's compensation)	Earnings-related orphan's pension (workmen's compensation)
		Medical care	Pro-rata partial disability (work injury) benefit (workmen's compensation)	Medical care
			Limited social assistance	
			Medical care	

NEEDY FAMILIES	THE SICK AND INJURED	THE UNEMPLOYED	METHODS OF FINANCING	RESPONSIBLE GOVERNMENT ADMINISTRATIVE AGENCIES
Lump-sum provident fund survivor's payment	Paid sick leave	Limited social assistance	Employer provident fund contributions	Ministry of Labour and Social Services (Social Welfare Department through networks of local offices)
Maternity benefit (provident fund members only)	Earnings-related temporary disability (work injury) benefit (workmen's compensation)	Medical care	Employee provident fund contributions	Zambian National Provident fund
Earnings-related survivor's pension (workmen's compensation)	Medical care		Government allocation	Workmen's Compensation Control Board
Medical care (workmen's compensation)			Direct provision by employers (workmen's compensation)	
Funeral grant				

COUNTRY	SERVICE PROVIDERS	THE AGED	THE DISABLED AND HANDICAPPED	CHILDREN AND YOUTH
Zambia	Central government administrative agencies	Homes for the aged	Residential care	Reform schools
		Geriatric centre		Adoption
	Regional government administrative agencies			Recreational clubs
				Homecraft training
	Voluntary agencies	Granny villages	Institutional care	Community pre-schools
			Training	Foster care
			Support network	Orphanages
	Private enterprise			Community services

NEEDY FAMILIES	THE SICK AND INJURED	THE UNEMPLOYED	METHODS OF FINANCING	RESPONSIBLE GOVERNMENT ADMINISTRATIVE AGENCIES
Counselling	Health education	Job-search programmes	Government allocations	Ministry of Labour and Social Services (Department of Social Development)
In-kind relief		Small industry promotion	User charges	
Food supplementation				
Emergency relief				
		Training programmes	Local government allocation	Social secretary
			Central government allocations	Ministry of Youth
				Ministry of Higher Education
			Government allocations	Department of Social Development
			Donations	Ministry of Education
			Employer finance	

COUNTRY	SERVICE PROVIDERS	THE AGED	THE DISABLED AND HANDICAPPED	CHILDREN AND YOUTH
Zimbabwe	Central government administrative agencies	Social assistance Medical care	Social assistance School fee subsidy Permanent disability (work injury) benefit (workmen's compensation) Pro-rata disability (work injury) benefit (workmen's compensation)	Income tax relief Additional social assistance Additional workmen's compensation for children
	Voluntary agencies	Funeral subsidies		

NEEDY FAMILIES	THE SICK AND INJURED	THE UNEMPLOYED	METHODS OF FINANCING	RESPONSIBLE GOVERNMENT ADMINISTRATIVE AGENCIES
Social assistance	Paid sick leave	Social assistance	Government allocation	Ministry of Labour, Manpower Planning and Social Welfare (Department of Social Welfare and of Occupational Health, Safety and Compensation)
Rent and fuel allowance	Social assistance	Rent and fuel allowance	Insurance premiums paid by employers	
Medical care	Medical care	Medical care	Direct provision by employers	
School fee subsidy	Temporary disability (work injury) benefit (workmen's compensation)	School fee subsidy		
Widow's allowance (workmen's compensation)				
Funeral expenses (workmen's compensation)				
			Private premiums	Ministry of Labour, Manpower Planning and Social Welfare (Department of Social Welfare and of Occupational Health, Safety and Compensation)

COUNTRY	SERVICE PROVIDERS	THE AGED	THE DISABLED AND HANDICAPPED	CHILDREN AND YOUTH
Zimbabwe	Central government administrative agencies		Institutional care	Welfare of children at risk
				Adoption
				Foster care
				Reform schools
	Regional government administrative agencies			Youth services
				Day-care services
	Voluntary agencies	Old folks homes	Training centres	Children's homes
			Sheltered workshop	
			Hostels	
			Rehabilitation	

NEEDY FAMILIES	THE SICK AND INJURED	THE UNEMPLOYED	METHODS OF FINANCING	RESPONSIBLE GOVERNMENT ADMINISTRATIVE AGENCIES
Counselling		Counselling		Ministry of Labour, Manpower Planning and Social Welfare
				Ministry of Health
				Local authorities
Referral services	Food supplementation		Per capita government grants	Department of Social Welfare
Self-help projects			Donations	Welfare Advisory Board
				Ministry of Health

INDEX

adoption
 Ghana 48; Kenya 113; Mauritius 157-8; South Africa 204; Tanzania 237; Zambia 250, 264; Zimbabwe 285, 292-3 see also foster care
aged, personal social services
 Ethiopia 14; Ghana 36-7; Ivory Coast 83-4; Kenya 110; Mauritius 145; Nigeria 174; South Africa 194-5; Tanzania 229; Zambia 258; Zimbabwe 289-90
aged, social security
 Ethiopia 13-14; Ghana 35-6; Ivory Coast 82-3; Kenya 110; Mauritius 143-5; Nigeria 174; South Africa 196; Tanzania 228-9; Zambia 258; Zimbabwe 290-1 see also elderly dependants (survivors) benefits
aged, the
 Ethiopia 13; Ghana 34-5; Ivory Coast 82-3; Kenya 109-10; Mauritius 143; Nigeria 173-4; South Africa 193-4; Tanzania 227-8; Zambia 257-8; Zimbabwe 288-9
agricultural settlements for handicapped
 South Africa 199; Zimbabwe 300
alcoholics, treatment of
 Ivory Coast 94

blind, welfare of
 Ethiopia 15; Ivory Coast 84, 85-6; Mauritius 149; South Africa 198, 199; Zambia 259; Zimbabwe 300, 301
brotherhood, spirit of
 Ivory Coast 69; Nigeria 164-5
burial grants see funeral grants

child labour laws
 Ghana 47, 51; Zambia 263

children and youths
    Ethiopia 14; Ghana 46; Ivory Coast 88; Kenya 112; Mauritius 154; Nigeria 177; South Africa 202-3; Tanzania 235; Zambia 261-3; Zimbabwe 291-5
children and youths, personal social services
    Ethiopia 14-15; Ghana 47-8; Ivory Coast 88-9; Kenya 112-13; Mauritius 155-6; Nigeria 178; South Africa 203-4; Tanzania 234-6; Zambia 263-4; Zimbabwe 291-4
children and youths, social security
    absence of in Ethiopia 15; Ghana 46-7; Ivory Coast 90-1; absence of in Kenya 113; Mauritius 154-5; South Africa 206; Tanzania 235; Zambia 265; Zimbabwe 294
children, welfare of abandoned
    Ethiopia 14; Ghana 48; Ivory Coast 88; Mauritius 156; Nigeria 178
children, welfare of destitute
    Ethiopia 14; Nigeria 168; Zambia 262-3; Zimbabwe 292
children, welfare of neglected
    Ghana 49; Mauritius 156; Nigeria 178; South Africa 204; Zambia 263; Zimbabwe 292
church missions see missions
collective spirit
    Kenya 101; Nigeria 166; Tanzania 220, 243; Zambia 248
colonialism
    Ethiopia 1; Ghana 22-3, 24; Ivory Coast 69, 76; Kenya 100-1 105; Mauritius 120, 23; Nigeria 164, 167, 168; Zambia 248, 249-50, 252
community-based welfare services
    Ethiopia 17, 18; Kenya 111; South Africa 186, 190, 191, 203; Tanzania 227, 232 see also community centres
community centres
    Ethiopia 17, 18; Ghana 26
communal spirit see collective spirit
constant attendance allowances
    Ghana 52; Ivory Coast 87; Nigeria 176; South Africa 196, 200
Coptic Church, influence of
    in Ethiopia 4
counselling services
    Ghana 26, 36; Mauritius 150; Nigeria 178; South Africa 195, 199, 203; Tanzania 227; Zambia 264; Zimbabwe 285, 286, 297

day care services
    Ghana 26, 45, 48-9; Ivory Coast 89; Kenya 112-3; Mauritius 156; South Africa 203, 205; Tanzania 236; Zimbabwe 285, 294

delinquents, rehabilitation of
    Ethiopia 14-15; Mauritius 156; Zambia 250, 262, 263-4

dependent child allowances
    Mauritius 153; South Africa 208; Zambia 273; Zimbabwe 302 *see also* maintenance grants, orphan's benefits

disabled and handicapped, personal social services
    Ethiopia 15-16; Ghana 40-2; Ivory Coast 84-7; Mauritius 149-50; Nigeria 176; South Africa 198-9; Tanzania 231-2; Zambia 259-60; Zimbabwe 300-2

disabled and handicapped, social security
    Ethiopia 16; Ghana 39, 52; Ivory Coast 86-7; Mauritius 147-9; Nigeria 176; South Africa 199-201; Tanzania 231; Zimbabwe 302-3

disabled and handicapped, the
    Ethiopia 15; Ghana 38-9; Ivory Coast 84; Mauritius 146-7; Nigeria 175-6; South Africa 197-8; Tanzania 230; Zambia 259; Zimbabwe 300

disability benefits *see* invalidity benefits

disability pensions *see* invalidity benefits

domiciliary services
    Ethiopia 17; South Africa 195

economic development
    in Ethiopia 7; in Ghana 27-8; in the Ivory Coast 76; in Kenya 102, 105; in Nigeria 169-70; in South Africa 189; in Tanzania 223-4; in Zimbabwe 283

elderly dependants (survivors) benefits
    Ivory Coast 90

emergency relief
    Ghana 36; South Africa 209-10; Tanzania 233

employer-based welfare services
    Ghana 32, 45, 48; Nigeria 172, 173; Tanzania 221, 226; Zambia 249, 250, 257

family allowances
    Ivory Coast 71, 91; Mauritius 136, 138, 155; South Africa 206

family, welfare role
    Ethiopia 13, 14; Ghana 23, 26, 34, 38, 42, 53; Ivory Coast 69-70, 84, 88, 91; Kenya 105, 108, 110; Mauritius 143; Nigeria 166, 167, 173, 174, 177, 179; South Africa 185, 193, 194, 202; Tanzania 219, 227-8, 231, 237; Zambia 249, 250, 257, 263, 264; Zimbabwe 288-9

famine
    in Ethiopia 4, 6, 18; in Kenya 111
fiscal welfare measures
    Ghana 45; Mauritius 126, 155; Tanzania 235; Zimbabwe 294, 295, 304
food supplementation
    Ethiopia 9-10; Ghana 44, 47; Mauritius 155; South Africa 209, 210; Zambia 264, 267
foster care
    Ghana 26, 48; Kenya 112, 113; Mauritius 157, 157; Nigeria 177; South Africa 202, 204-5; Tanzania 237; Zambia 264; Zimbabwe 285, 293 see also adoption
friendly societies
    Mauritius 127
funeral grants
    Ethiopia 17-18; Ghana 52; Ivory Coast 90; Kenya 112; Mauritius 131; South Africa 206; Tanzania 234; Zambia 260, 274; Zimbabwe 297, 302

handicapped, registration of the
    Ghana 40
handicapped, the see disabled and handicapped, the
handicap screening
    Ghana 42; South Africa 198; Zimbabwe 301
health care for aged
    Ghana 36; Mauritius 145; South Africa 196; Zambia 258
health care for needy families
    Ghana 44, 45; Mauritius 151; Tanzania 233
health services
    Ethiopia 2, 5, 18-19; Ghana 36, 44, 47, 49-50, 52; Ivory Coast 87, 93; Kenya 115; Nigeria 171, 173, 179-80; South Africa 199, 200, 211-12; Tanzania 231-2, 233, 237-9; Zambia 271, 273; Zimbabwe 288, 298-9 see also national health schemes
historical origins of welfare systems
    Ethiopia 7-8; Ghana 24-7; Ivory Coast 70-2; Kenya 101-3; Mauritius 125-8; Nigeria 166; South Africa 186; Tanzania 220-1; Zambia 248-51, 252; Zimbabwe 279-82
homes for the aged
    Ghana 36; Mauritius 145; Nigeria 174; South Africa 194, 195; Tanzania 221, 226, 229; Zambia 258-9; Zimbabwe 285, 289
hospital welfare services
    Ghana 53; South Africa 199
housing
    Ivory Coast 89; Zimbabwe 295

humanism
    Zambia 247-8, 252

ideological environment of welfare systems
    Ethiopia 1-6; Ghana 22-4; Ivory Coast 69-70;
    Kenya 100-1; Mauritius 123-5; Nigeria 164-6;
    South Africa 184-6; Tanzania 218-20; Zambia
    247-8; Zimbabwe 279-82
inflation
    Ghana 28; Ivory Coast 76, 78; Kenya 105;
    Mauritius 122; Nigeria 170; South Africa 189;
    Tanzania 224; Zambia 253; Zimbabwe 282-3
injured, the see sick and injured, the
institutional care for children
    Ethiopia 14; Ghana 26, 48; Ivory Coast 88-9;
    Mauritius 156; Nigeria 178; South Africa 205;
    Zimbabwe 294
institutional care for handicapped
    Ethiopia 16; Ghana 41; Ivory Coast 85;
    Mauritius 149-50; South Africa 198; Tanzania
    226, 231; Zimbabwe 300, 301-2
international relief agencies
    in Ethiopia 8, 9-11; in Kenya 112; in
    Zimbabwe 295
invalidity benefits
    Ghana 39; Ivory Coast 86-7; Mauritius 133,
    135, 148-9; Nigeria 176; South Africa
    199-200; Zambia 260; Zimbabwe 303
invalidity settlements
    Ivory Coast 87

job creation programmes
    Mauritius 159-60; South Africa 210; Tanzania
    241, 242
job-search programmes
    Ethiopia 15, 19; Ghana 57; Nigeria 179; South
    Africa 210; Zambia 270
juvenile delinquency
    Ethiopia 14-15; Ghana 25-6, 50; Mauritius
    156; Nigeria 167, 178; Zambia 262; Zimbabwe
    281, 285, 293

kindergartens
    Ivory Coast 89; Kenya 112-13; Tanzania 236;
    Zambia 264, 294 see also day-care services

local government welfare services
    Tanzania 221, 226, 227; Zambia 250, 253, 254,
    264; Zimbabwe 281, 286, 288, 294, 297

maintenance grants
    South Africa 206 see also orphan's benefits, dependent child allowances
maternal and child health services
    Ghana 47; Kenya 113; Tanzania 233, 237; Zambia 264
maternity benefits
    Ghana 47; Ivory Coast 71, 90-1; Mauritius 152; South Africa 206; Tanzania 235; Zambia 273
maternity leave
    Ethiopia 18; Ghana 44, 47; Ivory Coast 71; Tanzania 233; Zambia 273
mentally handicapped, the welfare of
    Ethiopia 16; Ghana 41; Ivory Coast 84, 86-7; Mauritius 150, 151; South Africa 201; Tanzania 231-2; Zambia 259; Zimbabwe 300, 301
minimum wages
    Ghana 45; Zambia 249; Zimbabwe 282
missions
    in Ethiopia 4-6, 7, 10, 13, 15, 16, 17; in Ghana 26, 49, 52; in Kenya 101, 109; in Nigeria 166, 167, 168, 174; in Zambia 249, 250, 258, 259
modernisation, ideology of
    Ethiopia 1-2, 6, 2; Ivory Coast 69; Kenya 100
mutual aid
    Ghana 23, 37; Kenya 110; Nigeria 166; Tanzania 219, 243; Zambia 246
mutual aid societies
    Ghana 26; Zambia 249, 269; Zimbabwe 280 see also friendly societies

national health schemes
    Kenya 106, 108; Mauritius 123 see also health services
natural disasters, welfare of victims of
    Ethiopia 12, 17; Mauritius 131-2; Zimbabwe 295-6 see also famine
needy families
    Ethiopia 16; Ghana 42-3; Ivory Coast 88; Kenya 111; Mauritius 151; Nigeria 178; South Africa 202-3; Tanzania 233; Zambia 265-6; Zimbabwe 295-6
needy families, personal social services
    Ethiopia 16-17; Ghana 45; Ivory Coast 88-90; Kenya 112; Mauritius 151; Nigeria 179; South Africa 203-6; Tanzania 233-4; Zambia 267; Zimbabwe 297

needy families, social security
    Ethiopia 17-18; Ghana 43; Ivory Coast 90-1;
    Kenya 111-12; Mauritius 150-2; Nigeria 179;
    South Africa 206; Tanzania 233-4; Zambia 267;
    Zimbabwe 296-7
nurseries see kindergartens, day-care services

occupational retirement benefits
    Ethiopia 13-14; Ghana 35-6, 37; Ivory Coast
    83-4; Mauritius 143-4; Nigeria 171, 172, 174;
    South Africa 197; Tanzania 229; Zimbabwe 291
occupational social security
    Ethiopia 13-14; Ghana 35-6, 37; Ivory Coast
    72, 79, 82, 83-4, 87, 90, 94; Kenya 106;
    Mauritius 126-7, 143-5; Nigeria 171, 172,
    173, 180; Tanzania 225-6, 228-9; Zimbabwe 291
old age settlement
    Ivory Coast 83
orphanages
    Ethiopia 14; Kenya 113; Mauritius 157;
    Tanzania 236; Zambia 264; Zimbabwe 285, 294
orphan's benefits
    Ghana 46; Ivory Coast 90; Mauritius 133, 136,
    148, 153; South Africa 206; Tanzania 234;
    Zambia 265, 273 see also maintenance grants,
    dependent child allowances
orphans, welfare of
    Ethiopia 14; Ghana 25, 49; Ivory Coast 88;
    Kenya 111; Mauritius 157
out-of-school care
    Ghana 50; Tanzania 236

personal social services, administration of
    Ethiopia 12-13; Ghana 31-2; Ivory Coast 79;
    Kenya 106-8; Mauritius 142-3; Nigeria 171-2;
    South Africa 190-1; Tanzania 226-7; Zambia
    253-6; Zimbabwe 285-6
personal social services, financing of
    Ethiopia 13; Ghana 33-4; Ivory Coast 82;
    Kenya 108-9; Mauritius 142-3, 149-50; Nigeria
    172-3; South Africa 192, 193; Tanzania 226-7;
    Zambia 256-7; Zimbabwe 288
physically handicapped, welfare of
    Ghana 41; Ivory Coast 84; Mauritius 149;
    South Africa 201; Zambia 259, 260, 301
political environment of welfare system
    Ethiopia 11-12; Ghana 27; Ivory Coast 72;
    Kenya 103; Mauritius 122-3; Nigeria 169;
    South Africa 188-9; Tanzania 222-3; Zambia
    251, 253; Zimbabwe 284

popular participation in welfare services
    Ghana 22; Zambia 250
private insurance
    Ghana 30; Nigeria 180; Zimbabwe 280, 299
provident funds
    Ghana 24, 30, 32-3, 35, 37-8, 39, 44, 46, 51, 56-7; Kenya 105, 108; Nigeria 171, 172, 173, 176, 179; Tanzania 225, 229, 231, 234, 242; Zambia 248, 250, 255, 257, 260, 265, 273
public assistance see social assistance

racial discrimination
    South Africa 186, 212-13; Tanzania 220; Zimbabwe 279
recreational facilities and services for aged
    Mauritius 145; South Africa 195
rehabilitation
    Ethiopia 15-16; Ghana 40; Ivory Coast 84-5, 86-7; Mauritius 150; Nigeria 176; South Africa 198; Tanzania 231, 232; Zambia 260; Zimbabwe 285, 301-2
rehabilitation aids
    Ethiopia 16; Ghana 41, 51; Tanzania 232; Zimbabwe 301
rent allowances
    Mauritius 143, 151; Zimbabwe 281, 297
retirement benefits
    Ivory Coast 83-4; Kenya 110; Mauritius 132, 134, 143-5; Nigeria 174; South Africa 196-7; Tanzania 228-9; Zambia 258; Zimbabwe 291
retirement deferral increments
    South Africa 196
rural welfare services
    lack of in Ethiopia 19; Ghana 22, 36-7, 47; Mauritius 158; South Africa 193-4, 202; Tanzania 221, 227, 233-4; Zambia 250, 264, 274

school welfare services
    Ghana 26, 31
self-help activities
    Ghana 23, 25, 53-4; Kenya 107; Zambia 248
self-reliance
    Kenya 101; South Africa 185; Tanzania 219-20, 243; Zambia 248
sheltered workshops
    Ghana 41, 42; Mauritius 150; South Africa 198; Tanzania 221, 227, 232; Zimbabwe 300
sick and injured, personal social services
    Ghana 52; Ivory Coast 94-5; Tanzania 240; Zambia 273

sick and injured, social security
    Ethiopia 18; Ghana 51; Ivory Coast 93-4; Kenya 115; Nigeria 180; South Africa 212; Tanzania 239; Zambia 273-4; Zimbabwe 299-300
sick and injured, the
    Ethiopia 18; Ghana 51; Ivory Coast 93; Kenya 115; Nigeria 180; South Africa 211; Tanzania 237-9; Zambia 271-3; Zimbabwe 298-9
sick leave
    Ethiopia 18; Ghana 51; Mauritius 151-2; Tanzania 239; Zambia 273; Zimbabwe 299-300
sickness benefits
    Ghana 51; Ivory Coast 71, 93; South Africa 212; Zimbabwe 300
social aid see social assistance
social assistance
    Ghana 23; Mauritius 125, 128, 131-2, 138, 147, 152, 157, 160; South Africa 190, 196-7, 206; Zambia 250, 253, 258, 269; Zimbabwe 280, 281, 286, 288, 291, 296-7, 298, 300, 303
social environment see socio-economic environment
social equity see social justice
social insurance
    Ghana 24, 59; Ivory Coast 71, 78, 80-1, 87; Mauritius 132-6, 138-40; South Africa 190-1, 192-3, 206, 208, 212; Zimbabwe 280
socialism
    Ethiopia 3; Mauritius 124; Nigeria 164, 165; abhorrence of in South Africa 185; Tanzania 218-19, 222, 243; Zambia 248; Zimbabwe 282, 303
social justice
    Ghana 22; Kenya 100, 105; Mauritius 123-4; Nigeria 165; Tanzania 219, 223; Zimbabwe 304
social security, administration of
    Ethiopia 12; Ghana 30-1; Ivory Coast 71-2, 78-9; Kenya 105-6; Mauritius 140-2; Nigeria 171; South Africa 190-2; Tanzania 225-6; Zambia 254-5; Zimbabwe 286
social security, financing of
    Ethiopia 13; Ghana 32-3; Ivory Coast 79-82; Kenya 108; Mauritius 138-40; Nigeria 173; South Africa 192-3; Tanzania 225-6; Zambia 257; Zimbabwe 287-8
social welfare education
    in Ethiopia 10-11; in Kenya 107-8, 112; in Zambia 250

socio-economic environment for welfare systems
    Ethiopia 6-7; Ghana 27-30; Ivory Coast 73-8; Kenya 103-5; Mauritius 121-2; Nigeria 169-71; South Africa 188-90; Tanzania 223-4; Zambia 262-3; Zimbabwe 283-4
SOS Children's Village
    Ghana 48; Ivory Coast 88-9
supporting mother's benefits
    Zimbabwe 296
survivors' benefits
    Ethiopia 17-18; Ghana 44, 52; Ivory Coast 90; Kenya 111-12; Mauritius 133, 135, 136, 138, 148, 153-4; Nigeria 179; South Africa 200, 206; Tanzania 234; Zambia 260, 273-4; Zimbabwe 296, 302 <u>see also</u> orphan's benefit, elderly dependants (survivors) benefits

trade unions, welfare role of
    Ghana 27; Mauritius 127
tribal societies
    Ghana 23, 26; Ivory Coast 69-70; Kenya 100, 101, 102, 105, 108, 110, 111; Tanzania 219; Zambia 247, 249; Zimbabwe 282

unemployed, personal social services
    Ethiopia 19; Ghana 57-8; Kenya 114; Mauritius 160; South Africa 210; Tanzania 242; Zambia 270; Zimbabwe 297
unemployed, social security
    absence of in Ethiopia 19; Ghana 56-7; Ivory Coast 92; absence of in Kenya 114; Mauritius 160; Nigeria 179; South Africa 209-11; Tanzania 242; Zambia 270; Zimbabwe 296-7
unemployed, the
    Ethiopia 19; Ghana 55; Ivory Coast 91; Kenya 113; Mauritius 158-60; Nigeria 177-8; South Africa 208-10; Tanzania 240-2; Zambia 267; Zimbabwe 295
unemployment
    Ethiopia 19; Ghana 29; Ivory Coast 77-8; Kenya 104, 105; Mauritius 158; Nigeria 170; South Africa 207, 208; Tanzania 240, 242; Zambia 268; Zimbabwe 283-4
unemployment benefits
    Ghana 56; Ivory Coast 92; Kenya 112; Mauritius 137, 138, 153, 160; Nigeria 179; South Africa 208-10; Tanzania 229, 242; Zambia 269; Zimbabwe 296-7
unmarried mothers and illegitimate children, welfare of
    Mauritius 156, 157; Tanzania 236

vocational guidance
 Ghana 31, 50; Mauritius 160
vocational training
 Ethiopia 19; Ghana 27, 58; Ivory Coast 89; Kenya 112-13, 114, Mauritius 160; South Africa 210; Tanzania 242; Zambia 264-5; Zimbabwe 294
voluntary agencies
 Ethiopia 13; Ghana 26, 31-2, 34, 36, 37, 38, 41, 42, 44, 47, 48, 50, 53, 57, 58; Ivory Coast 79, 82, 84; Kenya 107, 109, 112; Mauritius 127, 142, 149-50, 151, 156; Nigeria 166, 169, 177-9; South Africa 186, 191, 194-5, 198, 203, 207, 210; Tanzania 225, 226, 231, 235, 236, 238; Zambia 248, 250, 255-6, 259-60, 263-4; Zimbabwe 285-6, 289-90, 294, 297
voluntaryism
 Ghana 23, 25; Tanzania 232; Zambia 256

widows, welfare of
 Ethiopia 17; Ghana 44; Kenya 104, 111-12; Mauritius 153-4; Tanzania 234; Zambia 266
work ethic
 Mauritius 147; Tanzania 219
work injury benefits
 Ethiopia 16; Ghana 51-2; Ivory Coast 71, 87, 93-4; Kenya 115; Mauritius 136, 147-8; Nigeria 176; South Africa 200-1, 212; Tanzania 231, 239; Zambia 273-4, 302
workmen's compensation
 Ethiopia 13, 16, 17-18; Ghana 25, 31, 39, 46, 51; Ivory Coast 71; Kenya 106, 108; Mauritius 125, 137-8, 147-8; Nigeria 168, 171, 176, 179, 180; South Africa 190, 193, 200, 206, 212; Tanzania 220-1, 226, 231, 234; Zambia 249, 255, 257, 265, 272, 273-4; Zimbabwe 286, 287-8, 302

youth facilities and services
 Ethiopia 15; Ghana 50; Ivory Coast 89; Kenya 112; Mauritius 158; Nigeria 178; Zimbabwe 294
youth movements
 Ghana 26
youths *see* children and youths
youth unemployment programmes
 Ghana 50